Praise for There is No Finish

A great read for everyone! It was great t
origin of my own sport, and exciting t
episodes and emotions.
Merijn Geerts, former Backyard Ultra world record holder, Belgium.

Stephen did a tremendous job in bringing to life these cruel yet beautiful races, as well as the protagonists that made each one of them unique.
Hendrik Boury, 2022 Backyard Ultra champion, Germany.

A must read for any runner or any athlete who wants to reach their full potential! A Backyard Ultra can do just that, and this inspiring book explains why with great detail!
Amanda Nelson, 4X ultra record holder, Canada.

Every page of this book was a joy to read. Backyard Ultra is loved, and feared, by runners all over the world. This tells the story beautifully of how it started and how it became a global phenomenon. Backyard Ultra opens up a world for runners of a different kind. Anybody can go far. Finally a book about how we all can come last and win.
Jon Asphjell, 2022 Backyard Ultra champion, Norway.

The story behind Lazarus Lake and how Backyard Ultra came to life. The book delves into its early years with a lot of behind-the-scenes stories that make the book very personal.
Thor Thorleifsson, 2022 Backyard Ultra champion, Iceland.

The title of Stephen Parker's new book says it all. If you like finish lines, a Backyard Ultra is not for you. But if you like reading about the crazy antics that take place during one of these extended sufferfests, this is a true page turner!
Dean Karnazes, Ultramarathoner and NY Times bestselling author, USA.

This is a Bible for the Backyard Ultra passionates like me. It transported me to the key moments in the races.
Oriol Antoli, 2022 Backyard Ultra champion, Spain.

Well-researched and utterly captivating, this book really resonated with me on a personal level. I found myself reliving certain events, even feeling a bit of trepidation as it approached the difficult parts of my races.
Phil Gore, former Backyard Ultra world record holder, Australia

Stephen Parker captures the heart of Backyard Ultras and takes the reader through the history of this weird game in a way that makes it hard to stop smiling. Even if you are not a runner, it's impossible to not get caught up in the stories and characters, and the individual struggles. As well as a great story, it's also a great encyclopedia when it comes to Backyard Ultras!
Anna Carlsson, ultra running champion, Sweden.

I enjoyed reading it twice. When you think about it, a Backyard is the cruellest sport. It's a fight where you need a strong body a stronger mind, but where you curse your strong body and mind because it only means that you will suffer longer. A race without an end and only one finisher, the invention of a true evil genius. Thanks Laz.
Ivo Steyaert, former Backyard Ultra world record holder, Belgium.

Unveil the extraordinary journey through the world of Backyard Ultras in 'There is No Finish'. In these relentless races, runners face an unyielding battle against time, terrain, and themselves. Follow the gripping narratives of those who defy their limits, and meet the visionary behind it all, Lazarus Lake.
David Christopher, 2022 Backyard Ultra champion, Malaysia.

An in-depth read on Backyard Ultras and other ultramarathons. Stephen's academic background shows through with his focus on the granular details of events that unfolded over many races.
Sam Harvey, former Backyard Ultra world record holder, New Zealand.

Stephen Parker interestingly recounts the brief history of Backyard Ultras and provides insights into the future of the sport, highlighting the significance of the running community and support teams. The author's own competition experiences illustrate the beauty of the sport even for an ordinary runner.
Juha Seppälä, Nummela Backyard Ultra Race Director, Finland.

A gripping narration of the history and evolution of the Backyard Ultra. Whether you're an ultra runner or simply a fan of extraordinary human achievement, this book will leave you inspired and awed by the limitless potential of the human spirit. Packed with enthralling experiences, it is a must-read for anyone fascinated by the thrill of relentless races.
Ihor Verys, 2024 Barkley Marathons champion, Canada.

It's clear that Stephen has poured his heart and soul into creating this exceptional book. The result is a comprehensive and engaging guide that's a must have for anyone who loves Backyard Ultras. With its detailed history and insightful stories, this book is the ultimate resource for fans of the sport. A true tribute to the world of Backyard Ultras.
David 'Patto' Patterson, Backyard Ultra Podcast host, Australia.

Stephen manages to present the lore surrounding the Backyard Ultra and its organiser, Laz, in a comprehensive and engaging read which amplifies one's respect towards these remarkable athletes who relentlessly push their bodies in pursuit of testing their limits.
Niki Micallef, 2022 Backyard Ultra champion, Malta.

Captivating story for ultra running fans and people in general. Written in a fascinating way, it inspires you to go out and test your personal limit.
David Stoltenborg, Nordic Backyard Ultra record holder, Denmark.

This book is a reliable source of information for the phenomenon of the Backyard Ultra. The content includes reports, facts, data and statistics from all available sources. It's amazing how far we can go beyond the boundaries we create in our minds. To be completely honest, I'm proud to be even a small part of this passion story.
Bartosz Fudali, 2024 48-hour World Champion, Poland.

As an ultra runner, it was like traveling to Disneyland. I am grateful for the opportunity to learn about the origins of the Backyard Ultra, which I admire. Many people have lamented their misfortune, been devastated, and yet stood up and challenged. I pray that more people will read this book and become victims.
Akihiro Maeda, 2022 winner, Last Samurai Standing—Shimane, Japan.

This book shares the best ultra-stories of recent years, exploring the deep universe of the Backyard and other races founded by the king of superhuman limits - Lazarus Lake. It is about great effort, disappointment, and the ability to turn suffering into pleasure, where examples of ultras from around the world inspire us to confidently face our fears.
Viktoriia Nikolaienko, 24-hour, 6-day & Backyard Ultra champion, Ukraine.

From the humble beginnings of BYU to the latest edition of Big's BYU World Championship in 2023, the author has captured the highlights and key milestones of this amazing event with great detail and insight. From the battles among the sporting giants of this race to the struggles and quiet achievements of other aspiring runners, the author has captured their stories with wit and eloquence. Highly recommended.
Joshua Toh, 2022 Backyard Ultra champion, Singapore.

The story of the greatest and ugliest athletic event the sport of ultra marathoning has ever seen. A gift to the masses from the mind of Lazarus Lake the diabolical chain smoking hillbilly himself. This book expertly highlights the Backyard, the concept that shakes the toughest to their core yet keeps them coming back for more.
Dave Proctor, author of UNTETHERED and Trans-Canadian speed record-holder, Canada.

Laps? Who would want to run laps? The Backyard Ultra is a very unique type of challenge and one you don't really understand until you actually take part. There Is No Finish dives into the mind of those who attempt this type of race, what makes them tick and what drives them to run those laps over and over. If you want to go "Just one more lap" then this book will take you there.
Sean Sandiford, 2022 Satellite Championships Race Director, South Africa.

THERE IS NO FINISH
THE BACKYARD ULTRA STORY

www.runningforever.au

RF

STEPHEN PARKER

FOREWORD BY LAZARUS LAKE

There is No Finish: The Backyard Ultra Story

First edition.

Contents of the present edition, including text, editorial matter, notes and illustrations, Copyright © 2024 Stephen Parker.

All rights reserved.

No part of this book may be reproduced, or stored in a retrieval system, or transmitted in any form or by any means, electronic, mechanical, photocopying, recording, or otherwise, without express written permission of the publisher, except as permitted by copyright law. Reviewers may quote brief passages in a review.

No part of this book has been created using AI-generated images or words.

Editor: Gary Dalkin
Cover Design: Ben Taylor
There is No Finish logo: Charlotte Parker
Cover photo: Mike Trimpe
Author: Stephen Parker

ISBN: 978-1-7635863-1-4 (Print)
ISBN: 978-1-7635863-0-7 (Ebook)
ISBN: 978-1-7635863-2-1 (Audio)

First published in October, 2024 by Running Forever, Logan City, Australia.
www.runningforever.au

DEDICATION

To my first support crew, Doug and Ann Parker.

Almost forty years ago, my parents inadvertently prepared me for Backyard Ultras by encouraging me to run or walk what felt like endless laps of the cricket oval at Underwood Park. They would sit in the car patiently, occasionally call out encouragement, and satisfy my seemingly infinite desire for food.

Thank you.

CONTENTS

Foreword		1
Apologies		5
Prologue		6
Chapter 1:	Meet Lazarus Lake	9
Chapter 2:	The Birth of the Backyard	32
Chapter 3:	Accidental Innovation	55
Chapter 4:	Learning the Ropes	79
Chapter 5:	International Showdown	104
Chapter 6:	Dead Cow Gully	130
Chapter 7:	Big Dog's Backyard	153
Chapter 8:	Running Forever	188
A Final Note		206
Acknowledgements		207
A Plea for Help		209
About the Author		210

FOREWORD

my parents raised me with good values.
either that or i think they are good values because they are what my parents taught me!
and a key value was that we should make a contribution.
we should make a contribution to our family, our community ...
.
service is the highest goal.
to be of service to others.
.
it would be nice to say that backyard is the product of a dream.
but it was a product of serendipity.
all i set out to do was figure out a race that we could hold in our backyard
something that did not require a huge venue or a lot of resources.
something simple and fun.
.
when the first backyard was run,
my biggest hope was that people would enjoy it enough that we would have sufficient interest to hold a second....
.
13 years later tens of thousands of people will run backyards this year, in more than 80 countries.
the same factors that led to the first backyard give it universal appeal.
it is simple and inexpensive to hold.
all you really need is a watch and a 4.167 mile course.
backyards have been held with the only equipment involved being a single wristwatch.
.
there are a couple of other aspects of backyards that give it appeal.
one is the social aspect.
instead of the field spreading out
and runners sometimes never seeing another competitor for many hours
which is the nature of the long distance races
everyone sees everyone every hour.
there is a short time when everyone is together between yards
and with no real purpose in going fast,
anyone in the field can run a lap with anyone else.
.

the other has turned out to be a twist on the backyard rejection of multiple awards.
much of the focus is on the individual goals
and the backyard format is conducive to covering a lot of distance.
in the world of backyard
every runner who goes further than they have ever gone before is a winner.
.

and so,
the backyards have grown organically..
.

as the number of backyards grew
and the sport spread across the globe like some sort of invasive plant
i really expected the original race in my yard to fall by the wayside.
it was still the same home-grown event it started as
and i saw other backyards spring up with fancy websites
slick organization
and lots of swag.
.

but a funny thing happened.
the best runners in the world kept wanting to come and run at bigs.
.

well, what race director doesn't want to host the best runners in the world?
before i knew what was happening
we had to come up with a system for qualifying for bigs.
given the nature of backyards we hit on having golden ticket events.
in the backyard, no one can do well
unless everyone does well.
that was built into the rules from the beginning.
but if bigs was to become a true world championship
entry did not need to rely on having the resources to travel to one of the races where big yards were being logged.
.

and then in 2020 serendipity struck again.
covid stuck most of the big's championship field at home.
pretty much no one could travel.
and just to fill in the empty place we came up with the idea of having the team championships.
15 people from each country would simultaneously hold a race in their home country.
we would link all the results

every yard would count as a point
and the team logging the most yards would be the world team champion.
simultaneously each team race would count as a national championship.
each winner would receive a golden ticket to run at big's the following year.
.
the runners loved it.
if the backyard fosters unity in the field under normal circumstances
this team version increased it exponentially.
struggling athletes found themselves surrounded by supportive teammates
picking up their spirits and encouraging them to the very last hour.
it wasn't like any racing experience they had ever been a part of.
.
this is where my lifetime in athletics paid off.
with the help of like minded volunteers,
like alex holl, naresh kumar, bad mike dobies
and race directors around the world
we set up a qualifying system in which the athletes could control their outcome.
they could start with any backyard, anywhere
and if they won (or got big enough results)
they could advance,
and ultimately
they could make their national team.
.
win there, and they would have a place in the world championships.
.
there is a dream every athlete has from childhood.
one day they will wear their national colours in competition.
and my dream was that backyard athletes would embrace this qualifying system
and find the joy that comes with pursuing their own dreams.
.
it was sort of a gamble.
if no one cared it would have been a lot of wasted effort.
but nothing ventured, nothing gained.
.
and my dream has come true.
last year at the world individual championship

there were 30 languages being spoken in my yard.
the athletes that came were not there by chance
not there because they had the financial resources.
they were there because they had set out to qualify and make it to the top.
some had spent years working toward that goal.

.

when i saw athletes there who were just regular ordinary working people like me
who had devoted themselves to qualifying
and then their home community of backyarders had raised the funds to allow them to attend a world championship.
everyone involved in those athletes' presence at the race epitomizes what athletics are really about ...

.

all year i have been hearing from people who had qualified for their national teams.
about their pursuit of a dream.
how hard they had worked,
and the joy of finally achieving it.
but, whether they succeed or fail,
the real joy was in the journey.
the memories of that will always be there.

.

and my dream?
the dream of every sports organizer.
to provide a venue for people to find greatness in themselves.
it has come true.

Lazarus Lake
Founder, Backyard Ultras.

APOLOGIES

I've used a broad variety of sources for this book. I've interviewed athletes, race directors and support crews. I've listened to countless podcasts, contacted hundreds of participants, watched too many YouTube videos and read innumerable articles, race reports, and social media posts. I've used www.backyardultra.com, DUV and other race report services constantly. For the chapter on Big's, Tim Moffatt's statistical analysis was very helpful. This book might look more academically credible if it was littered with footnotes referencing these sources, but the sheer quantity would make it less readable. Sometimes I have relied on four or five sources for a single sentence, and citing them would distract from the fun of the story.

Also, if you are not used to British or Australian English, many of the words in this book may seem incorrect. Metre, colour, apologise, travelled and countless similar words would be written as meter, color, apologize and traveled in American English.

For distance, some measure a Backyard lap as 4.167 miles, others call it 6.7056 kilometres. Mostly I'll use the relevant country's preferred units, but I'll also reference significant numbers such as 100 km or miles where helpful.

A runner who completes the course has completed one lap, even if the course includes multiple loops within that one lap. However, Backyard Ultras commonly refer to these laps as 'yards', and each lap or yard can take a maximum of one hour only. Hence the words lap, yard and hour will be used interchangeably.

I have attempted to tell an accurate story. However, occasionally sources have differed, and why and how things played out can be subjective. When I asked participants to check that my information was correct, sometimes I found that the sources I had relied on were wrong. Sorting out the competing stories is my responsibility, so any remaining errors are mine.

For all of these issues, and for anything else that causes confusion, I do apologise.

Finally, to my family, and anyone else I neglected during my writing, I also apologise. Thanks for your encouragement and graciousness throughout this mammoth project. I hope that it has been worth it for the readers!

Prologue

It was dark. I was lost. It was wet. I wished it was raining; that would have been refreshing, a welcome relief. In fact, the drips I felt falling on my leg and chest were not from the sky, but my own body. By the end of my first lap early that morning, so many hours ago now, I was covered with sweat from head to toe. The small patches of moisture on my chest and back soon spread, covering not just my shirt, but my shorts and socks too. Occasionally I would reach down to my clothes, gather up some of the fabric in my hands and twist it. Any moisture squeezed out would soon be replaced by fresh sweat, but in the moment, it made me feel better to see the liquid ooze out of my clothing.

After an entire day of running in 30-plus degrees Celsius (86F), and 80-plus percent humidity, I had sweat more than most people would consider healthy. I was drinking well, about one litre per hour, some at the end of each lap, plus several cups throughout the course. Each time I drank it was a good excuse to walk for a while and ease the pressure on my legs.

By now, I was in pain. My injury-plagued body was not keeping up with my demands. The course was far more technical than I was used to, and the roots, rocks and rough ground offered too many tripping hazards. I'd fallen over twice, hard, earlier in the day. I had a cut on one knee, and loose dirt from the trail had stuck itself to my sweat-covered body. Both falls had come with a shock, and I laid on the ground for a while afterwards before I felt I could move again. I knew fatigue would make further falls more likely, and I feared a third one would take me out of the race.

Although none of the hills were significant, more often than not I was either running up or down some incline. I was starting to regret having done almost all my training for the last six months on flat and smooth tracks. It had felt like such a good idea at the time, training for a race on a flat course that had now been cancelled. But now I was here, running my Plan B race, and paying the price as the problems accumulated.

There was no support crew to help with all the logistics and problems throughout the day. I had developed a blister on my heel on the second lap, far too early to have that kind of problem emerge. My stomach had stopped wanting food or drink hours ago. And I was completing each lap by smaller and smaller margins, the finishing corral filled with runners eager for the next lap by the time I returned.

When we began there were over 100 competitors, each trying to do as many laps as they could. By now we were down to 25, and there were 23 in front of me. I'd been running alone mostly. Pete would run with me from the start of each lap, then head off at a speed that worked for him. Mark had stopped a few hours earlier.

By myself, a bit lonely on the trail, I thought it would be entertaining to run without turning my headlight on. I often enjoyed running in the dark, and soon enough my eyes would adjust to the blackness. It made me pay attention to the trail and run with more care. My other senses felt like they were heightened, and the challenge made running even more fun. I think I liked doing it as it gave me a sense of competence and control while everything else felt like it was coming apart.

There was a downside, though. As I ran down a hill, around a corner that felt unfamiliar, I stepped out onto a road. Although I'd been running the course all day, this was the first time I'd seen a road. With no one to follow, and no light to see where I was supposed to turn, at some stage I'd gone off the course. I had no idea where I was.

I have to admit, it all seemed crazy. What self-respecting fifty-year-old man would get into a mess like this? But to be frank, I was having the time of my life, loving every minute.

For years I've loved running long distances, particularly on the trails near my home in Daisy Hill Forest in Queensland, Australia. But more recently I've been exploring this fascinating new type of running event, the Backyard Ultra. I first heard about it while I was in Covid-lockdown, when I noticed thousands of people from all around the world were somehow racing against each other for days on end. It was incredible. Since then, I've had an absolute blast running in Backyard Ultra events, supporting friends as they've competed in them, and following a series of adrenaline-filled races around the world. I've found my time in this relatively new realm to be exhilarating. And the more I've dug into the story of how the race developed, my amazement has only grown.

So, what is a Backyard Ultra? In short, participants attempt to run or walk a succession of laps 4.167 miles or 6.7056 km long, and have up to one hour to finish each lap. If they take forty minutes to complete the lap, they then have twenty minutes to recover before the next lap begins. If they take 59 minutes, they have one minute. Those who want to keep going then line up at the start of the next hour and attempt another identical lap. If they don't finish on time, or choose not to start the next lap, they are eliminated. There is no set finish to the race, as competitors keep on running and walking until all except one drop out. That last person standing is the winner if they can complete one lap more than anyone else.

In the first thirteen years of the sport, it has grown from just two events in one country in 2011, to 484 (at time of writing) in 83 countries, in 2024. With epic battles, new stars emerging each year, an incredible series of world championship qualifying races, and records being pushed beyond the imagination, the Backyard Ultra is one of the most exciting athletic stories of recent times.

Over the last several years, this spectacle has earned a growing audience. Some races are live-streamed, so at any stage thousands of people will be watching real-time video. Countless others will follow on social media, debating why various things happened, offering their own interpretations and theories about what they think will happen next.

It's all a lot of fun, so strap yourself in, as I share some of this astonishing story. I'll get back to what happened in my race eventually, but before that, let me tell you about how it all began and then exploded around the world. You'll meet a fascinating cast of characters, encounter shocking episodes from amazing races, and discover, in the 2023 world championships, a series of events that made it one of the true sporting blockbusters.

It all begins, though, with an eccentric accountant from Tennessee known as Lazarus Lake.

1

Meet Lazarus Lake

RUNNERS CAN BE a strange bunch, waking up early and calling things *fun* that others would consider *punishment*. Ultramarathoners, who call traditional marathons a warm-up, can make standard runners look normal. Ultramarathon race directors, those who deliberately plan the pain for ultrarunners to endure, are a different breed again. And then there's Lazarus Lake, a retired accountant from Bell Buckle, Tennessee, who has led countless people to voluntarily endure suffering and pain for the joy of running.

Although ultrarunning has grown in popularity over the last decade, it remains outside the sporting mainstream. It wasn't on the Paris 2024 Olympic timetable. Most runners, let alone the general public, would struggle to name the organiser of a running event near them, let alone of an obscure race overseas. And then, again, there's Lazarus Lake, the former ultramarathoner who has organised the craziest, the most innovative, and the most popular ultrarunning events that you can imagine.

In 2016, Netflix added a documentary, 'The Barkley Marathons: The Race That Eats Its Young' to its platform. Based on the 2012 edition of an ultramarathon, the film introduced the world to Lazarus Lake. It was after the film started streaming on Netflix that non-runners started telling me about this amazing race and its even more amazing organiser.

By the time the broader world began hearing about Lazarus Lake, he was already a few years into organising his next big thing: the Backyard Ultra. The Barkley Marathons may have brought him fame, but Backyards may well be his lasting legacy. Although the sport only began in 2011 with a single race of 32 people, they have since then swept the world and exploded in numbers.

So, who is Lazarus Lake? Imagine you could make up a race director who embodied all the tropes of running combined into one person. Put together all the craziest ideas, the most iconic running stories, mix them together, and out would come Lazarus Lake. You name it, he's done it.

One common story is about the runner who tries to run every day for a month, or even a year. In 1975 Lake began a streak of running, at least one mile every day. Unlike many runners, he didn't stop after the first week. He didn't stop at the end of the year. No, he continued for close to a decade. Regardless of the weather or his physical health, for at least 3,500 days, he would run at least one mile. That's commitment.

Naked runs may be less part of traditional running, and more sophomoric prank. Lake still added one to his resumé as part of the Memphis Runners club in a late-night session.

Today, the method of alternating walking and running during marathons has been popularised. Although Jeff Galloway brought this technique into the public consciousness, Lazarus had been practicing and preaching it for years.

Early on in his running life he drew a series of maps and set himself the task of running every road in the counties near his Tennessee home. Later he would walk across America. In 2018 he averaged 27 miles per day, taking four months to go the 3,331 miles from Newport, Rhode Island to Newport, Oregon. He described the feat to Outside Magazine as a *kind of a pathetic attempt. I'm an old, beat-up man who doesn't have a lot left in the tank.* In 2019 he undertook another epic journey, this time from the Canadian border to the Mexican, in three stages. In 2024 he began his third crossing by a different route.

Despite his calling as an organiser of the fit and healthy, he's happy to fill his body with—for the running world—a far from optimal diet. He ate five ham sandwiches before running his first marathon. He used pizza as sustenance for his cross-America walk. He's been hooked on smoking for years and drinks beer at will, even using it as race fuel in one early event, albeit with limited success.

He's run without socks, been shot competing in a marathon, suffered hallucinations while running, and pulled his own teeth out.

To call Lake *amazing*, as I did above, is one of the less dramatic ways of describing him. As I read countless articles, I noticed how authors liked to outdo themselves with their superlatives. In a single paragraph of a 2016 article, Trail Runner Magazine described him as *ultrarunning's resident madman*, an *evil genius*, a *true artist*, the *Leonardo da Vinci of pain*, the *Rembrandt of mind games*, the *Lady Gaga of suffering*, and a *Master of sadomasochistic craft*. Later in the article, he was called a *savant*, *like some sort of hillbilly Santa Claus*, and the author wrote that *his words are like the beautiful poetry of a sadistic Thoreau.* In the same year, The Bitter Southerner added *The Bearded Saint* and *The Godfather of the Woods*. Deadspin pronounced him, with justification, as *Backyard's Emperor*. In 2023, Harvey Lewis preferred the simpler epithets of *Mastermind* and, with much affection, *kinda crazy*.

In his typical self-deprecating style, he calls himself *just an old hillbilly who lives in the woods*. He adds that this is nothing special, *because you can't swing a dead cat without hitting an old hillbilly who lives in the woods*.

When we met, I'll admit, none of the descriptions I've quoted above came to mind. He seemed like the classic grandfather: smiling, laughing, loving to tell stories. He knew of his fame, or a growing awareness of his exploits, but preferred to ignore it, to live a normal life. He enjoys his daily walks and cherishes spending time with his beloved wife of many decades, Sandra, and whenever they visit, with his grandchildren.

Within the ultrarunning community, though, his name is spoken of with awe, sometimes with a tinge of fear. As the founder, godfather and, in practice, supreme overlord of the world of Backyard Ultras, Lazarus Lake is renowned for his radical vision of a new form of running that has taken off far more than he ever imagined. Yet Backyards are just one of his event children, and to understand this one, it pays to start the story earlier.

The Backyard Ultra story begins not with Lazarus Lake in 2011, but in 1954, when someone called Gary Cantrell was born. Lazarus Lake, as the catchy alliteration may suggest, was not his birth name. In the 1980s, while crossing Tennessee on one of his 'journey runs', where he ran seemingly ridiculous distances from A to B, he happened to stumble on the name in a telephone directory. Doesn't everybody browse a telephone book while resting during long runs? There was a pastor and farmer of that name in Bolivar, Tennessee, and his name stood out.

About a decade later, to avoid having to use his work email, Gary signed up for his first personal email address. Wanting to preserve some privacy, on a whim he used the name Lazarus Lake, the memory springing from the hidden recesses of his mind. Something clicked, and he began using the name as a pseudonym for his race directing, and later, his social media commentary. Over time he came to be known as Lazarus Lake just as much as Gary Cantrell, and many of his runners would call him that, or just Laz.

Although Lazarus Lake may have been 'born' in Tennessee, Gary Cantrell came from Texas, though his family soon moved to Oklahoma. When he was twelve, they moved to Tullahoma, Tennessee, about 70 miles southeast of Nashville, where his dad began work as an aerospace engineer. Although Laz gives off rustic hillbilly vibes, Gary was literally the son of a rocket scientist.

Gary's running career began similarly to my own; because there was no other sport in which he excelled. American Football was his first preference, but any delusions of grandeur in that game did not last long. Standing just five feet tall, and weighing 70 pounds, he didn't have the size, strength, or speed to succeed. The wrestling team would not even let him start. He did, however, enjoy the run training with the football team, and did that religiously. He would also run with his dad and his friends and was elated when he could beat his father in the mile. As the first thing he was ever better than his dad at, the thought popped into his mind that maybe, just maybe, he was a runner. He joined the track team, and enjoyed training and racing with them throughout his school years, without ever being particularly helpful to their leaderboard.

By the time he was sixteen, though, he'd developed a love for longer runs, being discouraged by the results from the races he took part in, which were often on the shorter side. Even though he finished towards the front, he imagined that a longer, slower race would suit him better.

Around the age of nineteen, he ran the 1975 Andrew Jackson Marathon, his first event of that distance. His time was a creditable 3:20 (3 hours, 20 minutes). Afterwards, he wrote to a friend: *I felt so proud. I was so ecstatic, what a thrill, I had done it. A marathon, wow, incredible. You really ought to try it once, it is unreal, it was one of the highlights of my life.*

In his thrill at running his first marathon, Gary was getting swept up in a craze that was sweeping the USA and much of the world. Today long-distance running is recognised as a mass-participation sport, with over 800 marathons held annually, the number of finishers in the millions. However, it was not always this way.

Running as a mass-participation sport only took off in the 1970s. Much earlier, long-distance walking had attracted interest from the masses, not as something to participate in, but to watch. From the late 1770s, for just over a century, multi-day walking races became a spectacle, as crowds would both watch and gamble on whether participants would be able to walk certain distances, whether around the world, between cities or even around a tent.

In 1874, P.T. Barnum, the scandal-ridden promoter, decided he could make money from the walking craze. He somehow managed to convince thousands of paying customers to watch people walk 500 miles in six days around a 600-foot track inside his portable Hippodrome in Manhattan, New York. Whether despite or because of all the attention, running and walking long distances was considered a 'freak show' for years to come.

It was not until 1972, when the USA's Frank Shorter won gold in the Munich Olympic Marathon, that the American people turned their attention to running. Over the subsequent decade, battles between Frank Shorter, Bill Rodgers, and Alberto Salazar captured the public imagination, and more and more people began to lace up their shoes. In 1977, Jim Fixx's book The Complete Book of Running was released. It was a worldwide bestseller and helped encourage many more to join in the running boom.

The Boston Marathon, which began in 1897, had already experienced a surge of runners, rising from 197 in 1960 to 1,174 in 1970. Those numbers continued to grow, to 5,417 in 1980, then multiplying six-fold over the following four decades. The New York Marathon began in 1970 with only 127 runners, but now has over 50,000. Other cities began to follow suit. Australia's Gold Coast launched their marathon in 1979, London in 1981, and soon all major cities around the world would have their own marathon attracting tourists and prestige.

Having been hooked on the craze with his first marathon, Gary wanted more. The next year he ran 30 miles in training, technically his first ultramarathon distance. Over the next few years he ran more and more marathons and developed a strong training regimen; ten miles most days, thirty miles on alternate weekends.

Then came 1978, a year which would become pivotal in the world of ultrarunning, not for any new or exciting development, but for another of Gary's disappointments. After clocking up eight marathon finishes, Gary was keen to try his hand at an ultramarathon, technically defined as any running event longer than the marathon's 26 miles or 42.2 km. He decided that he would enter the Stone Mountain 50-mile ultramarathon near Atlanta, Georgia. It was just a few hours from where he was studying at Middle Tennessee State University in Murfreesboro and was the closest ultra that he could find. Even with the running boom, ultramarathons were still a rarity. Today, ultramarathoners can be spoiled for choice, with multiple events on successive weekends within easy driving distance. Not so in 1978.

Unfortunately, the Stone Mountain race ended up being cancelled. Even worse, the next closest ultra he could find was in Philadelphia, a good 800 miles away. In a classic case of making lemonade out of lemons, Gary talked a dozen of his running friends into organising their own ultramarathon. Although his friend John Anderson suggested they call it the Idiots' Run, Gary would call it what it is still known as: the Strolling Jim 40.

This would be the first of many races invented and organised by Gary, and the birth of an iconic career in race direction. Although he would run in his own races for a few years, he came to realise that running and directing the same event was just too difficult, and he turned his attention more fully to the organisational side of things.

1979, The Strolling Jim 40
The Strolling Jim 40, even as Gary's first race as organiser, would have many of the elements that would be seen in his later races. Wanting to run something close to home, he held it in his hometown of Wartrace, Tennessee, in May 1979.

The race's unconventional name broke with the common practice of calling races after geographical locations or features. Its namesake was a Tennessee Walking Horse, a breed developed in the American South. In 1939, a three-year-old horse, Strolling Jim, had become the first Grand Champion Walking Horse by winning a self-styled World Grand Championship, held in Wartrace. Given that Gary's friends called themselves the Horse Mountain Runners, Wartrace was known as the Cradle of the Walking Horse, and the race itself would finish at the supposedly haunted Walking Horse Hotel, it was an appropriate name. The '40', however, was less fitting, as the race's true length was 41.2 miles.

Gary's love of pushing runners to their limits was also evident early on. Although the course was mostly on road, it was difficult. He explained that its hilliness would make the race ninety percent a mental challenge, as the runners would have to push themselves beyond reasonable limits to continue. To taunt them on their way, at the beginning of features that gave every appearance of being hills, spray-painted signs would advise participants that 'this is not a hill'.

Peter Sulymna of Alabama was the inaugural winner in 4:31:46. Of 22 starters, twenty managed to finish, despite only two competitors having ever completed an ultramarathon beforehand. Mary Cantrell was the first and only female, finishing in 7:25:04. Just over ten minutes later was her husband Gary, coming second-last in 7:35:30.

Sulymna won the next two years also, and the race has continued to be held on an annual basis, with high-profile runners Harvey Lewis and David Goggins winning in later years. Its 45th race in 2023 attracted 149 finishers, and it claims to be the second oldest continuously held ultra in the USA. Most pivotally, it introduced a young Gary into the world of organising races. A new era of ultrarunning events had begun.

1980, The Nick Marshall Track Run
It did not take long for Gary to develop his next event. Only months after the first Strolling Jim, he held the Birthday Track Run. This was an outlier amongst his races, as it avoided any hills or other difficult terrain, and any element of uncertainty or need for navigation. As a classic track

run, competitors were to complete 50 miles by running laps of the Shelbyville Tennessee High School 400 m track. To add to the adventure, the race started at night.

In 1980 it was renamed the Nick Marshall Track Run, as Gary regarded Nick as one of the fathers of American ultrarunning. Nick had written an article for Runner's World, by then one of the key magazines supporting the running boom, about his exploits in a 62-mile Lake Tahoe run. It had stirred Gary's desire to consider running ultramarathons: *That sounds like fun!*

Only eight runners took the 1980 challenge, including Gary himself, but despite the lack of obstacles, seven dropped out. Gary stopped after 31 miles with a cramping back, while Jim Crompton won, the only finisher, in 6:47:56.

The following year Gary morphed the race into a 24-hour track run, this time held at his old high school in Tullahoma, where competitors aimed to complete as many laps as they could in the timeframe. Presumably a higher calibre of runner was attracted, as although only ten competitors started, all but two exceeded the race's minimum goal of 50 miles. Gary, in his second and final attempt, brought up the rear with 50 km, while Raymond Krolewicz finished with 114 miles.

Numbers almost doubled in 1982, to nineteen, remained at nineteen for 1983, then almost doubled again to 35 for the event's final outing in 1984. The eponymous Nick Marshall ran in the final two events, taking the win in 1983 with 122 miles. The last event served as the national 24-hour championships with a top class field. Ed Dodd took the win, despite being back in 16th place at the halfway point.

Gary's trademark humour was evident even at this stage. His 1980 entry form advised participants that the race *must be experienced to be understood (sort of like death)*. On his 1983 entry form, he promised *Glamour! Pageantry! Big Stars! Live TV Coverage! Throngs of Admirers!!! You too can avoid all these things by joining us.*

1981, The Last Annual Vol State Road Race

The genesis for this event, like so many of his ideas, came from his own experience. In October 1980 he had tried to run across Tennessee, over 100 miles from Alabama to Kentucky. All he took with him was some cash so he could buy food and drink along the way, hoping desperately that he would get to the next store before he got too thirsty. He ran 64 miles in twelve hours, motivated by his desire to get to a bar to watch a football game. After Texas beat Oklahoma 20-13, he continued until his 93rd mile, when a freezing rainstorm led him to finish early.

Hooked on the freedom and adventure of the quest-like run, 'journey runs' like this soon became an annual tradition, often with friends in tow. And if it was this much fun for Gary and his friends, surely, he thought, others would be interested too.

In July 1981, Gary launched what was first called the Cross-Tennessee Race. He charged only 25 cents to enter. The price may have appeared cheap, but all they got for their fee were course directions and starting line information. No prizes, aid, or finish line spectators. For the first year, runners went from Knoxville to Nashville. In 1983 it took runners from the Alabama border in the south, north up across Tennessee, passing through Fayetteville, Shelbyville, Murfreesboro and Lebanon, before finishing on the Kentucky border. In the 1983 and 1984 editions, only three people finished. In 1984, Gary completed it himself, giving himself a perfect record of participating in events that he had organised. It would be his last outing in his own races, though, until the much later Race for the Ages.

After 1984, the race was given its current title: the Last Annual Vol State Road Race. The name was another insider reference; 'Vol State' stood for Volunteer State, a nickname of Tennessee. As for the 'Last Annual', evidently Gary had scoffed at the tendency of wannabe race directors calling their inaugural events 'The First Annual …' as if they could predict or guarantee its success and continuation. Wanting to buck the trend, as always, he called his first event the Last Annual, and the name stuck. In the early years, the race changed course each time, so technically, each event was the last annual. The winner of the event would be lauded as King of the Road.

Over the years the course kept changing, and the distance kept increasing, until it officially settled on a pythagorian 314 miles or 500 km. From 2006 on, runners would begin their adventure on the ferry in Dorena, Missouri, crossing the Mississippi River into Hickman, Kentucky. After cutting across the southwest corner of the state, runners would move into Tennessee, which they would spend most of ten days crossing diagonally. They would finish in their fourth state at Castle Rock, on Sand Mountain, just over the border into Georgia.

Unlike in most other races, but true to Gary's form, participants would have no external support. There would be no aid stations, no pacers, no friendly volunteers, apart from those who picked them up when they quit. Runners, or walkers more often, were responsible for themselves. They might bump into other participants along the way, friends could follow their progress, and they would have to check in twice electronically each day. But apart from that, all their basic needs were self-provided. They would carry or acquire any food or drink themselves.

Accommodation could be a fancy hotel, a noisy motel, or even as basic as a park bench.

As the race progressed, participants found that non-runners along the way found out about the adventure and began offering assistance. Some would leave out portable coolers with food, chairs to rest in, even fold-out stretchers for naps. A few of these Vol State Angels, as they came to be called, took matters further, gifting runners with hot showers, warm meals and laundry services.

Other participants choose to enter the race as 'crewed', as opposed to 'uncrewed' or in Gary's vernacular, 'screwed'. The crewed could have their friends meet them along the way and offer food and other needs. Gary later lamented that he knew many who considered themselves screwed would still surreptitiously have friends lie in wait with sustenance. Despite knowing people were abusing the freedom of the format, he still preferred not to enforce the rules. In his words, *that is pathetic …missing out on the fun of doing it yourself is punishment enough.*

1981, The Idiots' Run
Only months later, Gary finally organised a race called the Idiots' Run, once again in Shelbyville. At 76 miles it was almost double the length of the Strolling Jim 40 and offered the bonus of even more hills: 37 of them. Of the twelve who turned up to race the inaugural event on 6 September 1981, only five finished, with Jay Birmingham winning in 12:22:13.

Although Gary was surprised even twelve had entered, he tweaked the race the following year to make it harder again. At 108.6 miles, it was the length of four marathons, and somehow, he managed to make it even hillier than before.

The Ultrarunning History podcast recorded Gary explaining
> *this is the single grimmest race held anywhere in the world. … The course is an almost continuous string of steep and treacherous hills, and if we've had rain the week of the run, there will be as many as 18 creeks and rivers to cross. We'll be going through some wild country, and much of it after dark. A run like this can destroy you, and simply tear you down.*

This desire to push participants to their limits continued to attract some runners, but numbers remained intentionally low. Gary had no desire for a massive field, as he knew that only people of a certain calibre and experience would be able to handle the race. However, instead of following the standard elite ultramarathon route of having stringent speed-related selection criteria, he attempted a different approach. Potential runners, as part of their race application, had to explain why they were good enough to take part.

In 1982, only six of the twelve runners finished. In 1983, it was just two of five, while for the final event in 1984, there were four finishers from seven starters. For the last running, Gary joined in the fun, crossing the line in 40:16 with Jack Fabian, who achieved his third finish, the most of any competitor.

By then a trend had begun, whereby people who had appreciated Gary's earlier races started coming back for more punishment. In the first Idiots' Run, of the five finishers, only one, Doyle Carpenter, had braved one of Gary's races before. However, of the twelve who finished between 1982-1984 all but one had previously run at least the Strolling Jim 40 or Nick Marshall. The numbers were still low, and Gary was not yet receiving pervasive acclaim in the ultramarathon world, but a positive trend was beginning to emerge.

1986, The Barkley Marathons
A few years later, Gary launched what would propel him into the stratosphere of event directing royalty, the Barkley Marathons. Decades before Netflix introduced the world to Lazarus Lake, Gary Cantrell had created an event with few peers.

The Barkley Marathons drew on many features from his previous races. The event would combine the hills of Strolling Jim 40 and the Idiots' Run with the longer distances of the Nick Marshall and Vol State . As with the signs in Strolling Jim, Gary would specialise in taunting the runners. Like the Vol State, the entry price was absurdly cheap. Like the Idiots' Run, entrants had to justify their admission. And as with them all, but in a more extreme manner, runners would be encouraged to push themselves to their perceived limits, and well beyond.

The race itself was named after one of Gary's friends, Barry Barkley, who sadly passed away in 2019. Barry helped behind the scenes in many running events and ultramarathons, including providing chicken during his namesake race.

The legends of the race itself form part of its charm. Back in 1968, the internationally renowned Christian minister and civil rights trailblazer, Martin Luther King, Jr, was shot in Memphis. His assassin, James Earl Ray, was jailed in Brushy Mountain State Penitentiary, adjacent to Frozen Head State Park, Tennessee. In 1977 he famously escaped with six other convicts into the park. Although countless stories have said he was the first prisoner to escape the jail, he was but one of hundreds to do so. In fact, Ray himself had absconded from his cell twice before, in 1971 and 1972. It was the 1977 escape, though, which brought him national attention. Time magazine even featured Ray on their front cover with the headline 'The Escape'.

After 54.5 hours on the run, Ray was recaptured. He was lying down, his body covered with leaves, in a vain attempt to throw the sniffer dogs off his scent. In over two days on the run, he had only travelled about twelve miles, and was caught just eight miles from the prison. Part of the reason for the short distance was because the convict hid during the day to avoid searchers, but it was also due to the extreme terrain of Frozen Head.

In 1985, Gary and 'Raw Dog' Karl Henn went hiking, as they had done many times before, through the park in which Ray had spent so long going so short a distance. Gary had been intrigued by Ray's pathetic escape, and mused that he could have gone 100 miles in the same time. As the two hiked and talked, the idea of a new race was formed, inviting runners into the area that Ray had spent covering so little ground. The following year, Gary turned that spark of an idea into reality.

It's a good story, isn't it? If you've ever read about the Barkley, you're sure to have heard that it was inspired by Ray's escape. Like many good stories, though, it's nonsense. Gary first hiked the trails there back in 1973, when it was known as Morgan Forest, and saw the trails on the map. He did comment after the 1977 escape that he could have made 100 miles in that time, but there was no inspiration from the failed attempt. As Karl and Gary hiked the forest's loop in 1985, they started to plan a race that could be held there, which would begin the following year. This was no escape re-enactment, but a unique running challenge.

Although for the first few years it employed three loops, now the Barkley Marathons invites runners to complete five loops of a rugged, mountainous, and heavily forested course in Frozen Head State Park. In theory, each loop is 20 miles long, but the actual distance is unknown. Many runners swear the loops are closer to 26 miles, which — if accurate — means each loop is the equivalent of a marathon, and the total 130 miles. Whatever the truth, runners are asked to complete something like five marathons, hence the name being the Barkley *Marathons*, plural.

When most people think of a marathon, what springs to mind is a flat, road-based course, with cheering spectators, aid stations every few miles, and a high chance of finishing. Think again.

Each loop of the Barkley pushes the runners up thirteen savage climbs, with a total of 12,000 feet, or 3.6 km, of climbing per loop. Anyone who finishes will have climbed the equivalent of Mount Everest, twice. By comparison, the Hardrock 100 Mile Endurance Run, renowned for its elevation, only asks 33,000 feet of runners in total. Complete five loops of the Barkley and you're around 60,000. However, all such elevation and distance measurements are estimates, as the course changes each year and GPS measurement is banned. It's that lack of measuring that allows runners to argue that the course must be longer than advertised, or longer than in previous years. Gary suggests the course being harder and longer is *just what the runners like to say. Do you want to admit that it took you 17 hours to do 20 miles*?

The running world is often perceived to be split into two camps. There are the road runners, those who frequent fun runs and standard marathons on some form of smooth paved surface. And then there are the trail runners, who prefer to run, and sometimes walk, in the bush or forest. They traverse uneven trails that often include severely challenging hills but compensate by offering remarkable scenery. Although there is a lot of overlap between the camps, with some runners enjoying both forms, they are distinct.

The Barkley would fall on the trail running side, with not a paved surface to be seen. But at the same time, it's not quite a trail race either. There are trails out there, even some old dirt roads in places, and runners will use them when they can. But those dirt roads and trails are rough, with many being overgrown or abandoned. For much of the course, runners will be off-trail, fighting their way through the forest. Depending on the weather, the course may have tiny streams, waist-deep water crossings or paths so muddy they steal your shoes.

Trail runs are also known for their trail markers, coloured flags that help runners to know which way to turn mid-race. Sometimes the markers are stolen or moved by local troublemakers, and consequently, runners have been known to spend miles heading in the wrong direction. For the Barkley there are no such trail markers available for pranksters to disrupt the runners. In this event, it is the jovial race director who is the troublemaker. Rather than providing a clear path for runners to follow, he hides a number of books on the course. Only hours before the race starts, Gary provides a course map with directions showing where these books are located. Runners then need to copy the directions and locations onto their own maps.

When they finally find one of the books, if they indeed manage to, the runners then remove the page from the book that corresponds to their race bib number. When they come back to the start/finish point at the end of each loop, they hand over their collection of pages. Runner 23 would, hopefully, have found around a dozen books, and would now be clinging to a dozen pieces of paper all numbered page 23. At the start of the next loop, runners are given a new bib, so on that loop, they have to collect a different series of page numbers.

The navigational skill involved here is not standard in trail races, let alone road runs. In longer, more arduous trail runs, competitors might be expected to take a map with them, just in case something goes wrong.

But to have no race markers to follow, and need their own map and compass puts this event into a new category.

Those from an orienteering background will have some head-start here due to their advanced map and compass-reading skills. However, the average orienteering event takes less than an hour to complete, and for the Barkley, runners have up to sixty hours.

Rogainers may have some advantage, as the lesser-known sport of rogaining is a longer-distance navigational challenge. Teams of two to five people are given a map with a series of checkpoints marked on it. After being given an hour or two to plan their route, the teams head out simultaneously in an attempt to find as many checkpoints as they can in up to 24 hours. As they are responsible for choosing which checkpoints to search for, they head off in different directions, with no two groups taking the exact same route.

In the Barkley, though, competitors have a much longer distance to traverse, more treacherous terrain to cover, and are often alone while trying to find those elusive books. What may make it even more difficult than orienteering and rogaining is that runners don't have the freedom to select whatever path they choose between books. There are specific directions to follow, and failing to follow them risks disqualification. It is this extreme, unparalleled difficulty that gives the race its mystique and leads to so many disaster stories.

Runners have a strict cut-off of sixty hours to run the 100 miles, or 130 miles, or whatever the real number is. However, most will never complete the five loops. In fact, the first full five-loop completion was not until Mark Williams in 1995. Even then he had little margin, finishing in 59:28:48, with just over 31 minutes to spare.

Of the well over 1,000 entrants over the years, by the end of the 2022 event, runners had only ever completed the five loops eighteen times, this by twelve different people. With 32 editions of the five-loop version of the Barkley by then, it was a low success rate, about one finisher every two years, none at all from 2018-2022. The last two years, though, have seen a massive increase in success. Three finished in 2023, and an incredible five in 2024, with three of those repeat finishers. Even with that surge in completion, there are still only a total of 20 finishers and 26 finishes by 2024. If you add a win from the original shorter course, it becomes 21 finishers, and 27 finishes from 37 events.

The difference between the number of finish-ers, and the number of finish-es, is because three finishers have multiple finishes. One finisher, John Kelly has so far managed three finishes, in 2017, 2023 and 2024, coming first once and second twice. Jared Campbell tops the leader board for finishes with four, in 2012, 2014, 2016 and 2024, with a second place, two firsts and a third. Brett Maune is the only back-to-back winner, finishing and winning in both 2011 and 2012. In 2012 he finished almost four hours ahead of Jared Campbell, in 52:03:08, three hours faster than the previous course record. Since 2012, no runner has finished within five and a half hours of Maune's time.

The first event finisher was 'Frozen' Ed Furtaw Jr, completing the third edition of the Marathon in 1988. His win came in the original three-loop era, a 55-mile event with a 36-hour time limit. Another runner had finished before Ed, but due to some course-cutting, was disqualified, and Ed became the first champion. Seeing Ed's success, Gary then adjusted the course parameters, introducing the current five loops. It was then another seven years until Mark Williams finished the new course.

With so few finishing, most starters know that they have a low chance of getting to the end. Given the conditions, even completing one loop is a massive achievement. If you manage to finish three loops in under forty hours you are declared to have completed a 'fun run', a satirical use of the term if there ever was one. Of the 38 years the event has been held – with a gap in 2020 due to Covid restrictions – the fun run has been completed 175 times. This means only just over one in five starters will finish it.

Whether they aim for a five-loop finish, 'fun run', single-loop completion, or just finding a single page, all entrants start the same way: not knowing what lies ahead.

It all begins with the entry process, itself shrouded in mystery. There is no website, no listing in running event calendars, no contact details provided for potential heroes to make inquiries. Runners have to work out by themselves, somehow or other, how to enter. Even the race date itself is not advertised. It is often near April Fool's Day, another joke on the competitors. The entry fee of $1.60 has remained unchanged for many years, although, in another break from standard race tradition, entrants must bring a vehicle license plate from their state and other random items, less as an entry fee and more as tribute.

When the application form is finally provided, runners are required to answer random questions or complete such tasks as: What is the most important vegetable group? What will be the 119th element on the periodic table? Explain the cause of the 'great unconformity'. Write the Gettysburg Address in Sawveh. What even number is not the result of two prime numbers? Who built the Khatt Shebib? If that's not enough, writing an essay is also a prerequisite, to show that runners have some understanding of the demands of the course.

Eventually, forty entrants are selected, and are told when the race will be. Even then, they are only given a rough possible start time, within a half-day period. This leads to uncomfortable situations of runners not sure whether to go to sleep beforehand, or whether to stay awake and alert before it all begins.

Finally, at a time Gary has known for the previous twelve months, he blows a conch shell. This signals that the runners have one hour until the start. After some last-minute preparation, nutrition, and agitation, they assemble at the yellow park entrance gate. No GPS devices, phones or runner watches are allowed. Everyone is given a cheap watch that does little more than tell the time. The runners carry all the food and much of the drink they will need for each loop, as the only 'aid stations' they will encounter are a few stashed jugs of water.

Gary greets the waiting competitors, for many, ready to attempt a race they have tried to enter for years. They know that just by being there they are part of an elite group, and that thousands of other runners would swap places with them in a heartbeat. Yet, at the same time, they know that unimaginable pain and peril await.

Gary's pre-race introduction is less of a safety briefing and more of a taunt: *This is your last chance to pull out. Make peace with your God!* When he decrees that it is time to start, rather than the more traditional bell, or firing of a starter's pistol, Gary lights a cigarette. Given the entrants are mostly health-obsessed, the irony adds to the amusement of it all.

And with that, they are off.

The race is kept small by intention, in part to minimise its environmental impact. Gary reckons that a year later, all traces of the previous event have disappeared. However, the limited numbers also suit the difficulty of the event, given that the average applicant, no matter how well prepared, inevitably gets pummelled by the course.

That pummelling of the competitors leads to a host of Barkley disaster stories. Perhaps the most agonising was that of Gary Robbins, a prolific ultramarathoner, race director and running blogger from Canada. In his first attempt, in 2016, he made it to the fifth loop, putting him into an elite group, and it looked like he might be able to finish the event on his first attempt. John Kelly and Jared Campbell were the only others who began the loop.

After finding his first two books easily enough, Robbins got lost looking for the third. He caught his toe and found himself with a face full of dirt. He lay there for five seconds, stunned. After two and a half hours he found the next book, but then wasted time going the wrong way towards the fourth. By now he was bleeding, had run out of water, and realised that he could not continue without more sleep than he had time for. Jared saw him, just as he was about to fall asleep, and encouraged him to keep trying for an epic first-attempt finish. Eventually he gave up the struggle and, five hours short of the cut-off time, persuaded two passers-by to take him back to camp.

In 2017, things got even worse. Again, Robbins got to the fifth loop. This time there was no getting lost searching for the books. He found all thirteen of them, and glory awaited him as the sixteenth finisher ever, probably with five minutes to spare. Unfortunately, with several miles to go, as he made his final descent, he didn't notice that he was heading south, rather than the intended east. Suddenly he hit a staircase, which was unheard of on the Barkley course. He had made a small mistake, but a disastrous one.

Checking his map, he realised his error and calculated that he had no valid way of finishing. Because runners have to follow the prescribed route, he could not take a direct path to the finish. But nor did he have time to climb the mountain again, descend on the correct eastern route and make it back before the sixty-hour cut-off. He decided the quickest and most exciting option was to aim to beat the deadline, albeit by the wrong route. He fought through the bush, crossed a raging 15-foot river, and pushed himself harder than ever to reach the finish line of the Barkley's fifth loop. This was a position few had been in before, including John Kelly, who had just become the fifteenth finisher.

To the shock of the eager crowd awaiting his return, Robbins arrived at the infamous yellow finishing gate, but from the wrong direction. Even more gut-wrenching, his time was sixty hours, zero minutes, and six seconds, agonisingly missing even his revised goal.

At the other end of the disaster-story spectrum comes Dan Baglione, the oldest competitor in the race's history. In 2005, at the age of 74, he attempted the Barkley. In ten hours on the course, he found the first book, but only the first. Undeterred, he entered again in 2006. Again, he found the first book, but again, no more. After his initial success, he soon found himself on the wrong trail, travelling too far in the wrong direction. When night came, his light stopped working, so he sat down on the mountainside to put fresh batteries into his flashlight. As he attempted the manoeuvre, the housing that held the bulb came loose, and he heard it sliding down the hill. He tried to continue, but slipped and dropped his water bottle that contained the last of his energy drink. By then his list of lost gear included the lightbulb housing, his energy drink bottle, his Gore-Tex hat and his compass.

He was then stuck for the night and tried to make himself comfortable by a tree, but the temperature had plunged. He tried to fight off hypothermia by continually moving his hands, arms and torso, which was not conducive to a good night's sleep. He nodded off for a few seconds here and there, but spent most of the night awake in a state of frustrated exhaustion. After 32 hours, eight of them huddled by a tree, he was at last rescued by some young men driving around the park. By then, the park rangers and other event finishers had been searching the course trying to find where Baglione had got to. It seems he had traversed well off the course map.

One of the race peculiarities is that officially distances covered are measured by the distance to the books found. Given that he had found the first book only, despite wandering for 32 hours, and clocking up who-knows-how-many miles, Dan was recorded as completing only two miles. This gave him the record both for oldest race starter, and slowest race pace, at sixteen hours per mile. For his effort, he was given the race shirt which advertised, 'Meaningless suffering without a point'. It matched well with his shirt from the previous year: 'Where your very best just isn't good enough'.

In between Gary Robbins and Dan Baglione were a host of other failures. With 24, Leonard Martin has the longest record of attempts at the race, his best effort being to finish two loops. He is notorious though for having a several-hundred-yard, mud and briar-filled 45-degree gradient on the course's east side named after him: Leonard's Butt-slide. The tale of this race feature's origin speaks for itself. Although Leonard is happy to re-tell this story to race newcomers, one suspects that the patronym for another race feature, Testicle Spectacle, would rather remain anonymous. Other named features include Rat Jaw, Needle's Eye, Zipline, Bobcat Rock and the ominous Big Hell.

Blake Wood and David Horton joined the 'should have finished' club in 2001. Both had impressive ultrarunning resumés. David was on his second attempt of an eventual three, Blake his fifth of eight. They ran mostly together, both finishing in 58:21, almost two hours under the cut-off. In what felt like a tragedy, they were both disqualified for accidentally leaving the official course and following a parallel route for just 200 yards. To add insult to injury, the wrong section they took had been part of the course in previous years, that both had completed before.

Karel Sabbe was the third finisher in 2023, and the slowest finisher then recorded, with 59:53:33. After his experience the previous year, though, this was a stunning victory. In first place going on to the fourth loop in 2022, with Greig Hamilton the only other person on the course, he nailed the first six books. But soon he took a wrong turn and became unable to understand his map and compass. He hiked west, eventually realised his race was over, so kept on going to a nearby town. He was cold, well beyond exhaustion, so at 3 am he asked a woman he saw on the street for assistance. Somehow or other, she turned into a trash can, and he realised he was hallucinating. He tried to get several cars to pull over and help him, which only resulted in the police being called. Fortunately, the police officer had heard of the Barkley, and Sabbe was returned to the race in the back seat of a police car.

Somehow or other, these disaster stories don't discourage potential runners from wanting to sign up. In fact, it is this element of 'failure porn', the addictive nature of watching people desperately trying to overcome the course, but failing, that brings the event its allure.

A classic case of overcoming failure was seen in the 2024 event. Jasmin Paris had first attempted the Barkley in 2022 and had completed the fun run. She hadn't finished in enough time to start loop four, so had to stop. Gary had suggested, with one eye on motivating a generation of women to defy him, that he did not think it possible for a woman to finish, as according to various statistics, they were about 12% slower than men in ultramarathon events. Courtney Dauwalter had tried, but only made one loop. Maggie Guterl had three attempts, but never got past one.

When Jasmin tried again in 2023, many were hoping that she would become the first woman to finally complete the five loops. This time she made it out onto the fourth, only the second woman to do so, and the first woman to complete the fun run twice. She found nine of the books before running out of time.

In 2024 she made her third attempt. She completed the fun run for an incredible third time. She then became the first female to complete the fourth loop, and despite vomiting and appearing to be at her limit of endurance, went on to the fifth. Over thirteen hours later, with only a few minutes until the 60-hour cut-off, four runners having already finished the five loops, beating the previous record of three, hopes for Jasmin had faded. The maths wasn't on her side.

Suddenly, she is spotted off in the distance, and the cry goes up: *Runner!* A mesmerised crowd watches as the exhausted athlete runs strongly up the final incline towards the yellow gate. She reaches the gate and does not just touch it; she drapes her body over it in a combination of triumph and collapse. She falls to the ground, while photographers race up to take shots which will go viral and be celebrated around the world. Jasmin's time for the five loops was 59:58:21, coming in with only 99 seconds to spare. Officially she now had the closest finishing time to the cutoff in history, but more importantly, was the first female finisher. Gary, and much of the world, were elated.

2014, The Barkley Fall Classic
Over the years, as the popularity of the Barkley Marathons grew, more and more people wanted to try their hand at it. One strategy to deal with all that pent-up demand was to create another event, the Barkley Fall

Classic, which Gary did with the help of his friend Steve Durbin. From September 2014 onwards, this would give runners a chance to dip their toe into the waters of the full Barkley experience, without the massive distance, steep cut-off times and limited field of only forty starters.

It does retain, however, much of what was challenging about the original event. The course map itself is not revealed until the night before, and it takes runners on steep climbs that make up part of the famous course. Runners are given a taste of both the Barkley Marathons and James Earl Ray's escape route. Although it is 'only' a 50 km event, the elevation ensures it remains a challenging run, and offers runners the sight of spectacular scenery, assuming that they can lift their heads up to enjoy it.

Again, no GPS, pacers, support crew or trekking poles are allowed. Runners need to follow race directions on a map, rather than be guided by trail markers. It still begins with a cigarette, but rather than only forty starters, 500 runners are ready for action. However, even with the higher numbers, a lottery is used to allocate entries from a waiting list of over 1,000 people.

Although the event is called a 50 k, again the true course length is unknown. Some speculate that it is up to 40 miles. Runners are also given the option of finishing after completing the traditional marathon distance of 26 miles, rather than the full course. At the 25-mile mark, the course takes runners within a mile of the finish line before heading further away again. They are then given the opportunity to take a shortcut back and complete 'just' the marathon distance. For those who venture on to the full course, once they pass that decision point, they cannot change their minds. If they pull out at any stage after that they are given a Did Not Finish, not a marathon completion. To receive such a DNF, as they are commonly called by runners, would not be pleasant, so they will only continue if they are confident of getting to the finish line.

For those at the faster end of the field, the race offers another potential attraction. Not only does it allow an easier and more accessible experience of the Barkley Marathons course, it offers an almost otherwise unattainable guaranteed entry to the event's bigger brother. For many, this is reason enough to take the Fall Classic seriously.

2015, A Race for the Ages
The following year, Gary's creative juices led in a new direction. This time, he created an event that suited the demographic trends in ultrarunning. Although most people hit a physical peak in their twenties, in ultramarathons, often the majority of the field will be in their thirties, forties and much older. Given that so much of ultrarunning is a mind

game, with accumulated knowledge and wisdom playing large roles, having high-performing older athletes makes sense. Despite these factors, there is an undeniable physical deterioration which eventually occurs in aging bodies. That deterioration might go faster or slower, and start later or earlier, but the trend is clear.

To level the playing field for the waves of older ultrarunners, Gary invented a race that offered them an advantage. The race itself is simple; the winner is the person who does the most one-mile laps of Fred Deadman Park in Manchester, Tennessee. The innovation, though, is that runners are given the same number of hours to complete as their age in years. A centenarian, for example, would have 100 hours to accumulate their miles. A 99-year-old would start one hour later, finish at the same time as the centenarian, and would, therefore, have one hour less of running time. When they hit forty hours to go, all the young'uns are given their chance, and everyone aged forty and under start their runs.

In the first year, 2015, 163 competitors trialled the new format. The average distance covered was 98 miles. The winner, aged 49, accumulated 200 miles in his 49 hours. This was Joe Fejes, who had been prominent in early Backyards Ultras, and so far is the only winner in the event's history to be aged under fifty. As you would expect with such an advantage, in most years it is the older runners who dominate. Of the nine events to 2023, only three winners have been under sixty. Bob Becker holds the course records from his 2019 win, when he claimed not just the furthest distance ever, with 230 miles, but also, at age 74, was the oldest winner.

2020, Great Virtual Run Across Tennessee

Despite it appearing in the race's title, this was the first of Gary's events not to require participants to travel to his home state. It was also his longest. This was an event that was born out of necessity, the Covid-inspired lockdowns that swept the world in early 2020. With trail and road races being cancelled everywhere he looked, Gary wanted to provide some way to get people out running, competing and enjoying life, rather than being trapped at home. With Steve Durbin, he developed an event that would invite participants to virtually travel across Tennessee. Given that they couldn't physically run that route, participants would run wherever they could, logging their distances online. If they were in Poland and ran five miles on May 1st, the day the event began, they would record that data. Runners in Kenya would log their runs, as would those in Peru, New Zealand and all around the world. Gary thought that he might get 200 runners, if he was lucky. By the time the race began, over 19,000 had signed up.

Their goal was to run the equivalent of crossing Tennessee in four months, from the start of May to the end of August. It was called a 1,000 km race, however, the rules stated that runners needed to record 1,022 km, which would cover the distance across Tennessee. This led to some runners stopping after 1,000 km, thinking that they had finished, still virtually 22 km short of the state border.

Many runners took it as a serious challenge, running whenever they could and accumulating massive totals. Some started strong and then dropped out, but overall, the participation level remained high. Some even signed up for a double challenge, running from one side of Tennessee to the other, and back again.

Although the runners did not physically cross Tennessee, they did reap the traditional race rewards. Somehow, Gary managed a logistical nightmare in arranging for finishers' shirts and medals to be sent out worldwide to the deserving thousands.

2020, The Last Annual Heart of the South

Starting only a month later in June, but finishing almost three months before the virtual race across Tennessee ended, this event began when there were registration problems with the Last Annual Vol State Road Race. Something had gone wrong with the Vol State booking process, allowing far too many people to register. With Gary forced to offer an alternative, The Last Annual Heart of the South was born. It would be a similar race to Vol State, with competitors having up to ten days to get to Sand Mountain. In this version, there would be no support at all, and the course itself changes each year. Competitors are kept in the dark about where they will start until the night before; and only then do they find out what route they must traverse to get to Sand Mountain. This uncertainty means that bending the rules by sending crew to offer support in secret is harder to engineer.

The day before the race, all competitors board a bus at Sand Mountain. The bus then travels the 300 to 350 miles of the course route. This allows the runners to see, out the windows, every hill, every long stretch between towns, every section of sun-absorbing bitumen that they will endure in the June sun. It allows them to make plans, such as where to buy food, where to sleep, where to seek occasional shelter. It also allows their pre-race fears to escalate, as they are confronted with the enormity of what they are about to begin.

In the first running, 49 of the 66 starters made it back to Sand Mountain before the ten-day cut-off. Diane Taylor was closest to missing out, finishing in nine days, 21 hours, 18 minutes and 27 seconds, with almost three hours to spare. At the other end was the husband-and-wife team,

Bev Anderson-Abbs and Alan Abbs. They ran together, enduring blisters, storms and navigation difficulties for almost five days. With three miles to go, the heavens opened, and they were absolutely drenched. The last mile was mostly slippery mud, slowing them even further.

Still, it only took Bev four days, 23 hours, 37 minutes and 30 seconds to complete the 340 miles. Bev and Alan got to the end together, but with the finishing rock being on the edge of a cliff, for reasons of safety, Gary would only allow one of them to approach it at a time. Not only did Bev get to win overall, she beat her husband, Alan, who was only able to touch the rock fifteen seconds later, seven hours ahead of third place.

Bev provided some interesting details about how the competitors, or at least those who would win, handled the various stops along the way. She explained that when she and Alan would get to a hotel, they would only be there for two hours. One of them would shower and rinse out clothes, which by then were not suitable for polite company, while the other would prepare food. Then they would switch, finishing off the food and doing their own cleansing. Fifteen minutes after arriving, they would be lying on the bed, feet elevated on pillows, and ready to fall asleep. After an hour and a half of hopefully quality sleep, they would be back out on the road.

Given that the winner of Vol State was called the King of the Road, after Bev's victory, Gary cheekily inquired of her what she would like the winner of this event to be named. She chose the similarly gender-specific Queen of the South. Subsequently, the male winners of 2021, 2022 and 2023 were honoured to be awarded that title.

2020, Circumpolar Race Around the World

Even Before the Great Virtual Run Across Tennessee finished, Gary and Steve Durbin were at it again. If that many people enjoyed running across Tennessee virtually, why not let them go around the entire world? This time people would form teams of ten, and together would race virtually across twelve pre-defined regions of the planet. They would not be restricted to running and walking either. For this event, teams could also ride, ski, skate, paddle, or use any other method so long as it was human-powered.

Entry would cost $40 per region per runner, up to $480 for anyone wanting to do all regions. The organisers promised to provide whatever passports, visas, international flights, ferries and even smuggling that was required. When an event is virtual, promises are easier to keep.

They applied a subversive methodology to mapping and geography, not using the standard circumnavigation defined by an east-to-west lap. Participants would start at the USA/Mexico border and travel to the southern tip of South America. A plane would 'take' them to Antarctica and the South Pole, before another flight to Australia. After crossing the continent south to north, they would then use planes and ferries to island-hop across Southeast Asia to Singapore. The route then took them through Pakistan, Ukraine, and Scandinavia, before flying them across the North Pole to Alaska. The final leg would take them south through Canada and the USA back to the start. Their innovative approach defied the common logic of a globe defined by standard maps, but it was certainly efficient.

Starting 1 September 2020, they would have up to two years to accumulate the 30,167 miles or 48,550 km required. Four years, and almost 54,000 participants later, people are still participating in the virtual event all around the world.

2023, The Last Annual Circle of Hell
The most recent addition to Gary's voluminous race direction resumé came in August 2023. This was another journey run, similar to both The Last Annual Vol State Road Race and The Last Annual Heart of the South. In fact, the only way to gain entry into this diabolic race was to complete both of the other two cross-Tennessee events.

This race was described as a graduate-level journey run. Participants were given the map several months in advance, so they could see which of the remote Tennessee roads they would take, which steep mountains they would climb, and begin to plan where they would access their resources along the way. The event attracted 25 starters, 21 of them coming in under the ten-day time limit. Jim Winn lived up to his name, finishing in 5 days, 22 hours, 30 minutes and 59 seconds.

2011, Backyard Ultras
If you're an observant reader, you may have noticed a convenient blip in the narrative where a race was skipped over. In 2011, Gary introduced the world to his greatest creation, the Backyard Ultra. Before explaining the origin of this event, there is another character to introduce: Big.

2

The Birth of the Backyard

BEFORE HE DIED in February 2023, a red, 100-pound, pit bull would attend every edition of the Backyard Ultra World Championships in Bell Buckle, Tennessee. His huge brown eyes would see each of the competitors go through their preparations, or just as often, ignore them all as he sat under the scoring table. He'd wonder who these strangers were, and why they were visiting his place. Each of the runners was indeed visiting the dog's property, and he was right, they were his visitors. The animal's name was Big, and in later years he was joined by a Jack Russell, appropriately named Little.

By the time Gary was planning his first Backyard event, he was known widely as Lazarus Lake. As with his own moniker, he wanted an eccentric name for the race. As with several previous events, he named it after someone he had affection for. And so Big's Backyard Ultra was born.

Big himself had a rough start to life. He had been abandoned by previous owners, shot, and left to die. The pit bull had crawled off into the Tennessee woods in agony, where Gary found him on his property while out for one of his regular walks. He'd been taught when young that you shouldn't let animals suffer, so brought the injured dog into his house to ease its pain and allow it to die in peace. Instead, the dog recovered, and Gary tried to find a new home for him. Soon enough, the dog came back to Gary. He tried again, and the dog kept on coming back, sometimes travelling huge distances to return.

Eventually, Gary realised that the dog was his, and accepted him as part of the family. For a time, he was referred to as just 'that big dog'. Soon he became 'the Big Dog' or often just 'Big'. Similarly, the key Backyard race would be called Big Dog's Backyard Ultra World Individual Championship, Big's Backyard Ultra, or even just Big's. This was part of the race's charm, that runners were not visiting some sterile race precinct, instead literally running around the backyard of a dog.

The property may belong to Gary and his wife Sandra, but Big and Little roamed freely around their domain. Gary built the walls and steps from stone himself, learning the skills of masonry as a rehabilitation exercise after a back injury. He also made trails in the woods to walk, and now, for ultramarathoners from around the world to test themselves on. He even designed a room on the second floor of his house for athletes to sleep in.

In theory, Gary was the one who rescued the pit bull, but he has often said that truly it was Big who rescued him, teaching him about perseverance, loyalty, affection, gratefulness and how never, ever to give up. *Best dog you can imagine*, says Gary.

There is delicious irony too in the Backyard Ultra format itself. With the way athletes push themselves past any previously known limits, Gary noted in a 2015 race update that *if we did this to dogs, they would throw us in jail*. Yet, in his 2011 Ultrarunning Magazine report on the inaugural Backyard, he noted that, in contrast to the illegal sport of dog fighting, *it seemed somehow appropriate that a pit bull should host an event where humans fight to the death*. It was poetic justice.

Of course, although Big Dog may have been the race's guardian and namesake, it was Gary who developed it. The first backyard was only in 2011, but the genesis of the race was in the early 1970s when the young Gary Cantrell was running track and cross country at high school. Although he had the occasional success, and showed significant talent as a runner, he knew even then that he was never going to be one of the fastest. What he did have, though, was the capacity to persevere, to endure punishment beyond most people's limits, and most importantly, to enjoy it.

Back then, before there was a Lazarus Lake, Gary dreamed of an event that would push runners to cover huge distances, but with no need for high speeds. It would be a pure test of stamina; whoever could endure the most would win. It would be open-ended, with nothing making the runners stop except their own limitations. It wouldn't need a massive course, as laps of around four miles would allow the distance to be accumulated easily enough. He didn't yet have Big Dog, nor a suitable backyard, but nevertheless, the seed was planted in those high school years for Big Dog's Backyard Ultra.

Over the years there has been speculation about the influence of novelist Stephen King. Back in 1979 King published his seventh book, The Long Walk, his second writing under the pseudonym of Richard Bachman. The thriller was set in an alternate, dystopian America, and bore some similarities to Philip K. Dick's 1962 novel The Man in the High Castle, as well as having elements which anticipated Suzanne Collins' 2008 The Hunger Games.

Each year a totalitarian military government selects 100 teenage boys at random from a massive pool of applicants to walk up to 450 miles. It is both a form of entertainment and a method of controlling the population, giving them a slim hope of improving their situation.

The boys must walk at a constant, difficult-to-maintain pace of four miles per hour, not much below the Backyard's 4.167 miles. The walk, and the teenagers, cannot stop until there is only one left. When the walkers cannot maintain the pace they are given a warning. After three warnings they are shot, making it literally a last man standing event. That last living teenager wins a large cash reward and the promise of being given whatever they want for the rest of their lives.

Huge crowds gather to watch the death-sport, but crowd members are forbidden to offer any assistance to the walkers. The contestants can bring whatever supplies they want to sustain themselves and are allowed to help one another. The walkers must never stop, not even for inclement weather.

The book became a national bestseller and is regarded as one of King's best novels. As recently as 28 November 2023, New Line Cinema announced that Francis Lawrence, who directed all but the first of the Hunger Games films, would make a film adaptation.

The similarities with the Backyard Ultra are obvious. The limited numbers, having to sustain a pace of about four miles per hour, only one person left at the end, no assistance from the crowd, bringing your own supplies. Those similarities raise an interesting question: was it really Stephen King who invented the Backyard?

However, the differences are also clear. Backyard Ultras are regarded as running events, despite walking being a common practice. The difference in distance might be small between the two, but it is still enough that most people cannot walk multiple Backyard laps without running. King's novel has contestants walking non-stop, having to sustain four miles per hour as a continual pace. Gary's race allows runners to go at any pace, as long as the required mileage is completed per hour. Unlike The Long Walk, most Backyards have zero prize money and, despite Big Dog enjoying the humans battling each other, there is strictly no killing of contestants.

The psychological drama is different too. There are certain races where the slowest runners are removed until there is only one winner. For the Backyard, though, participants will mostly quit voluntarily when they decide that they cannot continue or conclude that they've had enough. Almost all will later regret their decision and say that they could have gone further. The Long Walk, by contrast, has compulsory elimination, while the rewards for winning and consequences of quitting prevent most from giving up.

Similarly, although the crowd cannot assist the walkers, in Backyards each runner will have crew members who offer pivotal assistance. During a lap, they are banned from helping, but in between laps they can support their runner in whatever way is required.

The ability to rest without being shot may be the biggest difference between the two. In Backyards, competitors can rest anywhere between a few seconds and half an hour. During this time, they might sleep, eat, drink, enjoy massages, chat with the crew, or do whatever else they prefer. In The Long Walk, the four mile per hour pace has to be kept up in every two-minute block of time, giving no opportunity to rest. Walkers survive, supposedly, by occasionally walking in their sleep.

Gary had read the book, but says he had forgotten it by the time the Backyard was born. He told me in our interview that, having read it again, King *captures the mood and atmosphere of multi-day races well.*

The date of publication may settle the issue. King published his book in 1979, 32 years before the first Backyard Ultra. However, as mentioned above, it was in the early 1970s that Gary came up with his rough idea for his race. Yet the King-inspired-the-Backyard theory has another twist: although it was his seventh book published, it was his first written, the author completing the draft manuscript in 1966-67 while still an English college major. Could a young Gary have met King and read the draft manuscript? That's unlikely. Far more plausible is that the long-forgotten novel was one of the countless subconscious influences that led to the race's development, building on the foundation of those high school dreams.

Regardless of King's influence, it's fascinating that there was a forty-year period between Gary developing his crazy idea and its implementation in 2011 by Lazarus Lake. Like the biblical Moses's forty years of preparation in Egypt, perhaps it took forty years for Gary to be prepared for his iconic race.

Gary had his first attempt at creating a Backyard-style race in 2010, not long after moving to a 100-acre property in Bell Buckle, Tennessee. Ultrarunning Magazine recorded the race results under the heading of 'Lazarus' Backyard Ultra', but it was not what is now regarded as a Backyard. The 2010 edition was an 11-hour timed event, where 24 participants sought to run as far as they could on the hastily crafted trails in Gary's backyard. Will Taggart took the win with 61 miles, while Gary's son Case Cantrell ran well for eighth place and 40 miles. Leonard

Martin, of Barkley Butt-slide fame, ran for 33.5 miles. Also present, and with each completing 31 miles, were Carl Laniak, Mike Dobies, Mike Melton, Naresh Kumar, and Steve Durbin, each of whom would play prominent roles in organising future races.

With the limited resources on his property, Gary reflected on the merits of that 2010 race and considered what could be done to make for a good ultra on his property. It was from those ruminations, building on his high school dreams, that the final form of the Backyard was born.

There are other written hints about the creation of the Backyard Ultras. Not from Stephen King, but from Gary. Since 12 May, 1981, he has written 'From the South', later renamed 'View from the Open Road', a regular column for Ultrarunning Magazine. Read through these and you will discover a master wordsmith, a true storyteller who can take the reader with him on literary journeys. Read 'The Ultimate Aid Station' from July 2010, and you, too, will mourn the passing of the country stores of years past.

For those who have enjoyed Laz's social media commentary on Facebook, you will have noticed a distinctive lack of capitalisation, yet his writing remains readable, comprehensible and enjoyable. It is Laz's signature style. Not so Gary Cantrell, at least not in 'View from the Open Road'. Here the punctuation conforms to all the normal standards, and the readability, if anything, is even stronger.

In 2010, the year before Big's Backyard Ultra burst into the world, some articles gave a few clues as to Gary's thinking. In 'The Gauntlet', October 2010, he wrote of the necessity for hard work in training, and its link to our enjoyment of the sport:

> ... it is not always easy to see the fun when things become difficult. Always remember, the greater the effort, the greater the satisfaction and joy that is waiting on the other side.

With the benefit of hindsight, you can almost see the master organiser's mind at work. If greater effort leads to higher satisfaction and joy, then why not create a race that cranks up the difficulty?

In April 2010's 'Failure', Gary was lamenting the everyone-is-a-winner culture of youth sports where participation trophies replace merit awards and even keeping scores. He explained how failure was crucial to the development of athletes, and of people more generally. Yet by telling people who do not win, or worse, receive a Did Not Finish, that this is not a failure, well-meaning parents and coaches deprive competitors of having a measure of what success is. Without failure, there can be no success.

Instead, Gary advocated for coaches to

teach the youngsters about failure and success ... the joy of overcoming adversity ... acknowledging the failure, while expressing our belief that they are capable of finishing.

Again, there is a foreshadowing of the Backyard Ultras. If failure is a learning opportunity, and DNFs are helpful measuring tools on the path to success, then why not develop a race where almost everyone will get a DNF?

Not much earlier, in Jan/Feb 2009, he wrote 'One Day Out of Your Life'. In this column he explained that completing 100 miles in 24 hours was, for runners, a magical and compelling numerical achievement. It was akin to the ten-second hundred metres, a four-minute mile or three-hour marathon. Where the 24-hour miler differed, according to Gary, was that almost anyone could achieve it if they put in appropriate training and applied a healthy race strategy. This assumption would soon lie at the heart of the Backyard, where every 24 hours athletes would accumulate 100 miles, without the event being out of most starters' reach.

He also noted that such 24-hour milers should keep rest times to a minimum, as *any extended break will require some recovery time before you can get back into a running groove*. He advocated no more than five-minute breaks at a time and that, if needed, five minutes of sleep will suffice to rejuvenate you. Perhaps he was laying the groundwork for the strategy that would be needed for the Backyard.

It was in 2011 that Gary retired as Shelbyville's City Treasurer, giving him more free time for creative thinking and race directing, arguably his true calling. By then, he and Sandra had their Bell Buckle property equipped with sufficient trails for multiple options for a 4.167-mile race. The Barkley Marathons documentary (2012) had not been made, so his broader fame was yet to come, but years of organising a bevy of fascinating races had established his credibility as a race director, and developed his skills to a point where he could again experiment with something new. And although friends still called him Gary, increasingly he was now known as Laz, or Lazarus Lake.

The new event that Laz began was simple. Participants would attempt to complete laps of 4.167 miles or 6.7056 kilometres, no more, no less, and had one hour to finish each lap. Those laps, given that they were all run around his backyard, were called 'yards'. Someone who ran for twelve hours would be said to have done twelve yards.

At the one-hour mark, a cowbell would ring, telling the runners that they needed to begin the next lap. If they failed to complete the yard, or didn't start the next yard, they were eliminated, and the race continued until there was only one person left. Participation didn't require a fast pace or even high levels of fitness. For race organisers, the potential simplicity was a virtue. Armed with just a stopwatch, events could be put on almost anywhere that had a few runnable miles available.

For those who pursue their Backyard interests more seriously, it can be anything but simple. The format offers a potential world of complexity, psychological warfare, strategic planning and the opportunity for runners to go further than they had previously dreamed possible. Much further.

The rules are simple too. A whistle is blown three minutes before the start of the first yard. The competitors are then brought up to the start line, and the race director will typically use a can of spray paint to mark the perimeter of the starting corral around the runners. The idea is to create a defined area that all competitors must fit into at the beginning of each hour, and this becomes the area they must get into before the yard starts. The first event I participated in had only 21 participants, while one at the same venue the following year had 243, and the corral is meant to be just big enough for however many runners are there.

A minute later, the two-minute warning is blown. Another sixty seconds and it's the one-minute warning. More often than not, the race director will blow three times for the three-minute warning, twice at two minutes, and once for one minute. A verbal warning comes at thirty seconds, twenty seconds, ten seconds, nine, eight, … three, two, one – and they're off!

Hopefully. At the designated start time, the race director vigorously rings a cowbell. If a competitor is not in the starting corral at this time they are removed from the race and don't even get to start.

Those who are assembled in the corral then run, or as is often the case, walk, stumble or shuffle off, seeking to complete one yard. Once they head out, they are bound by a series of strict rules. These were established from the first event in 2011, but not codified until 2019. To be an official Backyard Ultra, a race has to be open-ended, with no maximum limit to how far runners can go. Slower runners need to give way to faster competitors, allowing them to pass by. In the narrower, 'single track' sections, only wide enough for one runner at a time, this is often useful. On pain of removal from the race, runners may not leave the course, with the single exception of visiting the restroom, until the lap is over.

No non-competitors are allowed on the course itself, including friends, support crew, eliminated runners, and most particularly, any pacers, although some events will have official aid stations mid-lap. This is part of the general prohibition against any external assistance being offered to runners out on the course, which is taken seriously. Runners are not even allowed to have trekking poles, which are common in ultramarathons. The courses do tend to be flatter, though, so most would not use them even if permitted. There is no 'personal aid' allowed during the lap, so — apart from the occasional cheering — supporters or crew cannot offer drinks, food or other assistance mid-lap. However, fellow competitors are permitted, and in fact encouraged, to assist one another throughout.

In the break between yards, the restrictions on assistance and leaving the course do not apply. Most runners will have a dedicated support crew who swing into action, assisting them through the event. For them too, it will be an endurance challenge.

At the end of each lap, the first thing competitors do is go to their own personal space. Most will set up a tent or gazebo for their private use beforehand, hopefully erecting it close to the starting point. The further away it is from the start, the greater distance they have to walk between the loops. If the runner's camp is 150 metres from the start, a 6.7056 km loop can become seven km from walking there and back.

Inside these runners' camps can be all kinds of equipment. Most will have a chair to sit on, some with a reclining feature so they can lie down and put their legs up while resting. All will have supplies of food and drink to replenish their energy. Portable coolers are often filled with ice. Changes of clothing and footwear, plans for each lap, medical supplies, massage equipment, and much more are also present. Some competitors will have curtains for privacy and darkened areas for sleeping, while others will be much more exposed to the elements. Occasionally, race organisers will provide indoor facilities, lowering concerns about the weather for both runners and their long-suffering crews.

The laps themselves come in several different shapes. They can be a single loop, where you leave in one direction and come back from the other, an out-and-back circuit, or more complicated configurations where the runners traverse multiple smaller loops and occasionally come back past the start before the end of each lap.

Some courses are dead flat, with almost no change in elevation throughout, usually on a smooth path or road. Others are more treacherous, with hills, uneven ground, gravel, tree roots, mud and other occasional obstacles to overcome. Temperature variations can be severe, with athletes experiencing both ice and sweltering heat in the same event. Some events have excellent support facilities, with running water, multiple bathrooms and ample shelter for all. Others are in more rustic settings, with portable toilets, and runners required to supply their own water and shelter.

What doesn't vary about the laps, though, is the length. Each yard, in every race, whether in Finland, Venezuela or Saudi Arabia, is an exact 4 miles 880 feet, 4.167 miles, or 6.7056 km in length. It's an obscure and head-scratching distance, whether in miles or kilometres. That said, if you measure it in feet, you do get a more normal-looking number: 22,000.

However you measure it, the runners all head out onto the lap, and they all begin with one goal. They must, at peril of disqualification, complete the lap within a one-hour period. If they are not back in the starting corral by the time the whistle is blown to start the next lap, they are officially declared a DNF: Did Not Finish.

Of course, it's not that hard to run just over four miles or almost seven kilometres in an hour. In the late Kelvin Kiptum's 2:00:35 world record at the 2023 Chicago Marathon, he ran at a pace of 4:36 minutes per mile, or 2:52 mins/km. That's 13.04 miles, or 20.98 km per hour. To complete the Backyard Ultra yard in the required hour, the required pace is a more achievable 4.167 mph or 6.7056 kph. Measured in the more common runners' formula of minutes per distance, that's still only 14:24 minutes per mile or 8:57 minutes per km. That's literally less than a third of Kelvin's pace. If you think about the popular parkrun, the free, volunteer-run five km events, the pace required for a Backyard would mean one could be completed in 49:45 minutes. I've tried walking at that pace, and although it's not comfortable, it's doable.

Most times, at the end of the first hour, the same number of people who start the lap will finish it. It's not that hard. The problem begins, though, at the start of the next hour, when all the competitors assemble once again in the starting corral. It's a social time, with laughter, boasting, and encouragement. Once again, the runners hear the three whistles to signify three minutes before the start. At this stage, some of the slower runners, or people who have walked too much, may still be out on the course. A minute later comes another two whistle blasts, and the stragglers start coming in. Then the single whistle for one minute, and those who are desperate to finish their first lap are racing in. On the hour, the cowbell clangs, sending them all out for another lap. This next yard is still the same distance; it's still not that hard, except this time, the competitors have done one lap already. And although the average healthy person could, without any proper training, expect to pull off one lap in one hour, doing two back-to-back is trickier. And with each successive yard, it gets harder. And harder.

Depending on the event's conditions, the athlete's fitness and preparedness, and a heap of other variables, people start to drop off. Some won't make the second lap; some won't make the third. As the total distance covered gets further, and the time endured grows longer, the cumulative impact of the previous laps starts to take its toll. What was an easy pace for one yard starts to become unsustainable.

Even with those who don't get far, there are often great stories of accomplishment. I've seen people with disabilities push themselves to their limits and finish one yard. For them, it's a stunning victory. For many who get to three laps, a distance just shy of a half marathon, that will be the furthest they have ever gone. For others, getting to seven yards is special, as at that stage they may well have completed their first ultramarathon. Technically, an ultramarathon is any distance greater than a marathon, and completing seven laps gives you 29.2 miles or 46.9 km. That's something to talk about at work on Monday!

The next significant lap is the fifteenth. In many races, the majority will have finished by now. For those who are still going, this lap often has the highest number of dropouts. In my first Backyard Ultra, two-thirds of the field had dropped out before this point, and almost half of those remaining finished straight after their fifteenth. Why are there so many dropouts at the fifteen-lap mark, apart, of course, from the exhaustion of running all day? It might not mean as much in the imperial 62.5 miles, but in metric, completing 100.6 km is a big deal. For races that start at 9 am, you have until midnight to get to this distance, and there is a certain symmetry and a massive sense of accomplishment in running 100 km by the end of the day.

Beyond this monumental mark, some of the participants will still keep going. For those who persevere, the next significant yard is 24. Running for an entire day, with only limited breaks, is always going to be a big deal. But what makes the 24th yard special is that, at the completion of this lap, runners will have completed 100 miles, assuming the course has been measured correctly. In the vernacular of the ultrarunning community, any run of 100 miles is known as a 'miler', and completing one puts you into an elite category. Although ultramarathons are often in the vicinity of 50-100 km, completing a miler is regarded as an amazing accomplishment, one that few ultrarunners manage to achieve. To complete one in less than 24 hours is astonishing.

To put this in perspective, I looked at the recent results of some comparable ultramarathons in Brisbane, Australia, close to where I live. In 2021-23, AAA Racing ran their Butter 24 event three times. Competitors are set the task of running as many laps as they can of a 400-metre athletics track in 24 hours. The course is flat, the obstacles non-existent. Support and flexibility are almost unlimited, as runners can rest, sleep, eat, drink, change shoes, or even get massaged every single 400 m lap. It might not sound exciting, but it's a fascinating experience for all the runners. Across those three 24-hour events there were 42 finishers. Out of those finishers, only fifteen in total completed more than 100 miles, or 160.9 km.

Not too far away from Butter 24 is the Brisbane Trail Ultra, which takes runners through the stunning bushland hills of Brisbane. Each year they have a broad range of races, from 10 km up to the pinnacle of 100 miles. The races remain on good quality track, albeit with serious elevation at times. Across the three milers of 2021-2023, in total 87 competitors finished. Of those, just sixteen finished in less than 24 hours.

Both these events are for serious ultramarathoners only. They aren't casual fun runs one signs up for on a whim. Yet out of all these elite starters, only 36% of the track runners, and 18% of the trail runners, managed to run 100 miles in less than 24 hours. In the world of distance running, those who do the miler in 24 hours are the best of the best.

However, the introduction of the Backyard Ultra in 2011 may well have changed that calculus. In the first official event the winner completed 18 yards. That 75 miles (or 120 km) was above the 100 km mark, but well short of a miler. The following year, at that same event, the winner ran 28 yards, with two others also reaching or exceeding the 24-lap mark. Each year, the number of people in Backyard Ultras reaching at least 24 laps, 100 miles, continues to grow. In the 2013-14 season there were seven people worldwide who completed 24 laps or more. In 2014-15 the number grew to twelve. Fewer events in 2015-16 saw a slight increase to thirteen, but the rate of increase accelerated in 2016-17 with thirty milers, then 82 in 2017-18.

The word exponential is often used too casually for any increase in numbers. Yet moving into 2018-2019, with the rate of increase rising, the growth was truly exponential: 208 people reached the miler. For 2019-20 it crept up to 221, before another leap to 691 in 2020-21. In 2021-22, there were 995, while in 2022-23, a mammoth 1,451 competitors ran 24 yards or more. Although exact numbers are difficult to calculate, Laz contends that more athletes will soon be completing sub-24-hour milers each year in Backyards than in all other miler or 24-hour events combined worldwide.

It does seem that the 100-mile mark has been engineered as the true measure of a Backyard Ultra. If you were wondering why the yards have the obscure length of 4.167 miles, just multiply that distance by 24 and the answer you get is 100 miles. This makes calculations of distance simple; if you've run for a full day, you've done 100 miles. If somehow you could run two days, you'd have run 200 miles. If you could stretch the limits of human endurance and run almost non-stop for three days, that would be 300 miles.

When the Backyard Ultra starts, the competitors have no idea how far they will run. Most keep on going until they cannot continue any longer. For some, they reach a physical limit; for others, it is mental, and each of them receives the dreaded DNF when they stop.

The exception is the last runner standing, the only one who does not pull out voluntarily. At the end of the race, this person still has no idea how much further he or she could have run. They have not reached their physical limits. They have not reached their mental limits. They are not yet, though, ready to be declared the winner. For in the Backyard, when the second-last person stops competing, the runner still going must complete one last lap to achieve the victory. This is not like most other sports, where once your opponent resigns, the remaining competitor automatically wins. In a Backyard, the event does not finish when the second-last person concedes. The final competitor does not win by ensuring they quit after the second-last person; they need to not quit at all. The rules are such that to win the event, the final runner must complete one more yard than the competitor who attains second place.

For the Backyard winner, this solitary sojourn is a true victory lap. Complete this last lap with no assistance and victory is yours. Of course, that also means that if you don't complete it, you too will lose. If the final runner is unable to finish for any reason, is too slow to complete the yard in under the hour, or — unimaginably — decides to quit mid-lap, they also will be declared a DNF. In this case there is no winner, and all are given a DNF. The final two runners cannot agree between themselves to have a tied or shared win. If they stop together, both are declared losers. The last yard matters!

And this is why no one can know when they will have to stop, as the winner is prevented from running further after all the others have dropped out. One lap more, no more, no less. The winner could be one hour short of claiming a world record, but if there is no one else to keep running with them, they still have to stop.

In every Backyard Ultra, the winner of the race is limited by what that last person to quit accomplishes. In the unique parlance of the Backyard, that second-place finisher is rewarded with a special title: the assist. They are still regarded as a loser, as a DNF, yet their role is considered crucial to a successful event. What makes the assist so important is that they set the limit for the winner, as the winner can only go that one more yard than the assist. Want to break a world record, or even just beat your personal best? Make sure that the event you are in has at least one other person willing and able to get to the previous mark with you. Without a strong assist, the race winner can't go far at all. Far more than just a second placing, the assist is responsible for the greatness of the winner.

In Backyards, there is seldom prize money, and almost never awards of gold, silver and bronze medals for the top three. The winner will often receive a token trophy or symbol of their success. The second-placed competitor will rarely walk away with silverware, but they will receive significant acclaim and great prestige as the bearer of a noble title: the assist.

This dynamic is responsible for some of the psychological interest of the events. In a standard running race, there is a start line and a finish line, and you win by trying to get to the finish quicker than the other runners. In the Backyard Ultra, though, speed is almost irrelevant. It doesn't matter how fast you run each yard; as long as you complete it within the hour, you still have to turn up to the start line of the next yard, at the same time, in the same place, as all the other runners. Your speed in one yard gives you no advantage over the others. In fact, finish too early and your legs have even more time to cool down, stiffen up, and not want to restart. The fastest runner in the world has no significant advantage over others, given slower runners can continue to crank out laps and stay in the competition all day long. Every yard, each runner starts in first place. Equally, every lap, each runner starts with the chance of dropping out and their race being over.

The importance of the assist, though, adds another variable to the mix. In any conventional race, runners hope to do better than their opponents. Most don't want them to fall over and get injured, but the way to win is by doing better than all the others. In the Backyards, for anyone to run far, they need to be surrounded by other runners who will run a long way. This means that for most of the race, the aim is not to demoralise your fellow competitors by running off into the distance. Often the better runners will encourage others to keep going, persuading them to run further than they thought possible. This both adds to the camaraderie of the event and helps each runner to go further than they would have otherwise.

Sometimes, this camaraderie continues until there is just the winner and the assist left. Each will encourage the other, hoping that whether they win or lose, they will at least run a number of yards they can be proud of, and might even achieve a personal record. At some stage, though, the relationship changes. Kind encouragement gives way to an unspoken: *Why won't you just stop?*

There are two ways the final two can find a winner. If one stops at the end of a lap, the other will go on to complete one more yard, effectively a victory lap. If they stop mid-lap, or not make it back to the finish on time, all the final runner needs to do is complete that lap to be declared the winner. That will be enough for them to have finished one yard more than the assist.

This can lead to some interesting dynamics. If the final two competitors are not running together, each time the first to finish crosses the line there is at least a chance that the other will not finish, or not get back in time to start the next yard. Unbeknownst to the remaining runner the assist might concede mid-lap and hobble back to the start line. Or they might try to finish, but not make it back in time.

Imagine you've been running for longer than you ever have before. You're one of the final two and manage to cross the line first. You look around to see if the other runner has already finished. Then, while trying to rest, just in case another lap is required, you keep one eye on the finish line, hoping against hope that the other runner doesn't return and force you into another lap; if they don't get back within the hour, victory will be yours. All of this adds to the drama, which can be exhilarating to watch.

The fact that there is always just one person left at the end leads to Backyard Ultras sometimes being called Last One Standing events. Some event directors extend the title further, and use the initials of Last One Standing Endurance Race to spell out L.O.S.E.R., the accolade bestowed on all except the winner: It's a clever insult to remind almost everyone that they have fallen short.

Although the Backyard was a new race, it drew on elements of Laz's previous competitions. Like most of his earlier events, there was the eccentric title, this time being named after an animal, Big Dog. There was pushing runners beyond their perceived limits, now taking that to extremes. Laz's specialty in race creation was in framing events so they were just short of impossible. He's argued that it's simple to create an easy race, and simple to create one that is impossible, but to devise one that is horrendously difficult, but just possible; that is the true art.

As with the Strolling Jim 40, Laz would taunt his runners throughout. There would be no external assistance whilst on the course, as per the screwed cross-Tennessee events and Barkley races. For many, proximity to Laz's home had been a feature; it made sense to locate them in areas that he knew. For the latest event, he'd take that proximity to a new level, hosting it in his own backyard.

Although not an element in all of Laz's races, uncertainty has played a pivotal role in many. In The Last Annual Vol State Road Race, The Last Annual Heart of the South, and The Last Annual Circle of Hell, runners have to work out for themselves where and when they will acquire food, drink, sleep, and other basic needs. Like the Barkley Fall Classic, Barkley Marathons and The Last Annual Heart of the South, the map was only revealed the night before. In many of the races, although official distances were provided, often the real distance was different, and normally greater. Runners would begin the race uncertain as to how far they would need to go.

In the Barkley Marathons, they didn't even know when it would begin. Laz explained to me that the hardest thing for Barkley runners is uncertainty, and competitors are not sure about things until it is too late to do anything about it. They don't know what to pack as you don't know whether you'll be out in the dark or day, whether you will complete your first lap in the daylight or need to take gear for the night.

In contrast, all such details would be known well in advance for the Backyard Ultras. Some competitors know almost two years in advance that they have a starting berth at the following World Championships. They know where the race will be, what the course will be like, and the exact time at which it will begin. They know the distance of each lap, the number of competitors, and can plan their packing well in advance. They can arrange to have patient friends serve as crew, who can cater to their every whim, once they've completed each lap. They can even predict their hourly pace.

In the Backyard, though, the element of uncertainty resides in the hands, or perhaps the legs, of the athletes. This uncertainty is simpler, but so much harder to navigate, and it comes down to: how long will they run for?

In any conventional race, competitors know how far they will go before it begins. In the Backyard, except for those who plan to finish at a designated time, every runner starts not knowing when they will finish, or how many miles they will accrue along the way. All but one of them will stop when their mind or body gives way, which cannot be known in advance. And one of them will stop just one lap after the assist finishes, which cannot be known in advance either. This uncertainty is unique in the world of ultrarunning and is a key part of the Backyard's attraction. When you approach the starting line, how far will you go?

The competitors at the first Big Dog's Backyard Ultra, on 22 October 2011, had no idea how far they would go. One by one, when they failed to be ready for the next yard, their names were rubbed off the whiteboard on which all the starters were listed. The course was all trail, with multiple tricky sections, all going through the woods of Laz's Bell Buckle property. There were no extreme changes in elevation, but there was some special scenery.

Later, they found it more difficult to complete each lap running in the dark. With the only lights being those they carried, their lap times worsened, some fell on unseen hazards, and soon the numbers competing fell too. Four dropped out on yard 12, the first of the night loops. Case Cantrell was back for the first official Backyard, as he would line up for the first half dozen such events. He was one of the falls at 12 laps and 50 miles, tying for seventh place. Of the 32 starters, only five made it to the 15-lap, 100 km mark.

Then Tim Englund pulled out a faster lap and broke the spirits of the remaining runners, and not much later he was able to win with 18 yards. David Carvey was the inaugural assist with 17 laps. In equal third with 16 was Joe Fejes and Tim's future wife, Lisa Bliss.

Interest in this new race format grew, and slowly the attendance limit was expanded until Laz capped it at 75. Even before the first running of the event, there was curiosity elsewhere. Another run director in nearby Jackson, Tennessee, had asked about whether he could organise a Backyard Ultra too. No problem, and a few months later the second Backyard was run. The third event jumped overseas to Norway. In August 2012 the Røde Huset Backyard Ultra attracted thirty competitors. It may not have begun by following the standard Backyard rules, as Kim Johannesen was awarded the win despite being one of three not starting yard 11. However, it was met with tremendous feedback, and the event continued to be held.

For Laz's second Backyard, in 2012, he changed the course and introduced a new innovation. The trail remained for daytime hours, but once night arrived, runners were diverted onto an alternate road course. This would allow competitors to have a much safer, faster and flatter course, and would avoid the previous year's problem of the trail being too difficult to traverse in the dark. It also added a new tactical dimension to the race, as now runners could plan to run the easier night course at a faster pace, and then have sufficient time between laps to sleep, however briefly.

In 2012, with the now easier conditions, seven of the runners got to 100 km, and four exceeded Englund's winning total. Joe Fejes took the win in 28 yards, Marcy Beard, the assist, on 27. During the 28th yard, Marcy turned back without completing it, which Joe didn't know until he finished his lap. When he saw her waiting at the end, he ran towards her and the two competitors hugged. Laz had to remind him to take the last few steps to cross the line and make his win official.

Englund came back stronger in 2013 to win again in 35 yards. Keith Knipling was the assist, with Marcy in third place, in a higher total of 29 yards. By then there were too many people who were wanting to race, so half the field was selected based on their running credentials, the other half by a lottery.

When I asked Laz to tell me about a remarkable race, he immediately went to 2014. Big's that year brought the drama up to a new level, with an epic battle that has entered the annals of Backyard history.

It began with the full contingent of forty runners. Eleven dropped out before seven laps, falling short of an ultramarathon. Only seventeen got to the 100 km mark, and by the time Charlie Engle stopped after 31 yards, there were just three runners left. Jeremy Ebel, Johan Steene and Joe Fejes only had four laps to go to reach Tim Englund's world record of 35 yards. For six laps the three of them ran, together passing the record, until Joe decided to stop. At 37 hours, he still had the physical and mental capacity to continue, but he had to go to work. With the previous record only 35 hours, and his own best 28, he'd assumed prior to the race that 37 yards would be more than enough.

Jeremy and Johan ran together for some of the next laps, sharing stories and laughs with one another. Earlier, Jeremy had been running as slowly as he could, finishing with the smallest of breaks so as not to waste energy, but now he increased his pace to match Johan. He also shared with Johan his creative sleep strategy; instead of racing to finish early and have a brief nap in the break, he would close his eyes for twenty or thirty seconds while running. He didn't quite fall asleep, but would enjoy the relaxation, refreshment, and rest that came with having his eyes closed. Eventually, they split up, and they spent most of the night running alone. Johan went back to finishing his laps in around 51 to 52 minutes, allowing four to five minutes of sleep each night lap, while Jeremy kept finishing at around the 58-minute mark, evidently getting his rest while running.

From the first Backyard Ultra, Laz had posted hourly updates online for anyone to follow. It was this 2014 event, though, that saw the first substantial rise in people following the race. There was something compelling about these two running giants competing one-on-one for so many hours. The Backyard had become a spectator sport, albeit a virtual one mediated through the internet.

At the 43-hour mark, Jeremy was in trouble. He had gotten colder throughout the night, and thought it made sense to put on some warmer running pants. Most people know, at least when they are lucid and not sleep-deprived, that if you want to change the pants you are wearing, you should take your shoes off first. That's what Jeremy's support crew told him to do. But in a hurry, not wanting to remove his shoes from his aching feet, and possibly not functioning at his optimal cognitive capacity, he tried to pull the pants on over his shoes. Unsurprisingly, they got stuck halfway. They would not come up, so he tried to remove them, but they would not come off either. Still inside his tent, he ignored the one-minute whistle. He ignored the 30-second warning. With fifteen seconds until the start of the next lap, it looked like Johan would win due to Jeremy's foot being stuck inside his pants. Suddenly he broke free, sprinted to the start line and crossed it as the cowbell rang. The race could continue.

As the number of yards climbed into the mid-forties, another problem emerged. Johan was the CEO of multiple companies in his homeland, Sweden, and he had urgent business to get back to. His flights were booked, and he had to stop running at 48 hours, which would be a mammoth 200 miles. Like Joe, given the previous efforts to date, he'd assumed he had allowed himself more than enough margin.

Johan explained the situation to Jeremy, who then convinced him to run just one more lap, so they would complete 49 yards and 204 miles. That would still give Johan just enough time to catch his flight. They agreed to run the final lap together. Johan would stop as the assist, while Jeremy, who presumably had nowhere else to be, would run the obligatory solo lap and take the win.

They finished the 49th yard together, beating the previous world record by 14 hours, and congratulated each other on a terrific shared contest. Now all Jeremy had to do was run one final 4.167-mile lap, and he would be the winner, world champion, and solo world record holder.

Laz blew his whistle to indicate there were three minutes to go, and Jeremy entered the starting corral. Next came the two-minute whistle. The one-minute whistle. The 30-second warning. On the start of the hour, Laz shook his cowbell to signify that the lap would begin. The watching crowds, present and online, waited to see Jeremy begin his fiftieth and final lap of victory. Jeremy, however, stayed inside the corral, refusing to step onto the course itself. This led, naturally enough, to his disqualification, and so the race ended. Jeremy explained:

> I didn't go. It wasn't the right way to end a race like this. He still had a lot left in the tank and so did I. Even if I made that last lap, I wouldn't have won. Steene just had someplace he needed to be, so I just let the clock run down.

And that was it. Both shared the world record. Despite their heroics, for the first time in race history, there was no assist, and no winner. Both were given a DNF. For some time there was talk of a re-match, but it never happened. Jeremy was lauded for his sportsmanship. Johan was grateful, and would come back stronger in the future.

In 2015, due to storm damage on Laz's farm making the facilities unsuitable, there was no Big's. In fact, the only recorded Backyard that year was in Norway.

2016 became the year when the race really took off internationally. A new U.K. event began in February, the Last One Standing Castleward. Two events began in Sweden, which would be the start of an explosion of Backyards there. Somehow or other, the concept took root, and in a country of only ten million people, there were 27 Backyards recorded in 2023, with over forty planned for 2024. This may be because running and organised running events were already big parts of Swedish culture. According to a 2016 report, 40% of Swedes considered themselves runners, and Backyards provided a helpful format in a social setting.

Sweden was also the site of a fun innovation. Because of the Backyard's nature, runners will often go well past their previous longest distance. The forced rest between laps, the normalised slow pace, the social aspect, the ready supply of food and drink, the regular rejuvenation provided by massages and anything else that might happen back at their tents, all these contribute to helping competitors exceed their previous performances and perceived limits.

At the Lurs Backyard Ultra, the Swedish organisers' innovation was to encourage runners, when they surpassed their previous best distance, to loudly ring a cowbell. Runners, particularly the vast majority who were almost guaranteed a DNF, would see this as something to aim for. Ringing the bell was a source of joy, an accomplishment and celebration. Nearby spectators would join in, cheering in response and adding to the atmosphere. Other runners would hear the bell and be encouraged that someone was making massive progress. It was a great way to move the focus from purely the winner and allow the many who surpassed their previous best to be acknowledged. Soon the practice began to spread to other events.

Big's returned in 2016, with Babak Rastgoufard, thanks to Andy Pearson's assist, winning with 29 yards. It was the first time that the winning time at Big's was not higher than at the previous event.

In 2017 Babak ran 29 yards again, now only enough for fifth place. Johan was third with 37 laps, while Harvey Lewis burst onto the Backyard scene as a 58-lap assist to Guillaume Calmettes, who established a new world record. This time the final two ran together for an astonishing 21 hours.

In 2018, Last One Standing England was held for the first time. It would be renamed in 2020 as the Suffolk Backyard Ultra, the venue for many epic battles to come.

Big's 2018 was an iconic race for several reasons. By now, there were nine countries represented in the field of 61 competitors; it was becoming a true international event. It also provided restitution for an earlier star of the sport. And it was a rare event where Courtney Dauwalter, one of the best distance runners ever, lost.

Courtney was renowned not just for her running ability, but for her positive energy, kindness and all-round joy, all of which she brought both to the trail and her life in general. She would go on to win the famed Ultra-Trail du Mont-Blanc three times (and counting!) and had already amassed 33 wins in ultramarathons as the fastest female. Ten times she had beaten all the men too. The previous year she had won the Moab 240 Endurance Run overall, beating the second-place finisher by nearly 10 hours. Ultrarunning Magazine would name her the *2018 Ultrarunner of the Year*, the first of many such awards. But in the bizarre world of Backyards, in 2018 she would lose, receiving an accolade most runners detest, a DNF.

She had already run for 67 hours. In nearly three days, she hadn't stopped for longer than sixteen minutes. In this format, no one had ever gone further. By then she had run 279 miles, more than double the distance any other female had ever run in such an event. Five years earlier, Marcy Beard had run for 30 hours. The best male effort to date had been a year earlier when Guillaume Calmettes of France had set the world record in 59 hours.

Only 23 hours beforehand, the second-last female, Maggie Guterl, had finished with 44 hours, a new female record. At that point, there were five athletes left in the 2018 race. Guillaume, the defending champion, was there, along with Johan Steene, Courtney, Greg Salvesen and Gavin Woody. The other seventy runners had called it quits, but these five had kept running for the next ten hours. For another 41 miles, they kept going, effectively running a five-person ultramarathon after they had already run 183 miles.

At the end of the 54th hour, though, the 2017 winner and world record holder was out. Guillaume had only just snuck in to finish the 52nd lap with eighteen seconds to spare, pain in his right foot impeding his movement. He improved in the 53rd but fell in the 54th on a flat section of trail. He finished the lap, but by then he'd had enough and succumbed to his injury, withdrawing from the race.

And then there were four. Two laps later, Salvesen was done, not getting back in time to start the next lap.

And then there were three. Courtney, Gavin and Johan ran for another nine hours. This was yet another elite ultramarathon, this time 37 miles, entry to which was only available to those who had run the previous 56 hours. Four hours into this three-person challenge, they passed Guillaume's world record, together moving into uncharted territory.

Gavin Wood was the next to disappear. He finished his 65th yard with almost five minutes to spare. His physical condition would later be described by Laz: *his feet were sacks of broken bones and bruised meat and his leg muscles turned to blocks of unresponsive wood.* Nevertheless, he lined up with Courtney and Johan for the start of the 66th yard and headed off into the darkness. Minutes later, he stumbled back to the start line. His friends rushed to him and carried him back to his chair, where he collapsed in tears.

And then there were two. Johan may have had the experience in this format, as the 2014 equal furthest finisher, but he'd arrived exhausted from lack of sleep. His original flight from Sweden had been turned back due to mechanical issues. He caught a later flight, missed a connection, and finally arrived at nearby Nashville just before midnight, only hours before the start of the race. After a quick visit to Walmart for crucial race supplies, he was pulled over by the police on the way to the start. It wasn't a great beginning.

It was Courtney who was regarded as the probable winner, and she had been consistently beating Johan back to the finish each lap. Courtney's problem, though, was that her lap times were getting gradually slower. In the 64th loop, she finished almost two minutes ahead of Johan, the last time she finished before him. Then every successive lap took her longer. Johan, perhaps sensing an opportunity, went faster each time. He finished lap 65 more than a minute in front, 66 almost three minutes, and for 67 he put his foot down and took almost a ten-minute lead.

By now every part of Courtney was hurting; even carrying a cup of water was hard. Her body felt like it was becoming more and more broken, with nothing left to give.

She had planned to take naps between the overnight laps but had been too excited to fall asleep. She closed her eyes and tried to lay still, but never rested enough to feel refreshed. The lack of sleep was messing with her mind too. In one lap, she saw a twelve-foot cowboy; in another, an ice castle; entertaining hallucinations for sure, but not signs that things were going well.

Towards the end of their battle, Courtney said *Johan, you know you can end this whenever you want.* He was having none of that, replying *I don't know how.*

For Courtney, the accumulated pain, her perception of Johan's likelihood of going indefinitely, and her desire to simply stop running, all led to what felt like a sensible decision to finish the race.

Just before the start of the 68th yard, her resources spent, she walked over to Johan and shook his hand. *Go get those last four miles,* she encouraged him. And with that, she conceded defeat, accepting the ignominy of a Did Not Finish.

The starting bell rang, Johan began his final lap, and Courtney, finally, after nearly 67 hours of running, could rest.

When Courtney shook Johan's hand, wished him luck and nudged him out onto the course, he knew that all he had to do was complete this one last lap. Surprisingly, he reported no joy in this moment of pending triumph. Rather than exalting at the victory over a magnificent opponent, he felt the pain of losing a companion. In a Facebook post, he lamented:

> *At the moment when Courtney congratulated me and remained in the corral as I jogged away alone into the Tennessee night I didn't feel joy. I felt empty and without purpose. You can not carry the illusion by yourself. It takes at least two to play. Thanks Courtney Dauwalter for taking us this far. We are good at playing this game.*

And so Johan—encouraged by Courtney's nudge—headed out into the darkness of early Tuesday morning to complete one final lonely yard. For the first time since Saturday morning, there was no one accompanying him. In exchange for the company of the other runners was the tranquillity of the night. All that could be heard was the shuffling of his own feet and the occasional rustling in the undergrowth.

Johan completed his last lap in 48:35, a little faster than his average of 48:51, showing he still potentially had more to give. But, once crossing that line in the early hours of Tuesday morning he was the new world record holder, beating Guillaume's year-old record by nine hours. For him this was restitution from having to pull out in 2014 and accept a tied DNF.

Now the race was finally, over. After 67 hours, 48 minutes and 35 seconds, Johan could stop running. It was over. He had won! And along with his victory, the accolade of the assist came to Courtney. To receive this in her first Backyard was a worthy accomplishment. Calling it a loss is technically true, but as with all assists, it was only due to her perseverance that the winner was able to get as far as he did.

This all raises some obvious questions. What sort of race has the person who comes second classified as a DNF? What sort of race has someone go, in the space of seconds, from breaking a world record to, a handshake later, a DNF? What sort of race allows someone to run further than every other woman, not just in this particular race but in the format's entire history, and still be called a loser?

The answer is simple: only a special, perhaps twisted, yet oh-so-fascinating sort of race. This was the world of Backyard Ultras that Laz had created.

For Big's 2019, Laz developed a new system. The runners had begun referring to his event as the de-facto world championships, the race that all Backyarders wanted to take part in. Now Laz would make that more official. Rather than the previous selection by a combination of track record and lotteries, ten events around the world were given 'Golden Ticket' status. The winners of each of those events would then be guaranteed a berth at Big's. This led to a massive expansion in the international nature of the field, with twenty overseas runners selected for 2019.

Will Hayward of New Zealand was the assist, but with 60 yards Maggie Guterl became the first female winner of the now World Championships of Backyard Ultras. It was a significant year for female runners, and New Zealand too. Earlier that year, Katie Wright had become the first female ever to win a Backyard outright, with 30 hours in a race in New Zealand.

In the same year, there were over 100 Backyards scheduled in 33 countries. The sport had become a global event in only eight years.

For 2020, Laz planned more further expansion, with a record 24 international gold ticket races, and thirteen in North America. However, although that expansion happened the following year, it did not pan out the way he had planned. The most serious global health crisis in a century was about to sweep the planet.

3

Accidental Innovation

IN MARCH 2020, as the Covid-19 coronavirus spread around the planet, it felt like the world went on hiatus. For some people, at first, isolation was voluntary, as they began avoiding busy or crowded places. Then before long, lawmakers worldwide responded to the disease by prohibiting public gatherings.

The arts closed down quickly. Whether you wanted to see Rage Against the Machine in North America, BTS in South Korea, or Taylor Swift anywhere, their concerts were cancelled, along with countless others. Broadway disappeared overnight. No one could watch Hairspray, Frozen, Moulin Rouge, or any other musical live. Cinemas, art galleries, operas, comedy gigs, any sort of festival, gone, gone, gone.

At first, the sporting world tried to modify its practices. The NBA recommended their players give fist-bumps instead of high-fives. Two days later, the English Premier League banned the traditional pre-game handshakes between opposing teams. In Australia, Rugby League and the AFL kept playing, but without any fans present. Soon enough, the restrictions skyrocketed, and leagues began to be cancelled. The NFL, MLB, NBA, golf, horse racing, wrestling, soccer, tennis, NASCAR, you name it, they all stopped.

Far more importantly, at least to my world, running events began to be called off. The Boston Marathon was cancelled for the first time in its 124-year history. Even my local Underwood Park parkrun, all organised by volunteers, was unable to continue. The trend continued, and before long almost every running event worldwide would be closed. Even Sweden, renowned for its lack of compulsory Covid restrictions, cancelled Backyard Ultras.

It was a devastating time. Millions of people died. Even more suffered from the effects of the virus, many taking months to recover. It took me a good month to be free of 'brain fog' after my infection. And in most countries, people suffered under debilitating lockdowns, preventing the free movement of people. It turns out that we humans are made for community, and when we're deprived of social interaction, all kinds of other problems develop.

However, as with most tragedies, there was good lurking beneath the surface. People responded to the restrictions and perceived dangers with innovation. Artists began plying their craft online, offering concerts and other performances to virtual audiences. Many grandparents learnt the art of video calling; when it became needed to spend time with family, they were happy to become digital immigrants. QR codes suddenly became a convenient way to direct people to websites, and all kinds of other technologies were developed to help mitigate the crisis. Given that necessity is the mother of invention, people were now inventing ways to connect, exercise, and thrive, despite the restrictions that were in place. But with mass gatherings banned, what workaround could help the runners deprived of their regular events?

Dave Proctor had been planning an incredible expedition called Outrun Rare. His ten-year-old son had been diagnosed with relapsing encephalopathy with cerebellar ataxia. Now Dave wanted to do whatever he could to support other families affected by similarly rare diseases. His plan was to run 7,200 km across Canada in 65 days, beating Al Howie's 1991 record by a week. At 111 km per day, it would be a difficult challenge, and he had a team of volunteers lined up to assist him. He had attempted something similar in 2018, but a herniated disc in his back stopped him a third of the way through. Even so, Dave had raised $311,000 that first time, and now he hoped to reach $1 million. Then, like most other events, Outrun Rare had to be cancelled due to Covid-19. It seemed his months of training and preparation were to be wasted.

Enter Travis and Ashley Schiller-Brown of Personal Peak, an endurance coaching company based in Calgary, Canada. They were Dave's running coaches, and the three developed the crazy idea of creating an opportunity for runners around the world to compete together despite all the restrictions. They particularly wanted to enable runners to enjoy the social aspects that come with the best races. They sought to encourage those trapped at home to not give up on their health and engage in some athletic pursuit. And they wanted to give those mourning the loss of every other event the opportunity to still experience the joy of competition.

How could they do all this with a pandemic raging? Dave had run at Big's the previous year, finishing in third place with 52 yards, and realised that the Backyard format offered a unique opportunity for the isolated to participate in. They brought together an amazing team of volunteers: Stephanie Gillis-Paulgaard, Daniel Bowie, Ryan Kershaw, and many more, and the team developed a new version of a Backyard that almost anyone could participate in. There would be no cost and no barrier to entry, apart from having internet access.

This new event, beginning on 4 April 2020, early in the pandemic, would be called the Quarantine Backyard Ultra. Ironically, just like the virus that led to its invention, it would be one of the catalytic events that made the Backyard Ultra itself go viral.

The rules were simple. Like any other Backyard, runners had one hour to complete 4.167 miles. Those who finished on time could attempt another lap at the start of the next hour. The race would continue until there was only one person left, who would have to complete one lap more than the assist. All would receive a DNF except the winner.

Where this varied from a standard Backyard was that the competitors, due to the coronavirus restrictions, would not all be able to gather in the same starting location. Instead, each person would develop their own 4.167-mile course. For many, the default was to use a treadmill at home. Others would run a single physical loop outside. Some, forced by lockdown laws to not travel far from their home, ran multiple smaller laps. Across the world, thousands of runners all had their own different restrictions and risk factors to deal with, and developed their plans accordingly. Wherever runners could make it work, they set up their own mini events.

The key to it all was the online component. Whether you were running outside or inside, each lap would be recorded on some kind of GPS device, then at the end of the lap you would point your camera at the device and take a digital photo to prove that you had completed the required distance. If you ran on a treadmill, you would photograph its measuring tool. Partly the system relied on honour, but the hourly check was important too.

A series of Zoom meetings would be set up for runners to join, which would allow them to see how many others were still going, chat in comments, and follow the in-race commentary. There were four pages of Zoom meetings filled with runners for public viewing, with the top page being for elites. YouTube streams would highlight summaries of the Zooms and other relevant information. As one elite runner would drop out, the next best, or next most popular, would then be added to that page. As well as the Personal Peak team, the organisers had also invited Laz and Sandra to be honorary race directors, watching and occasionally commenting on the proceedings. As always, Laz provided Facebook followers with his uncapitalised comments on many of the laps.

Groups of runners signed up for the Quarantine Backyard Ultra, as it became an opportunity to do something together for a day or more. Some of these groups would establish their own private video calls in parallel to the official Zoom streams so they could chat to one another throughout the race.

As with any other Backyard, runners were responsible for their own crew, nutrition and rest. This led to people creating their own aid stations in garages, nearby parks or their actual backyards or gardens. Lounge chairs were moved into place for convenient rest breaks between loops. Cupboards were raided and massive varieties of food and drink were assembled to allow competitors easy access to whatever they wanted to consume throughout. Salt tablets, paracetamol, caffeine pills, anti-blister pads, bandages and any other medical supplies were similarly assembled.

For some, the technological setup was rigorous. In their starting corrals, speakers were put in place to allow runners to hear what was happening. Multiple screens enabled competitors to see the official Zoom meetings, YouTube streams, their private group and other messages. Those running outside could only access these in the lap breaks, those on treadmills could see them constantly. Some set things up so they could continue to work while they ran, others had music blaring.

Family members and housemates were cajoled into becoming impromptu support crews. In a normal race, runners find people who either care about them or the event and persuade them to provide ongoing support. Here, runners had to convince whoever they happened to be living with that catering to their every need while they ran all day would be fun.

The entire concept was intriguing. What would happen at the intersection of one of the oldest sports—running—with some of the world's newest technology? It was a massive experiment with thousands of participants, and any problems would have to be resolved live.

The odds were against the event from the start. The organisers only gave people two weeks to sign up, or, perhaps more importantly, to find out about it. They relied exclusively on social media, which has its limits. Personally, at the time I'd never even heard of such a thing, and only found out about the event once it had already got down to the final two. If I knew about it earlier, I suspect I would have joined in.

There was also no real prize, and because the runners could not see each other except via screens, it would not be an official Backyard. It was free, though, and for many, it was the most interesting thing to do that weekend of lockdown.

In Calgary, the event began at 7 am. By start time 2,413 participants had signed up from all around the world. Due to the different time zones, people began at various times of day, but all were synced together so every runner began at the same moment. Runners in London began at 2 pm, in New Delhi at 6:30 pm, and in Brisbane it was 11 pm. Many of them had never heard of Backyards until this event.

It was not just the average runner who turned up. Maggie Guterl, Courtney Dauwalter and Sally McRae planned to run it 'together'. Greg Armstrong, who had won the Last Vol State 500k took part, as did future Backyard champion Merijn Geerts, and many other elites such as Pete Kostelnick and Olivier Leblond.

One runner who I'd never heard of, but would discover later was an ultrarunning phenomenon, was Harvey Lewis. The 44-year-old was just starting to make his mark on the Backyard world, finishing as the assist to Guillaume Calmettes in 2017. This would be his second attempt, although his ultrarunning journey had been going for quite a while.

A public-school social studies teacher at Cincinnati's School for Creative and Performing Arts, Harvey's running story began when he was in high school himself. He was nick-named 'Chunk', after a chubby teenager in the movie The Goonies, and was often teased for being both fat and in special education classes. Years later he explained that *the only running I typically did was if I chased down the ice cream truck on my street*.

He tried out for football but was only ever third string. However, he found that, unlike most of the team, he enjoyed the lap running part of football training. He tried out for track and as part of that had to run two miles per day. Although he says he was inconsistent, and never scored much for his team, he was slowly building a foundation for a life of running.

He tried his first marathon aged sixteen, as a freshman in high school. He had always been curious about challenges, and when he was younger had noticed that occasionally the Cleveland Marathon replaced his Saturday morning cartoons on TV. He suggested to his track coach that he could run the marathon. The response was dismissive: *I ran a marathon, and it was miserable*. Only eight or nine days before the event, he asked his Mum if he could run it. Despite him never having run more than eight miles, she said yes. Now there's a good mother!

For the first eight or ten miles he had no problems, but then he started thinking *I'm going to die!* He was exhausted and had to walk a lot, but when he finally finished, after over five hours, he started seeing the world in a different way. It felt like he could do anything. He went from being a D student to getting As and Bs. In 2023 he shared that now he *tackled difficult tasks, learning the power of time and effort.*

While at college, he tried an even longer event, the FANS 24-hour race, where competitors aim to go as far as possible in one day. He was elated to run 82.25 miles and sensed that he had discovered a true passion in ultrarunning.

Success still did not come easily, or early. It took Harvey five years of running marathons before he finished one in under five hours. In 2004 he broke his neck, and any further running looked unlikely. Just being able to walk felt like a bonus at that stage. He tried to qualify for the Boston Marathon, but it took him seventeen years before he finally was fast enough to get in. It took him thirteen years of running ultras before he won his first, in 2009.

Eventually, though, the wins began to pile up. From 2012 to 2017 he won two ultramarathons almost every year. The exception was 2016, the year he turned forty, when he settled for three second-places and a finish of the Marathon des Sables, a six-day race across the Sahara Desert.

Turning forty appeared to have an impact on him, though. Instead of succumbing to the supposedly inevitable decline of middle-age, Harvey instead went to a new level of success. From 2018 to 2020 he won three ultras each year. From 2021 to 2023 he would improve again, each year winning four.

Most prominent of those results were his efforts at Badwater, billed as 'the world's toughest foot race'. Runners start in the ominously named Badwater Basin in Death Valley, California, 85 metres below sea level, the lowest point of elevation within North America. They then follow a highway for 135 miles before finishing at the trailhead to the summit of Mt Whitney, which takes you to the highest point in the contiguous United States. Somehow, Harvey has managed to run every edition of this elite, invitation-only, event since 2011, including a win in 2014.

Although he gives it an intense level of commitment, for Harvey running isn't a chore. It's not something he endures to achieve a goal; he adores it! When you listen to him talk about running, you can hear his passion. He told The Necessary Entrepreneur:

> *I love running, the elevated heart rate, it's like dancing. I like connecting with people, I like being out in nature. I feel most alive when I'm doing an event like this. The wild animal in me comes out. The shirt comes out. I'm not trying to show off, I feel connected with nature.*

Beyond his running, though, Harvey gives every impression of someone you'd love to hang out with. He's possibly the nicest teacher you'll ever meet, the kind of person you'd want to have teaching your high schoolers. Other runners tell stories of how he, despite being their competitor, frequently encourages them along the way. In interviews, he is affable, generous, self-deprecating, and keen to learn. Most noticeable, though, is his positive mindset. He knows this is one of his key assets as a runner, and in life in general. It allows him to enjoy his experience even more, and in races helps him to go further than would otherwise be achievable.

Harvey is always looking at things positively, rather than getting trapped in the despair and uselessness of worry. In an interview with Trail Runner Magazine, he said:

> *Everything you see that could be a challenge, just turn it around and make it a positive. It's the way you frame your mind. If you feel some sort of negative thought, you have to find some sort of way to get rid of that negative thought and turn it into a positive.*

As an example, he suggested that if it's hot, remember that everyone has to endure the same heat. Then, try thinking about how the beach is hot too, and going to the beach is fun, so the weather you're experiencing right now similarly has to be fun.

In some races, he would read a series of cards written by friends or students, which would fill him with encouragement. Sometimes, while running, he would think about others in his life, or even picture himself running along with them. As he reflected on the difficult situations some of them had experienced, he was able to put his own troubles in perspective. *Running is just so easy relative to that sort of thing*, he explained.

It's a great way of approaching life in general, and I loved it. Harvey was a great addition to the race.

The Quarantine Backyard Ultra (QBU) started like any other Backyard, with a three-minute whistle, two-minute whistle, one-minute whistle and a cowbell. As with every other Backyard, once that cowbell was rung, competitors had to start their lap immediately. The finer points of this rule would later become a big deal.

Unlike other Backyards, the cowbell was rung by the Personal Peak team, with runners hearing it through the streams on Zoom and YouTube. Unlike other Backyards, the cowbell ring did not lead to a rush of runners leaving one large starting corral, drawn to match the size of the field. Instead, every competitor would begin each lap on whatever course they had designed, wherever they were. The treadmill runners would take the first step on their treadmill, those running a physical lap would start on their own track.

If you were watching their feeds, you could see the treadmillers all throughout their running time, but in their breaks they might step out of view. For those running loops, the situation was usually reversed.

You would often only see them as they left their starting position, but then see more of them during their breaks.

Unfortunately, it didn't take long for the first wave of problems to hit. There were issues with runners' video feeds, software updates, computers crashing, and power outages. At the beginning, the organisers warned all competitors in the pre-race briefing not to have music audible on their video streams. Despite this, and it not being difficult to mute a microphone while you're listening to music, enough people disregarded the instruction that YouTube's anti-copyright infringement algorithms repeatedly stopped the live streams. Those watching from home had to play 'chase the video feed', as one after another, new YouTube streams were attempted, until, finally, streams of the race were banished from the platform altogether.

Many of the runners dropped out quickly. Quite a few never made it to the start line, good intentions not translating into sufficient preparations. In the end, 1,577 people recorded a result. There were 45 running loops inside, 263 on treadmills, 1,345 running outside, and 76 employing some combination of running inside, outside and on a treadmill. There were most likely more participants than this in practice, but Personal Peak could only record data from those who provided it.

Of those who started, eight did not finish their first lap. Another 46 ran only one lap, 84 stopped after two, 106 after three, 134 after four, and 130 ran just five. By the end of the sixth lap, over half had stopped. However, although the numbers may have been low by some Backyard standards, many of the runners had achieved their longest distance record. Each of the 1,322 who ran four laps or more had completed a creditable 16.7 miles or 26.8 km. In total, 952 people managed to complete seven laps, which meant they officially had run an ultramarathon.

Maggie Guterl was one of the earlier casualties. As one of the big-name stars, with a win at the Backyard Ultra world championships and three attempts at the Barkley, it was a surprise when she stopped after nine laps. The reason was that she had picked up her first real injury during the event. Her SI joint was damaged enough that she didn't run again for another two months.

An unexpected star was triathlete Rinat Mustafin. Because of the strictness of Dubai's lockdown rules, he was forced to develop a course inside his own apartment's living room. He would run a figure eight around the couch and through the hallway, even having options for occasional variations. On some laps his children joined in too. Although he wasn't considered one of the elites, those watching online pressured organisers to add Rinat into the main feed. The hashtag #livingroomguy began to trend on social media, and his popularity grew with each successive lap. Eventually, he finished after 20 laps.

Courtney, who kept watchers amused by sharing a joke between laps, and Sally McRae both finished after 24 laps. They could have gone further, but hitting the magic 100-mile mark was enough. Although only nine runners had dropped out in the previous three laps, eighteen others finished with them. It seems the carrot of a miler was helpful motivation for many.

Ben Tidwell, from the small town of King George, Virginia, ran just one more lap than Courtney and Sally before he stopped. What made this newsworthy was that, at the time, he was only thirteen years old. He was clearly following in his family's footsteps; younger sister, Anna, had previously run 46.5 km as a nine-year-old. Anna, older sister Becca, Mum Kris and Dad Rob, all ultrarunners too, served as Ben's support team. Perhaps his success was aided by having his mother in the crew and eating what he was told; his race diet of tomato soup, sandwiches, pasta salad and shrimp does seem healthier than average. Rob had begun running with his son, but started to struggle and stopped after seven laps of their neighbourhood. He then switched to crewing Ben for the next 18 hours.

Richard McChesney, a Kiwi living in London, was a bit different. As a competitive long-distance racewalker, he had a decent resumé against runners, having won the Last One Standing England in 2018. He was a rare person who might have handled the event in Stephen King's The Long Walk. For the QBU he planned to walk the entire event around the streets of London. However, no sooner had he signed up than the UK Government tightened their lockdown restrictions, so residents were only allowed out of their houses once each day for exercise. He toyed with setting up his car as an outdoor aid station, technically only leaving his house once to exercise, one very long exercise session. However, with media stories emerging of neighbours informing on each other for supposedly exercising too often, he decided that wasn't the best option. As an alternative, he found a nearby second-hand treadmill, some rubber to deaden the noise, and was now ready for action.

Richard was feeling great when, at lap 24, he began to smell something burning. He completed a faster lap, in 54:08, which was a particularly impressive walking time given it coincided with the completion of 100 miles. This allowed his wife and son to use the break to attempt some treadmill diagnosis and repair. They adjusted the treadmill's belt but discovered that the motor was probably overheating. His son bought a fan online and raced to the shop to collect it, hoping to cool the treadmill down.

A few laps later though, Richard was struggling to go on. His shorter rest time between laps, due to walking being slower than running, and the need to sustain an incredible walking pace, meant tiredness and pains accumulated with less time to manage them. Soon he could hardly keep up the pace, was mentally exhausted, and was only just staying on the treadmill. Then, midway through lap thirty, which would have seen him complete 125 miles, his machine suddenly stopped, and he was jerked forward into the dashboard. Fortunately, his family quickly unplugged the machine, but it was game over. Once recovered, Richard realised he could have gone outside and completed the lap, but his despair, exhaustion and agony weren't conducive to such innovative thinking in the moment. His 29 laps were still a magnificent effort.

Harvey Lewis ran his first lap with Carly, his beloved dog. He thought one was enough for her, so left her behind when he ran off for the second. She disagreed, jumped out the kitchen window after Harvey started and chased him down the road. Later he discovered that Carly's exploits had been captured for posterity on his Zoom stream for all the world to see. Harvey managed quite a few more laps than Carly, finishing on 35. That put him into fifteenth place, even with a distance significantly shorter than what he had made before. A trend was emerging — that some of the stronger runners were finishing earlier than expected.

Matt 'Shep' Shepard was one of the coaches for Personal Peak, so with the help of some inside knowledge, had become the first person to sign up for the QBU. He had planned to run around his cabin, but unrelenting snow and wind made it nearly impossible to maintain a trail for more than a day. Instead, he used the front entrance of his friend's Tall Tree Coffee shop in Valleyview, Alberta as his starting corral. Shep used to live in Alaska, so was well used to running in the cold, but for his first few loops before sunrise the temperature was as low as -30C/-22F, and his lips began bleeding as a result. Photos show an ice goatee forming on his beard, with stunning thick snow surrounding him.

The daytime was not as cold, but after 15 hours of running he moved into the coffee shop itself. Like countless other businesses, it was closed due to Covid restrictions, so Shep could run there instead. Like most coffee shops, though, there was not that much space. He created a 25-metre course around the stacked tables and chairs, requiring about 269 circuits to complete each Backyard lap. Every 500 m he would change his direction.

The virtual watching crowds began calling him Coffee Shop Guy, with the hashtag #shepspresso, and he soon became one of the fan favourites. His staple food consisted of Japanese omelettes, candy, chips and pizza.

A new problem arose. Because of all the sharp turns, Shep would occasionally kick his own ankles. To avoid this, he adjusted his stride, which itself then resulted in knee pain. After 32 laps, he'd had enough. His solution, surprisingly, was to remove his shoes and run on the hardwood floors in his socks. He found being closer to the ground helped with his movement and had the advantage of polishing the coffee shop floor. It may or may not be related, but he also reported experiencing delirium and sleep deprivation. He found that when he tried talking to his crew, what he thought were coherent thoughts kept coming out as misunderstood gibberish. He eventually stopped shortly after the beginning of lap 42, finishing in sixth place overall.

Greg Armstrong, a teacher from Tennessee, was one of the elite runners. He ran on his treadmill inside, presumably hoping to avoid some of the uncontrollable variables that come with running outdoors. In his spare time, he was also the founder of Run4Water, a non-profit that raises awareness and funds to help with water crises. He, along with Harvey Lewis and Maggie Guterl, were using their participation in the ultra to raise funds for the charity to assist people around the world to access water. A committed Christian, he spent much of his running time praying for the medics and those suffering from the pandemic.

As he ran, he was mostly enjoying his own self-induced suffering from the ultra. Twice, though, animal emergencies intervened to almost wipe him out of the race. At the sixth hour, his wife Shelley frantically told him that Dolly was moaning and on the point of death. Dolly was their goat. Wanting to ease the animal's pain, he ran the lap as fast as he could to buy some margin. The lap completed, he sprinted to Dolly, euthanised her, buried her as quickly as he could, and got back to his treadmill with minutes to spare.

Two hours later came another call of the wild. This time Shelley screamed. Greg had earlier asked her to open the door to let the cool breeze in. Unfortunately, along with the breeze, in had slithered a 4.5-foot snake, which then climbed the wall near the treadmill. Greg leapt off the treadmill, took the snake outside, and resumed his lap. It turns out the indoor running was not as variable-free as he had hoped, and he ran the rest of the time with the door closed, minus the friendly breeze.

After he completed his 43rd lap, tired and sore, he thought he could do just one more. At the two-minute whistle, he was still undecided. If you look at the video, you can see him thinking about it. He stands up, walks towards the treadmill, and turns towards the screen where he can see the other three runners. He looks over, continues thinking, then suddenly the cowbell rings while he is off the treadmill. No more contemplation required, he is instantly disqualified and out of the race, in fourth place.

Anna Carlsson of Sweden made it two more laps for 45 in total. An accomplished runner and one of the pre-race favourites, the conditions were not optimal for her. She had to snowplough her course twice beforehand, which was on top of a frozen lake. Her start/finish area was a sauna hut to keep her warm during breaks, as where she ran, 300 km north of the Arctic Circle, the air was well below freezing. She was forced to stop after lap 45, in third place, despite still feeling strong and wanting to continue. Her reason was different to most – the weather had turned, and the snow made further progress untenable. As it turned out, not one of the last four stopped because they wanted to.

For the next seventeen hours, the final two runners ran, alone but also together. Radek Brunner and Mike Wardian were both accomplished ultrarunners. Radek was a three-time podium finisher of the 246 km Spartathlon, the famed ultramarathon where runners would retrace the legendary steps of Athenian Pheidippides, who sought support from Sparta during the Battle of Marathon. Now his route was less exciting, running on a treadmill in the Czech Republic. He had no interest in running at Big's, wasn't thinking about winning, and nearly didn't make the start line. Two days before the race, the weather was good, so he ran 54 km with a friend. He thought it would be better to do another shorter run on Saturday instead, but at the last minute decided he would join in after all. He had never used Zoom before, and only installed it on his laptop an hour before the start.

Mike Wardian was running laps of the block he lived on in Arlington, Virginia. He had to run ten of the laps to complete one official yard. He began with just a small box of food, but after a while, his wife Jennifer noticed on Instagram that Maggie Guterl had a full aid station set up. She flew into action and created a table suitable for the next couple of days. Soon many of the neighbours realised this guy was bizarrely running past them ten times each hour and began coming to offer their own support. Some set up lawn chairs, tents, and hoses, to make their sport — of encouraging Mike to run — more comfortable.

Once Mike had made the top five, at 42 hours, he told his wife that he didn't want to go on. He hadn't been sleeping at all, using a lot of his rest time to answer questions and engage with the community online. Fortunately, she didn't accept his decision: *That's not a really good excuse.*

Once it got down to the final two, the online chatter went to a new level. Perhaps the idea of these two titans battling it out, while the rest of us were stuck at home doing nothing, grabbed our attention. For myself, it was now that I first heard about it all. Not just the QBU, but the whole field of Backyard Ultras.

Whenever I logged into Facebook, multiple people were sharing links to this crazy race where a guy on a treadmill was competing against someone running laps of his block. Occasionally I thought I saw someone that looked like that bloke with the beard from the Barkley Marathons. And along with me, just watching along, many others were engaged in chat about every detail of the race. Meanwhile, lap after lap, Radek and Mike kept plugging away.

Although they weren't proper friends, they had bumped into each other before; Mike had travelled to Greece for the Spartathlon, where he had had problems mid-event. A freak hailstorm had made him hypothermic, and he chafed from his neck to his knees. He wasn't in a good mental state and was about to quit while he was in one of the aid stations. Radek had seen that he was doing poorly and attempted to persuade him to get out and keep moving. *C'mon man! You're fast! You can do it!* In the end Mike DNF'd, but the support was appreciated. Now again, in this Quarantine Ultra, Radek was bringing out the best in Mike, and Mike was doing the same in return.

Suddenly, in front of a watching audience of thousands, it all fell apart. From laps 56-62, Radek had started to have small naps in the breaks to replenish his energy. Because the other runners kept on chatting, he hit mute on his laptop so they wouldn't wake him. He was wearing a smartwatch, but was using it, connected to a foot pad in his shoe, only to measure his distance.

At the start of the 63rd hour, both remaining runners looked strong. Neither were complaining, neither were toying with stopping. Both knew that Johan's world record of 68 hours was within reach. Who knew how far they could go together? It was this tension that was equally drawing the online audience and motivating the runners to continue the battle.

Watching the video stream, the audience could see everything unfold live through the four rectangles on-screen. The cowbell rings for the 63rd time. As you watch, in the top right-hand corner, the timer clicks over from 00:00 to 59:59 and starts counting down again. Mike is in the bottom right, heading off to begin the first of his ten block laps.

In the top left is Radek, standing on his treadmill, stationary, staring down at his tablet, occasionally fiddling with it. For nearly two minutes he stands there with no trace of panic or desperation. There is no hint of resignation or defeat. He looks strong and confident, but still, he stands there without starting the lap.

In the bottom left were Laz and Sandra, watching in horror. The online crowd held their collective breath. After 62 hours, seventeen with just the two of them, how could it end like this? Why would it end like this?

Travis and Ashley, off-screen commentators and event directors from Personal Peak, urge him to start. *Radek, the bell just went, you gotta get going. Radek are you on mute? The bell just went. Radek, can you hear us?*

Laz knows the rules; he wrote them. If you don't start when the cowbell goes, it's game over. He declares *I think he's done. I think he's done.*

At no stage does Radek show any awareness that he's done anything wrong. Then, after almost two minutes, with no sign of anything out of the ordinary, Radek looks up from his tablet and steadily begins walking, oblivious to the online turmoil. Sandra comments that he's looking very calm.

Less than a minute later, a friend brings him a phone, and someone from Personal Peak tries to explain the situation to him. He looks over to his laptop in confusion, and keeps walking.

Five minutes after the lap started, with the result obvious, Laz and Sandra log out. Radek doesn't stop. Instead, he starts running, just like he had every lap. Travis and Ashley join the feed on camera. Travis is apologetic, tearful, stumbles with his words, occasionally breaks down while still talking.

> *It's really difficult to say this, I don't want to say this, but, I don't want to say this, we've got to call the race here, because it's pretty cut and dry in the Backyard rules, we've got to do, got to do the right thing, you've got to leave the corral at the time you have to leave the corral and be moving onto the course. So we're going to have to stop the race here, which we really, really don't want to do.*

Making what's happening more surreal, as Travis struggles through his explanation that Radek is disqualified, a friend of Radek's comes across to his laptop, smiles comically, pats his dog, and begins to dance with it. All while Radek keeps running, Travis keeps crying, and the world keeps watching.

A fresh voice emerges. It's Jennifer, Mike's wife. *Can you clarify what Mike needs to keep doing, does he need to finish this hour?* Travis replies that yes, he has to finish the lap to get the win, and in the background excited cheers are heard from his household.

Mike keeps running for his victory lap. So, too, does Radek, but no one watching knows how to process the fact that he is still going.

The lap ends up being Mike's fastest, completed in 31:05. A convoluted discussion ensues, as Travis and Ashley try to explain to him that Radek has done the wrong thing, so the race is over. Mike looks confused, Jennifer sounds puzzled. Somehow, in the confusion, the fact that Mike has won is ignored until, finally, Jennifer asks for clarity. *Can you at least say congratulations?*

Mike still seems befuddled by the fact that Radek hasn't stopped running. How can Mike be the winner if Radek is still running? He offers to re-do the lap so the race can continue; it does look cruel for poor Radek. After 63 hours it feels unfair to both that they have to stop. Neither wants to finish; both are keen to keep going. It's a devastating way for the event to finish for the runners, organisers and viewers alike.

Mike asks if he can run on to get the world record, which is now only five hours away. He's feeling strong physically and mentally. Travis explains that the rules of the Backyard are such that the winner can only do one more lap; it's news to Mike. Finally, he's able to show his gratitude, thanking all the organisers, competitors, support crew and more. *It was a real honour and privilege beyond my imagination.* As his prize, he is awarded a golden toilet paper roll, apt in the era of Covid-induced toilet paper shortages.

Radek finally stops and approaches the camera, telling Travis and Ashley in English that he is there. To rub salt in Radek's wound, their computer chooses that moment to glitch. They try to fix it but are unable to give Radek the opportunity to speak, or to listen. The feed disappears, robbing the audience of any closure, then pops up elsewhere with a new link.

So, what happened to Radek? Why didn't he start on time? Why did he keep on running? Like many farces, the explanation was benign. That lap, instead of relying on his laptop to see the countdown timer, he had picked up his tablet and watched the Facebook stream there. What he didn't know, and had no reason to know, was that the tablet's feed had an almost two-minute delay. So, when the lap started, and Mike started running, and the organisers ask Radek to get moving, and the online audience begin their commenting, he had no idea that any of this was happening. When the timer ticked over to the hour, he did the right thing and started running, as he has done every time. From his perspective there was no problem, no tragedy, nothing to see here.

Less than a minute later, he had been surprised to hear his phone ring. It was Personal Peak attempting to explain, in English, what had happened; it was confusing, to say the least. When he tells the story, Radek says that he explained that his tablet was delayed, and he was told to continue running. So then, after following that advice, to be informed that the race was over despite him having run the lap and wanting to continue, was devastating.

If only he hadn't clicked mute on his laptop while trying to sleep those last few laps. If only he hadn't used his tablet for the countdown. If only he had a watch that showed the actual time remaining. If only a crew member had taken responsibility for his timings. If only the rules were different. If only the organisers could just ignore the rules.

All these possibilities raged, not just in Radek's brain, but around the world. For those watching, although the race was over, the saga continued with a flurry of discussion. In all kinds of forums, people who had been following the Ultra began to debate what had just happened. Accusations flew, and it all got ugly. Fingers were pointed at Laz and Sandra for declaring the race over so quickly and leaving the feed. People made fun of Travis and Ashley's looks of confusion as they stared at the camera, trying to fix the latest tech problems, unaware they were still live. Not congratulating Mike earlier was a big deal.

But mostly the discussions were about whether Radek should have been disqualified or not. People who had never heard of Backyards became instant armchair experts with opinions that they simply had to share. Whatever position people took in the debates, all agreed that it was a tragedy.

Some suggested that because Radek shuffled his feet on the treadmill, this could be understood as him having started the lap. Others accused Mike of cheating, as in an earlier lap he had begun running on-time but forgotten to re-start his watch, making his GPS data give the impression he too had started late. People pored over the video, looking for things to dispute, anything that would undo the outcome. Some argued that Greg Armstrong should have been disqualified for leaving his treadmill course to remove the snake. He suggested in response that it was the equivalent of a runner on a standard Backyard course picking up a snake and taking it to the side out of the way.

Amidst this sea of certainty, with each person convinced things would have been better if they had been in charge, Laz took a different tack. In his Facebook summary, he mused: *maybe I am the only person who is glad not to be in charge.*

In a Facebook post, Personal Peak defended Laz from the blame storm.

> To confirm. Lazarus Lake did not make the final call on the outcome of the Quarantine Backyard Ultra. He and Sandra were invited as honorary race directors, and a[s] such the decision was entirely that of Travis and Ashley of Personal Peak.

And although Travis and Ashley did struggle with some of the communications technology, theirs was a difficult hand to deal with. This was unknown territory for all, involving logistics and complications never faced before, yet despite being sleep-deprived and facing a barrage of technological issues, they amiably engaged with their online audience for days on end. Their accomplishment in creating the event and managing it as well as they did, bringing joy to countless thousands, was worthy of praise.

It's also easy, in hindsight, to judge the online spectators, with their airs of superiority and continual criticism of those who had volunteered so much of their time. But this was early in the Covid-era, at the peak of the lockdowns. We were all frustrated at the numerous restrictions on movement. In the absence of real community, things occasionally got nasty. This would not be the only example of people responding less than optimally.

Despite all the fighting though, it had been a magnificent event. For the emerging story of the Backyard Ultra, it was particularly significant. Not only did it add new tales for the annals of Backyard history, it introduced many more people to the concept. The numbers involved, the creativity of the logistics, the online engagement, the titanic struggle between the competitors, the farce of the conclusion, even the post-race disputes, all these helped to grab attention.

It was not only through this first QBU that Covid helped stimulate the development of Backyards. Three months later, many of the same volunteers organised a sequel. Another 1,200 runners competed, with the USA's Jon Noll winning in 51 laps.

The real innovation, though, would come from Laz. As usual, Laz had planned to have Big's in October that year. The growth of the format, and previous results, indicated that 2020 would have the strongest and most international field ever assembled. By the Fall, Tennessee's Covid-19 restrictions had loosened enough that he could offer the race. However, the complicated array of hopefully virus-halting international border closures meant that most of those hoping to travel to the USA would be unable to do so.

Once again, necessity led to some remarkable innovation. In conjunction with struggling race directors in other countries, Laz developed another version of the Backyard. Instead of having only a limited field travel to Laz's property, as in the previous eight years, he created a satellite system of Backyards around the world. One event would be held in each of 21 countries, each capped at fifteen runners, all beginning at the same moment. It would draw on the best of the QBUs, with live simultaneous feeds all being watched over by Laz back home. The winners in each country would then be invited to the proper Big's course for the, hopefully post-Covid, 2021 edition.

To make it even more exciting, there were to be three levels of competition happening at once. Each country's event was regarded as its own Backyard Ultra. The normal rules applied, and the winner could only do one more lap than the assist. There would be 21 such winners, each declared national champions. There would also be an overall winner declared. Whichever of the 21 national winners finished with the highest total number of yards would be the world champion.

Finally, the cumulative yards for each country would be added together. If, for example, fifteen runners from one country ran twenty laps each, they would finish with a national team score of 300 yards. The country which finished with the highest number of laps would be declared the winner of the team event.

A team event had been considered before at Big's, but capacity constraints — a maximum of 75 entrants — had prevented any serious team competition. Now Covid had provided a marvellous solution.

In practice, the winner of the individual world championship would also only get their win because of their team. The overall individual winner would not necessarily be the person who could run the furthest, but rather, the person whose assist — also from their country — would go the furthest. The winner could only do what their assist would allow.

The event would alternately be called the Team World Championships, the Satellite National Championships and 2020 Big's Backyard Ultra: Satellites.

The stage was set for a great international battle, which led to a wave of activity around the world. Runners in each country where Backyards had taken a foothold had to work out what they would do in response. Courses were created, selection criteria were developed, and runners desperately strived to qualify. If you could be one of the top fifteen in your country, you would be part of the national team, an international representative. All of this encouraged Backyarders to try to run further than ever, and ultrarunners who had not tried a Backyard yet were pushed to test this novel format. All this international expansion, and the explosion in participation numbers worldwide, was happening only nine years after the first Backyard.

It all began at 7 am Central time on 17 October 2020. In Tennessee, Laz arranged for the racers' tents to be situated separately, so runners and crew could socially distance for this still-Covid-afflicted race. The various events around the world all had their own starting times and their own distancing regulations. All would begin at the same second, but for some it would be late at night, others in the heat of the day. With daylight saving starting at different times between states and across countries, coordinating the logistics was made even more difficult.

Laz predicted before the race started that Johan's world record of 68 hours would fall. It was a quality field that had assembled, and the runners would not begin already exhausted from competing in too many other races. On the other hand, fewer competitions and the impact of lockdown on training might have dulled some runners' competitive edges. Key international contenders were Guillaume Calmettes from France, Dave Proctor and Matt Shepard from Canada, Katie Wright from New Zealand, Anna Carlsson from Sweden, and future Barkley finisher Karel Sabbe from Belgium. The American team was stacked with talent: Big's 2019 champion Maggie Guterl, previous assists Harvey Lewis and Courtney Dauwalter, and an imposing group of peers.

Each country would have their own Zoom stream, and all would be combined into a single Facebook feed that the general public could watch. More importantly, every runner could know what was going on in every race at any moment. They could be aware of what was at stake, how many other competitors were left, how many laps other teams had compiled, and much more.

Although teams could have up to fifteen members, not all reached this cap. France, Russia and Belarus each had just thirteen runners, while Japan only had ten, and India nine. Unsurprisingly, the smaller teams fared worse in both the team event and the overall competition. France was an exception, finishing in fifth place with 464 team yards. Pivotal to their success was their top eight all making it further than any other team, with 36 laps each. India was last with a total of 145 laps, the country's best performance coming from Kartik Joshi with 21. Belarus reached 174, Aksana Sulimchik getting 26. Russia had 270 laps, Tatyana Maslova the top-scoring on 28. Japan collectively ran for 291 laps, Akio Ueno winning with 43.

The rest of the countries had full teams. The USA, Canada, Belgium and Sweden were the big threats. However, Singapore, Mexico, Finland, Spain, Germany, New Zealand, Australia, Ireland, Ukraine, Switzerland, the UK and Denmark all had excellent runners and strong depth in their teams, with many capable of running big totals.

Mexico was one of the most fascinating teams. Anyone who has read Christopher McDougall's 'Born to Run', his tale exploring the origins of running, will be familiar with the Tarahumara or Rarámuri people. (Anyone not familiar should stop reading this and find that classic). The Mexico team featured local Rarámuri, and the event itself was held in the Copper Canyons that they live and run in, deeper and wider than the Grand Canyon. Their course had so much elevation that after the event the organisers retired it for one that was slightly less challenging.

Most of Mexico dropped out early, and did so in clusters. Their first to fall was Maria Modesta Ayala on the ninth lap. At that stage, only six others worldwide had stopped, five of them from Belarus. Maria stopping triggered a domino effect, with others stopping after laps 10, 11, and 12. The fallouts stopped briefly until another on lap 15, then a cluster at laps 22, 23, 24, then three together on lap 30. One more dropped out on 43, leaving only three remaining. That small group were then one of only seven teams left, and it put them into the top twenty runners worldwide. After Andreas Loeffler from Germany finished on 50 yards, Mexico were the only team left with three runners.

The Rarámuri have a saying *When you run on the Earth, and when you run with the Earth, you can run forever,* and it looked like they were taking it seriously. The three Rarámuri had been running together the entire race, the only trio to do so for more than 50 laps. Together they did 18 laps after their fourth runner finished, and 31 after their fifth. Finally, with only seven runners left worldwide, the last cluster of Mexicans finished, but only due to injuries. Juan Contreras finished after 61 laps, then was taken away in an ambulance. Miguel Lara Viniegra became the assist with 63, when persistent shin pain became too much to ignore. Pedro Parra took the win, and fifth place worldwide, with 64. Despite the trio's amazing run together, their team finished only in eighth place, a consequence of the earlier exits of their teammates.

Ironically, Sweden's last runners fell just before the three Rarámuri, but their overall team strength put the Swedes into fourth place. They employed some non-traditional strategies, singing songs together, hiding in trees to scare each other, and generally trying to have fun. When one person was struggling, a stronger runner would accompany them for a while, providing crucial psychological encouragement.

All except for two made it to the 24-lap miler. Ten made it to 125 miles, when a steady progression of drops began at laps 30, 31, 32, 32, 33, 34, 37, and 37.

By then there were only two Swedes left. Tobbe Gyllebring was only six laps short of his previous best. Anna Carlsson had hit 45 on her frozen lake at the QBU, and wondered how far she could go without a snowstorm interrupting her progress. Stomach problems plagued her after the first day, but she resolved to go as far as she could. The two got to Tobbe's best of 43, then past Anna's 45. By then only 18 runners were left worldwide, but Anna was deteriorating physically. It was only her mental strength that enabled her to continue. Later she told Runner's World: *I decided I wasn't going to quit. Just keep running until I was out of time or my legs didn't work anymore.*

Anna and Tobbe set out together for the 55th yard, but finally, Anna's body made the decision for her, despite her thinking that she could go a lot further. She passed out while running and fell to the ground. Janne Svärdhagen, the race director, found her out on the course, carried her back in, and off she went to hospital. Tobbe finished the lap, winning the Swedish race and coming ninth overall.

In Big's Backyard in Tennessee, online viewers were deprived of seeing Mike Wardian back in action following his last-minute withdrawal. He'd planned to run, but had injured his back one week earlier at the Spartan Games. In addition, several of the United States team did less well than they would have hoped. First to leave was David Johnston, his nine far off his best of 43. Joe Fejes was helpful with 24, but well short of his previous 44. Maggie Guterl ran a magnificent 39, but as the 2019 Big's winner with 60 laps, was disappointed not to go further. The strength of the American team, though, came from their third to sixth-placed runners. Third-placed Jacob Conrad ran 49 laps, beaten only by two other countries' third-placegetters. Sarah Moore and Gabe Rainwater's 48 for fourth and fifth, plus Maggie's 39 for sixth, were not beaten by any similarly placed runners.

Their departures left Harvey and Courtney locked together in an 18-hour battle between the previous runners-up. After the Mexicans finished, their only remaining competition was Karel Sabbe and Merijn Geerts, running across the pond in Kasterlee, a small Belgian town near the Dutch border. Both Americans wanted to win, but they were also motivated to push the other on to the highest total they could reach; it was a team competition, after all. And for both, Johan's world record of 68 beckoned. Although they mostly ran their own races, each were renowned for their positive attitudes in running, and life in general, so were able to spur one another on.

As the Tennessee night fell, exhaustion hit new levels. They set out on lap 68 knowing that all they had to do was complete it to be part of history. Finishing the lap would make them equal world record holders, even if only temporarily, with each other, with Johan Steen's existing record, and, if they also finished the same lap, with Karel and Merijn in Belgium. For Harvey, it was not to be. Not long after starting, he turned back, accepting his second assist, leaving the glory to Courtney. All she had to do now was complete that final 4.167 miles and the triumph would be hers. To the relief of all, she made it back. Her race, and the American race overall, was now over.

Courtney was the equal world record holder, the American champion, and the second successive female winner of Big's. She had battled off hallucinations, where she swore she saw a giant Mickey Mouse on a circus stage offering T-shirts to the crowd, but for some reason, not to her. She had changed her shoes and socks every twelve hours, husband Kevin doing the dirty work for her. All had been endured with minimal sleep, about four to five hours in total across the 64, just eight to ten minutes per lap on the second and third nights. Despite it all, she never had a scare that she wouldn't get back in time, her slowest lap 55:13, more often than not having a good ten minutes to rest. And now, she could rest for as long as she wished.

Along with Courtney's victory, the Americans could also celebrate coming second in the team race. Belgium's depth gave them the win. Although Christophe Lamotte ran only 11 laps, all the rest hit at least 24. Eight of them stopped in the thirties, two in the forties, and the other two, well…

As Courtney celebrated her win and temporary world record, the international race continued, albeit now in one location only. Courtney and Harvey had finished third and fourth overall, leaving only Karel and Merijn to keep running in Belgium.

Their race had not played out as smoothly as they hoped. In his first experience of Backyards, Karel found the noise in the race venue louder than he'd hoped, and was unable to sleep the first night. The second night, he attempted a new strategy, knowing that to go deeper into the race would require some unorthodox thinking. As he got close to the finish, he stopped running and turned his headlamp down to its lowest setting. He closed his eyes and walked with great care back to the finish line for the last five minutes, allowing his body to start getting ready for sleep. By the time he got back, he only had to walk twenty more metres to his bed, where he quickly fell asleep. Pleased with the success, he started doing this every yard, even continuing into the daylight. Unlike most Backyarders, who, if they aim to sleep at all, only plan to do so at night, for the last 40 hours, Karel also slept each lap in the day.

By the third night, another problem developed. After the race had started, Belgium entered a new wave of tightened Covid-lockdown restrictions. Consequently, the course had to be restricted on the third night. Instead of only one loop, the runners would do an almost one-kilometre circuit seven times, the antithesis of what ultrarunners want. Still, they pushed on, outlasting the Americans, the Mexicans, the Swedes and everyone else. As soon as Harvey pulled out, they knew Courtney would have to stop and the win would be theirs. They were delighted, but knew the camaraderie between them would now be replaced by a competition to see who would win overall and claim the world record. Merijn had been battling problems with his Achilles, and

Karel thought he might just do one more yard and finish. Yet on Merijn went, lap after lap.

Both finished the 74th lap and set out on the 75th, but only Karel completed it. Finally, it was all over, not just in Belgium, but worldwide. Karel was the winner, not just of the Belgium championships, but of the World Satellite Championships. He alone was the world record holder, while Belgium was declared the winner of the team championships.

Around the globe the event had been a stunning success. Of the 21 overall winners, seven were women. In local international rivalries, France finished just ahead of Germany and Spain, as did Australia over New Zealand. Sweden easily beat Finland and Denmark. Ireland was pleased to defeat the United Kingdom, and Ukraine was ecstatic to beat Russia and Belarus.

The Backyard Ultra had truly gone international, and excitement was building for what was to come. A pattern was now developed for rotating events. Henceforth, the satellite world championships would be held biennially, and the next one in 2022 would bring an incredible series of dramatic events. On the alternate years, the Big's Backyard Ultra World Championships would be held in its traditional home, Big's literal backyard.

Between the QBU and the Satellite World Championships, 2020 was a great year of innovation for the format. It led to an explosion of interest from competitors and spectators, and the beginning of a fascinating era of international competition.

The following year, with the world heading toward a semblance of normalcy, Big's was able to return to its standard individual competition. Michael Wardian finished the 2021 event early, with 36 laps. The two previous winners, Courtney and Maggie, also finished sooner than expected, with 42. The field's strength was high, with nine runners getting to 50 hours. Any of those nine would have beaten Johan and Jeremy's tied world record at Big's in 2014. However, the overall field was still restricted due to international travel restrictions. Only nine runners were able to attend from outside the USA and Canada, and the field had its lowest ever number of competitors at 34.

The top three were Japan's Terumichi Morishita, Missouri's Chris Roberts, and Ohio's Harvey Lewis, who had won Badwater for the second time only months earlier. By then Karel's winning record of 75 had been beaten by John Stocker in the Suffolk Backyard Ultra. As they ran lap 81, to potentially equal John's record, Terumichi tripped and fell. He lost consciousness for an unknown period, eventually picked himself up, tried valiantly to get back to the start in time, but fell short by thirty seconds. Those watching found it heart-breaking to see the warrior fall short after such a battle. On the 85th lap, Chris finally pulled out, knee problems getting the better of him.

Now Harvey had his triumph at Big's. On his third attempt, after being the assist twice, in 2017 and 2020, at last he got the win. He was now also the world record holder, with a formidable 85 laps. He'd hold this title for another 211 days, until Merijn Geerts won The Race of the Champions – Backyard Masters in Germany with 90 yards. That race served as a kind of surrogate world championship for those who had been prevented from travelling to the USA in October 2021.

It was not long after this race that my own Backyard story began. But before we get there, there is someone else to meet: Andrew Southwell.

4

Learning the Ropes

I'M NOT SURE where I first met Andrew Southwell. We have multiple mutual friends, and I recall one of them telling me for years that we'd get on well. In practice, though, I mostly know him through our Facebook interactions. Despite that, I regard him as a friend and, strangely enough for someone I've rarely seen, an informal mentor.

None of this is deliberate, but repeatedly I've decided to do things that Andrew had already done. Back in 2016, my friend Mark Morton and I toyed with the idea of starting a new parkrun. We'd been enjoying running to our nearest event at Wishart, a suburb in Brisbane, Australia, but by the time we ran there and back, it was a 20 km run to do a 5 km race. It made sense to create something more local that would benefit our community, so I started asking about how such things worked. We found that another bloke, Darren Ryan, wanted to start a parkrun too, so we joined forces, and another friend was made.

I'd also seen on Facebook that a guy I knew was serving as an event director for a parkrun on the other side of town, so I sent him a heap of messages. Andrew was keen to help and encouraged us to give it a go. He offered all kinds of advice, most of which, many years later, is still being implemented at our Underwood Park parkrun.

I then noticed, again through the joys of social media, that Andrew was getting into ultramarathons. Mark and I had been doing adventure races, rogaines, and trail running for a fair while, and I'd often thought that moving up to ultras would be the logical next step. I saw that Andrew had run Blackall, a 100 km race through gorgeous scenery in Queensland's Sunshine Coast hinterland. Runners would pass creeks, waterfalls, and lakes while running up and down the Blackall Range. It seemed like a lot of fun to me, but the distance was a lot greater than we'd run before, never having gone further than the 42 km of a marathon in a race. As fate had it, Mark bumped into Andrew at a party, listened to his Blackall adventures from the previous year, and soon enough, we'd signed up for the 2018 event.

Again I asked for help, and again Andrew shared his wisdom. I recall towards the end, when I was struggling to continue, repeating to myself his instruction: *you just gotta find a way to keep moving forward.*

The next thing that I noticed popping up on Andrew's Facebook was this unusual event called a Backyard Ultra. I'd never heard of it before, except for the QBU, which at the time I didn't realise was part of a broader network of events. I assumed the format had been invented just for Covid.

From 2020 onwards, each August I would notice Andrew running huge distances at the Clint Eastwood Backyard Ultra races at Rocklea, not far from where I lived. The event promoted itself with a picture of a surly Clint Eastwood asking *Do ya' feel lucky?* It was a pointer to the fortune that runners would need to endure the pain ahead.

The 2020 race began at the unearthly time of 1 am, and it looked like an incredible experience. Andrew ran 100 km, and only taking 15 hours meant he'd done it faster than either of us had managed for the — admittedly much more mountainous — Blackall 100. The winner was Ryan Crawford with 37 yards, an incredible 248 km. I was intrigued and told him that I'd love to try something like that. By the time I saw his comment that entries were already open for the 2021 event, all 250 places were filled.

In 2021, although I'd missed out, Andrew took part again. He turned up to the venue the day before to set up his supporters' gazebo. Unfortunately, while putting it together he hurt his hamstring, and that restricted him to just 12 laps. That was still an even 50 miles, particularly impressive with a dodgy hammy. Kevin Muller won with 42 yards. Again, I expressed my jealousy, and again I didn't think about signing up for the next event before it too was filled.

Things were different in 2022. Andrew did his best yet, running for 17 hours, 114 km. That was even further than Blackall, so I was impressed! Ryan Crawford took the win for a second time, his 59 hours the new Australian record. By then I was keen to try it for myself. I'd missed out on signing up for the 2022 event, but then I noticed that the organiser, AAA Racing, was offering a similar event in October. The course would even be the same as the Clint Eastwood. It was called the States of Origin, and was billed as a team event where people would compete in groups based on which state they had been born in. This was inspired by the epic State of Origin Rugby League battles between my home state of Queensland and New South Wales. It sounded like a good idea to me.

As it turned out, not many people agreed, and on the morning of 1 October 2022 only 21 of us turned up to run. I'd tried to recruit others for a four-person team, but for some reason, most people I knew didn't want to try running as far as they could before they collapsed. I had only managed to persuade Mark and my sister, Rachel Robinson.

I'd hoped that Andrew would be able to compete with us too, but with Blackall a couple of weeks later, he didn't think it was a great idea. As was now my pattern, though, I asked him for all the tips that he could offer. I watched a video he'd made running the event to give me a few ideas, and then sent a lengthy list of questions. *What training do you need? What food do they supply? What do you do in the breaks? Can one of my daughters run along with me? Can you sleep in-between laps?* On and on my questions went as I sought anything to help me through the daunting challenge ahead.

After watching Andrew's video of his experience, YouTube's helpful algorithms suggested some other videos I should watch, and soon I was down the rabbit hole of Backyard videos. Rachel mentioned that she had listened to some podcasts discussing the races and found them helpful, so I started doing the same. I had no idea what to expect in the race and was keen for any insights.

The most memorable video I saw was about another event in Queensland, Dead Cow Gully, which had taken place only a few months earlier. The production quality was great, and the story was gripping. I recognised Ryan Crawford from his Clint Eastwood wins, and he'd won the previous Dead Cow Gully too, but this time he only finished third, with 34 laps. An unheralded Josh Duff was the assist with 36, while Barry Loveday, who'd come second in the 2020 Satellite Championships for Australia, took the win.

One of the more interesting aspects of the documentary was the story of the winning female runner. Nicole Jukes was a lawyer, mum, and an emerging leader in the local Backyard scene. She smashed her previous best, out-lasted established stars like Kevin Muller and Chris Murphy, and, with thirty yards, set the new female course record. It was inspirational to watch, and I was starting to get hooked.

The podcasts were fascinating too, and I picked up information that would prove useful. Of course, as with anything, much of the shared wisdom was subjective, and the various experts offered contrasting perspectives. Some insisted that sleep was essential to go far, others that it was a waste of time. Some would swear by listening to their bodies and eating on a whim, others advocated for a rigid, scientifically-justified eating plan.

My favourite was Josh Duff's Smurf and Smurfette podcast. He'd driven almost a thousand miles from Cairns in Far North Queensland to race Dead Cow Gully, and used the podcast to recount his experiences. In his first race he'd run 150 miles and came second, which was a great performance.

Even more compelling to me was how he recounted the various phases of the race. Josh explained that multiple times he would experience some kind of difficulty. At one stage, it would be nausea; another time, his foot might be hurting; later his mind would be telling him to stop. He found that each of these phases would last for a few hours, and each time it would feel almost unbearable, and he'd wonder if he could get through it. But each time, again and again, whatever that particular difficulty was, it would pass, with some help from an incredible crew who would make adjustments to his plans. Unfortunately, the problem would then be replaced by a new concern not too much later, which still didn't sound like much fun. But what he learnt, and I was keen to learn too, was that a problem that felt overwhelming at any one moment would most likely resolve itself if he persevered and made appropriate adjustments. Once this realisation clicked in, the next time he felt some situation that he feared would stop him, he was able to remember the previous complaints, and how they eventually passed. *I guess if it happened every other time, no matter how bad it feels right now, this too shall pass.*

For someone about to run his first Backyard event, this was gold. I didn't know it at the time, but I'd reflect on this wisdom repeatedly throughout my run.

The other thing I learned from the podcasts and various videos was the importance of preparation. At one level the genius of the Backyard is that you can just turn up on the day with no preparation, just with your running gear and a water bottle. In practice though, many runners spend a lot of effort getting themselves ready, with detailed plans, equipment and a support crew. This latter proved a difficult thing for us to arrange, as we had no idea how far we would go.

Rachel, Mark and I planned to handle the first couple of hours alone, then have Sandi Canuto, a friend and coach from our Runners Jam club support us until mid-afternoon. Runners Jam was a great running group to be part of; we'd see a lot of friends from there over the next day, and they would then patiently listen to our stories about the race for months to come.

We assumed that once we'd been going for a while, I'd need some encouragement, so the plan was for my wife, four daughters, and niece to come along after Sandi left. Then, my brother-in-law Neil Bowles would come from six until midnight. He was training to be a chiropractor, and offered to bring his massage table, which sounded great. Cameron Pope, from Runners Jam, would take over for the gruelling midnight to 7 am shift. If, by some chance, Mark or I happened to still be going after seven, Rachel assumed that she would be finished and could look after us.

Of course, none of these kind people had crewed a Backyard before, and none of us had ever run one either, so I compensated by over-preparing. Drawing on the finest wisdom I'd gathered from Andrew, YouTube, and the podcasts, I created a guide for our crew. I explained what they could do while we were running: prepare food for us to eat on our return, remove the fizz from our Coke, make electrolyte drinks, charge our devices, update social media, and tidy our gazebo. Then when we arrived at the end of each lap, depending on the needs of the hour, they would fill our hydration bladders with water, offer us ice, and give us whatever clothes or gear we needed for the next lap. As we left, they were to help us out of our chairs, give us food to eat along the way, make sure we had lights and appropriate gear for the lap, take any extraneous clothing and put it away, and most importantly, make sure we didn't miss the start.

I also wrote down strategies for how they could handle different complaints we might have. Whether we came in whinging about sore feet, injuries, cramps, chafing, or tiredness, I gave them suggestions for what they could do to help. My thinking was that, once we'd been going for a while, our brains wouldn't be functioning at full capability, and with exhaustion and limited time between laps, we would be unlikely to be able to articulate what was optimal. I expected my communications would be more along the line of *It hurts, I want to stop!* Hence as much as possible, I tried to pre-empt such issues by having the support crew's responses elaborately planned.

The most important matter was, what would they do if we said we wanted to quit? Here the instruction was clear: if we wanted to quit, we were to be encouraged, pushed, and cajoled out of our chairs. *Just do one more lap!*

That may well be the mantra of the Backyard Ultra: one more lap. No matter the situation, a runner can probably do one more. And if they get through that, they can probably manage another one. And another. And another. If we could just get out of the chair and start each lap, hopefully adrenaline and muscle memory would take over, and we'd get back in time, ready to be bullied into one more lap. At least that was the plan.

In the podcasts and videos I'd heard several interviews with a West Australian runner, Phil Gore, who sounded like he knew what he was talking about. Phil had an hour-by-hour plan for races, so I created a spreadsheet listing what our crew should offer and when. It included sunscreen, hot food, Vaseline, stretching, battery charging, pain relief, magnesium tablets, sweaters, buffs, lights for the night, hats for the day. I knew I'd forgotten things, but I think we were as prepared as you could hope to be.

When we finally gathered our gear, I was amazed how large the pile was. There was, we hoped, enough food for three people for several days. It wasn't just about quantity, we needed the variety to cater for our changing appetites throughout. We had a big pile of healthy food: apples, pears, mandarins, oranges, bananas, cherry tomatoes, boiled eggs, sultanas, and cranberries. Under that, though, there were chocolates, lollies, chips and popcorn, energy gels, and protein bars, balls and powder. For drinks, we had electrolyte powder, beetroot juice, Coke, ginger beer, and tea bags. I liked the idea of sitting down to a nice warm cup of tea early in the morning.

The consumables were just the start. We also had a box with cups, cutlery, crockery, and storage containers. To keep our bodies going, there was ice, cramp-fix, surgical tape, band-aids, pain relief drugs and creams, insect repellent, and massage roller, ball, stick, and gun; I wanted all bases covered. Add in some adaptors, chargers, headphones, batteries, chairs, tables, portable coolers, a gazebo, tarp, and we were almost done. Then there were bags for race gear, dry clothes for afterwards and multiple potential changes of shoes and gear during the race.

Whether we would need the detailed plans, support crew and enough food for a full day, was another question. Rachel's furthest run to date had been 50 km at the 2018 Blackall, though after a few hours rest she had come back and run the final 10 km to help me finish. Mark and I had run the 100 km at Blackall. He'd done it easily, but I'd struggled, with cramps preventing any downhill running for a few hours.

When I reflected on it, I realised that I'd struggled in all of the few ultras I'd taken part in. I'd run the 2020 Guzzler 50 km, on steep terrain in stinking hot weather, the race Covid-delayed from its normally cooler time. At one stage I hadn't bothered refilling my hydration bladder, and soon I ran out of water and went an hour with no liquids. Shortly after, I began cramping and it kept getting worse. Soon I was stuck on a steep slope; one of my legs wouldn't bend and I couldn't get the balance to grip the loose dirt on the hill. I must have looked a mess, as a volunteer called from the top of the hill and offered to get a medic. Pfft! No rescue for me, thanks. I finished, and thoroughly enjoyed it, but it was an ordeal. Perhaps signing up only a few days beforehand might have had something to do with it.

With Mark and new friend Peter Jones we had run the 2021 Scenic Rim 65 km, which again was struck by unseasonal heat. This time the mercury hit 31C/88F, and there was little shade. I began to get massive headaches and debilitating cramps. My pace dropped, and, in a brand-new experience for me, I stopped enjoying the run itself. Once more, Mark did it easily, while Peter showed us how it was supposed to be done, finishing sixth. Technically, Mark and I only ran 61.61 km, as the race had to be abandoned when a small fire swept through the course minutes before we reached that point.

With a record of three ultras for three 'struggled to finish' results, I admit that my expectations were not that high. My training, while never extensive, had, due to a new injury, been less than usual. I thought I'd finally moved on from a series of persistent problems over the years: a persistent hamstring injury, some planta fasciitis post-Blackall, bone bruising from the Scenic Rim Ultra, and knee damage after a 24-hour rogaine a decade earlier.

Then, in what, with hindsight, I regard as one of my less intelligent moves, at Easter 2022 I played a game I'd never heard of before: Gaga Ball. Like a Backyard, it's a last person standing kind of event, where players in a round enclosure try to avoid being hit by a ball until there is only one person left. The way to get others out was to reach down and flick the ball onto a nearby player. It was a lot of fun, so I kept playing for several hours.

The next morning, I woke up and discovered that the repeated, unnatural reaching down movement had given me pain in my left glute. I didn't go for a run that morning, due to the pain, or on many days over the next few months. For far too long I couldn't run properly, which was frustrating given the States of Origin was coming up in October. Once the initial injury abated, I discovered that I could run long distances again, but only if I kept to a shorter stride length and held my pace slow.

My family soon grew tired of hearing about my sore glute, and my daughters began to affectionately refer to my injury as *Gaga Butt*. Even at the time of writing, two years later, I can still feel it most times I run.

With my previous ultra difficulties, injuries and limited training conveniently serving as excuses for a poor performance, I had no idea how far I could go. I hoped to run until midnight, which would be 100 km. For me, that would be a win and show that my aging, injury-wracked body could still manage the distance, even though Blackall had been so painful. Maybe I could then try some longer runs again. At the same time, I also dreamed of running through the night for the miler, and if I could go one lap more than 100 miles, then at 9 am I was hoping to take my phone with me and watch my church's live-streamed service.

My wonderful wife, Ruth, had not enjoyed me running Blackall. The more I told her my stories of incredible pain, the more convinced she was that I never should have done it, as she'd originally suggested. What I perceived as tales of personal heroism and perseverance, she saw as compelling arguments that I should have quit. One of my hopes in doing the States of Origin was that, if I could manage 100 km, admittedly much easier on a flat course, it might make her feel more comfortable about me trying for longer runs in the future. And it would make me feel better about them too, as I was starting to have doubts as to whether my body was up for such distances.

My core goals were to hit 100 km and then 100 miles, and not achieve too much less than Mark. But, given my situation, if I could at least run ten laps, that would be 67 km and a bit more than the Scenic Rim. That would be a decent pass mark. The bare minimum for me, to finish with some semblance of self-respect, was seven laps, as then I'd have run an ultramarathon. In reality, what I wanted was to run as far as I could. The race was a great format to discover what I could do, and perhaps my best chance of running my longest distance ever.

Finally, after years of following Andrew at the Clint Eastwood, after months of planning, it was time to get to the course. For the previous few weeks, I'd been worried that the event itself would be cancelled. I knew that 250 places sold out quickly for the Clint Eastwood, but had not seen much advertising, and even less online chatter, about this event. They couldn't cancel at the last minute, could they?

We pulled into the carpark at Oxley Common in the suburb of Rocklea. It was a picturesque, flat wetlands area in the middle of an industrial zone, with the Brisbane Markets selling fruit, vegetables and flowers across the road. We were relieved to see other tents already set up, and fit-looking people wandering around nervously. We went over and introduced ourselves to Alun Davies, the race director. I later discovered that he'd organised the event for the 2020 Australian team's Satellite Championships and knew a few things about the sport. He did a good job of calming our nerves, explaining how everything would work and telling us stories of other events. Evidently, in one race in Western Australia a competitor had been disqualified before he'd even started, because he left the course to get something from his marquee. Memo to self: *Take the rules seriously*!

The real question in the back of my mind as we talked was: *who else is in the race?* Despite my limited abilities, I've discovered that, although we tell everyone that it's most important that you try hard and enjoy yourself, races are more fun if you win or do well. The positive side of a small field would be possibly limited competition. What if everyone who came was doing their first event?

I'd checked the results for the previous race in 2021, and the winner had run 'only' 22 laps. I saw it was Ryan Crawford who'd won, and he could have gone a lot further. Hmm. If Ryan hadn't turned up, the event would have been won in 21 hours. That sounded like a stretch, but not outside the realms of possibility.

When Alun finally mentioned that Ryan was not running, it might have been small of me, but I was elated. I asked if he knew what was the lowest winning Backyard total in Australia, and he said he thought it was probably 21 yards. Again, I was intrigued.

It was then we found that the field itself was small, with only 21 runners. Excellent. Enough to not be cancelled – phew – but not so many that we'd expect to find the cream of the ultrarunning crop assembled. Alun started talking about the strong female field, and that no female had ever won such an event in Australia. He mentioned Tamyka Bell, who Mark and I had met in a few other races over the years. She had a daunting running resumé of six-day races, overseas events and all kinds of wins. It looked like second was the best we could hope for.

Then Alun mentioned another strong female runner contender, Nicole Jukes. She was the one who I'd just watched that week in the Dead Cow Gully documentary. On a harder course she'd run 30 yards, so who knew what this flatter one would allow her to do? We realised that we might see history and have not just the first female victory, but women in first and second, with us playing for third.

Of course, even that was just a dream, as we had no idea of what it would be like or who else would be running. Alun didn't mention that Susannah Harvey-Jamieson was there too. She had run at the venue as part of the 2020 Australian Backyard team, had completed scores of ultras, with more wins than I had events. If we had known that, we would have been aiming for fourth at best. Perhaps they could have a separate male category so we would still have a chance.

We set up our Runners Jam gazebo, and proudly took a photo of Rachel, Mark and myself, with it as our background. We looked fresh, excited, ready for action, and, for the last time that day, clean. Time was getting away from us, so we hurriedly prepared our tables, supplies, and all the rest of our equipment. Before we knew it, it was time to start.

We moved over into the starting corral, making sure that we were there when the three-minute whistle blew, the only time we'd be there that early. We saw Tamyka, Nicole, and the other sixteen people who would be our companions for the day.

The two-minute whistle blew, and we started to get a tad nervous. I prayed desperately for help. The one-minute whistle sounded, and I couldn't wait to go. The cowbell rang to start the race, and all of a sudden we burst into action. We stepped from the corral, across the starting line, onto the course and …. Mark and I slowly began strolling across the grass as we watched Rachel and the other eighteen competitors run off into the distance.

You see, we had a plan, and running at the start wasn't part of it. I'd spent ages trying to work out the strategy that would work best for us, and there were several factors to consider.

Even with my injuries, I could still run at a pace of 6:30 mins/km. That was relatively easy, and I could sustain it for a while. If we ran the 6.7 km course at that slowish pace, it would only take us 43:35, leaving us with 16:25 to rest. To me, that was a problem.

There were several times when I was sure that I'd been injured because I'd run without warming up properly, or re-started after resting too long in a training session. It looked like my legs reacted poorly to times of inactivity. In fact, when I first heard about the Backyards, I thought that perhaps they would be the worst event possible for my injuries. The enforced inactivity between laps would cool me down and lead to more injuries, as if I didn't have enough already. Having sixteen minutes of break time seemed like a recipe for disaster, so early on we planned to introduce several walks into each lap. If we walked for 400-750 m three times each lap, that would still give us between five and eight minutes of rest each time around, depending on our various speeds and length of walks. As I researched the race I'd found that most people would walk multiple times each lap, so it wasn't a novel idea.

Rather than being the worst possible race for me, I started thinking that it might be the ideal. Given that I was never that fast anyway, and injuries were making me even slower, an event that valued endurance over speed might be my cup of tea. If good race strategy was to go slowly, then I was your man!

I was also concerned about the start of each lap, as we transitioned back from inactivity to running. That would be the riskiest part for me, as our now cooler muscles and joints started reactivating.

Since I'd had my Gaga Butt, I'd found that runs were best when I had a rigorous starting routine. For any run, I'd spend a few minutes inside at home doing an active warmup, trying to activate my muscles, particularly my hips, glutes and hamstrings. I'd walk the first 200 m, run another 200 m, then move into another series of exercises as I ran: high knees, butt kicks, sideways and backwards running, and other such warm-ups. Occasionally, Mark or Pete would come along while I was doing all this, and I'd feel silly, but somehow or other, it worked for me.

Several times over the last couple of years I'd gone for runs without this lengthy warmup, and the results were grim. My injuries would flare up again, and I'd need to back off my training for a few weeks. Perhaps those times were just a coincidence, and I didn't need all those warm-ups, but I wasn't taking any chances — you don't mess with success.

I'd done my warm-up in the starting corral, then when the race started, we began with the now-standard walk. After a few hundred metres, I slowly went through all my other exercises, hoping they would prepare me well for what was to come. Mark was relieved that I didn't insist on doing all this every lap. However, we still would begin every lap with a walk to segue our bodies back into action. And during most laps we would then do another one or two walks, depending on how we were feeling.

The first two laps were intended to be different in another way too. I've often found that I feel better, and run better, after I've stretched properly. However, most research suggests that either stretching is of no value before a run, or any benefit is only realised when you have warmed up. I had no desire for a lengthy run before the race began, so decided that I'd treat the first two laps as warm-ups. We would walk the start, then run the rest without breaks, faster than we'd expect to for the rest of the day. That would then give us 15-18 minutes of rest between those early laps, just enough for some good stretching of now warm muscles.

All in all, I thought it was the perfect plan, at least for me anyhow, and Mark was gracious enough to go along.

Rachel was more concerned with her running speed, which had slowed over the last couple of years. She had good endurance, having run several ultras, half a dozen marathons and numerous half marathons. But now she feared not finishing the laps quickly enough, so began each hour by running ahead of us. This became unintentionally helpful, as each lap, we would catch up and run with her for a while. It broke up the laps nicely as we chatted and offered each other the occasional encouragement.

The course itself was great to run on, though the most annoying section was the start, where there was 100 m of thick grass. It had been cut, but relatively high and recently, so soon we would collect small amounts of grass all over our shoes, socks and legs. From there we joined a smooth rock and dirt trail through fields and wooded areas. It was pleasant, and we would sometimes see families going for a stroll, or photographers studying the local birdlife.

In places the course followed Oxley Creek, and the occasional sighting of water each lap was a highlight. The lap was out and back, starting and finishing at the same spot, with a dogleg in the middle. This allowed runners to see the entire field at three different places in the course, which made the event a lot more social. Given that everyone else was ahead of Mark and I most of the time, this was our only opportunity to see most runners.

For the first few yards, I wasn't convinced that my brilliant plan was as good as I'd imagined. My knees were aching, my hamstring pains had come back, and I had some worrying new groin soreness. On the bright side, my Gaga Butt seemed to have taken the day off, which felt like a miracle.

Even better, after a few laps, those initial niggles went away and none of my previous injuries returned throughout the race. We ended up running faster, and walking less, than we'd anticipated, and soon were taking 9-to-11-minute breaks most laps, which appeared to work well. I was having a lot of fun, and finished each lap with a massive smile on my face.

The first hint of trouble came earlier than we hoped; though Rachel was slowing each lap, she was still getting around the course with about five to six minutes to spare. However, some recent injuries–they seem to run in the family–combined with her long hours working with at-risk young people, meant that she had not done many long runs in the months leading up to the event. By the end of the fourth yard, we'd clocked up 26.8 km, further than Rachel had gone for quite a while, and now she thought she should stop. She was running fine, but was hurting all over, which after running such a distance, was fair enough. We encouraged her to do at least one more lap — that was the rule, right?

On the fifth lap, once we caught up with her I got an even stronger impression that she was ready to stop there and then. She was having some serious stabbing pains and knew that she was close to her limits. Mark ran ahead, while I started jogging along with my sister.

As we ran along together, I started to experience one of the moral dilemmas that arise in such races. You see, I love my sister, and always want what's best for her. Often you think, particularly about someone you love, *I don't want you to be in pain*. Pain is, well, painful. People take their hands off hot surfaces to stop the pain. They take medicines to suppress it. A normal person might be inclined to say *If it hurts, stop*.

But neither of us was normal; we were runners! As we'd run together over the years, one of the patterns we'd often fall into was that Rachel would complain about having to keep running, and I'd encourage her to keep going. She'd keep going, keep complaining, and afterwards express gratitude for the encouragement. Strangely enough, if I wasn't there, she'd often run through any pain with no need for my support. Or if she ran with someone else, she'd take on the persona of an encourager rather than a complainer.

Soon, though, I started to see that these were not her standard complaints, and that she was suffering badly. The stabbing pains continued and I could see them reflected in her face. What brother wants to prolong pain in his sister? Perhaps quite a few, but it made me feel awful.

On the other hand, we'd all had conversations beforehand about how we wanted to push each other to keep running. *Ignore my complaints. Don't let me quit in the chair. Make me keep going until I drop. Don't let me pull out unless there's a bone protruding through my skin.* Okay, we weren't quite serious about that last one, but we'd heard that line from Phil Gore in a podcast and liked it.

That's the real dilemma, not knowing what's best for the person you're with. Do you act based on what they're saying right now, or on what they've previously said? Do you allow them to stop and relieve their pain, because that has to be a good thing? Or is there greater valour in triumphing over the pain, in persevering, so the greater good is in encouraging them to keep going? What was the loving and right thing to do?

I knew that Rachel wanted to go as far as she could, and I was pretty sure that she could push through. But the pain was too much, and a few kilometres in we slowed to a walk. It was about 1:20 pm.

As we walked, I started thinking about how it was a big deal that our daughters were coming soon. Previously, when we'd run races, our families had not been able to come and watch. If the race was two hours away, and we were running for ten hours or so, it wouldn't be that much fun for them to drive for hours, wait until we came along, see us for a few minutes while trying to evade our sweaty hugs, then watch us run off again. It's not a great proposition, so I'd never pushed it before. Having said that, several times while running an Ultra I'd fantasised that my family came along as a surprise to cheer me on at an aid station. Bizarrely enough the thought cheered me up each time I approached the stations, even though I knew they would not be there.

For this event though, the calculus was all different. The venue was only half an hour away from home, and our families knew that every hour, on the hour, we would be there for five or ten minutes. The girls were all keen to come. They'd asked about how best they could support us, what they should say, how they could help. They were happy to trip up the other competitors, provide inspirational music, or do whatever we wanted. I loved it. The idea of having them come along for the first time like this was a huge part of the attraction of the race to me.

However, all of this joy, all of my excitement, was now a problem. In my planning, I'd underestimated how soon Rachel would need to stop running, and our daughters weren't planning to arrive until 3 pm, at the end of the sixth yard. This was only the fifth lap, so if Rachel did not finish this one on time, or stopped at the end of it, then the outcome would be one of massive disappointment. Rather than the girls coming along to proudly see their mum and aunt run, and to encourage her to keep on going, they would instead find her seated waiting for them, her race already over.

I thought that was a compelling reason to keep going, so I pitched the idea to Rachel. She saw the point and started running again. Of course, winning a mental battle doesn't necessarily change the physical side of things. The stabbing pains continued, and we had to keep switching back to walking. When we did run, it was still slowly, and I was aware by then that we were going to struggle to get back in time. I tried putting my hand behind Rachel's backpack and pushing gently as we ran, hoping to make running at a slightly faster pace easier, but I'm not sure how helpful that was.

Although she was in a lot of pain, and it felt like I'd caused that suffering, on one level it was among the best parts of the race. I got to run and chat with my sister, which was always a win. I felt supportive, and there's something about helping others that makes you feel better yourself. I hardly noticed that I'd run over 30 km by then and was completely distracted from any complaints that I might otherwise have had myself.

It was also great to see the other runners as they went past us too. Three times each lap we had to run past the entire field and react to the runners coming towards us in some way. Depending on the person coming, what conversations were happening, and our own feelings at the time, the reactions ranged from exuberant greetings to perfunctory nods or even completely ignoring the person approaching. Usually, we would try to offer some comment and exchange a grin, but a lot of the time people just stayed focused on their own pain.

During this lap, though, the other runners saw that Rachel was struggling and might not make it. The people who would normally run straight past without saying anything suddenly turned into a cheering squad. Clearly, they knew she was at risk of stopping and were genuinely trying to push her on with their encouragement. It was fun to be there for, and I was happy to steal as much of the encouragement for myself as I could.

Still, our pace remained slow, and by the halfway point it looked like we'd get back with just a minute or two to spare, so we tried to pick up the pace. It was hard to know exactly how far we had gone, as our GPS watches were recording the distance from when we began the course at the start of the day, and we didn't know how far it was until the finish line each lap.

Rachel appreciated me being there, I'm pretty sure, but kept asking me to leave her. She was horrified at the idea of me DNFing so early and it being her fault. I wasn't keen on that either. Fortunately, Mark was a maths teacher, and had earlier put his skills to good use. He'd calculated the distances of various legs of the course, so as we ran back, I was able to work out roughly where we were, what our pace was and how far we had to go. If my maths was right, it looked like we still had two to three minutes up our sleeves to avoid not getting back on time for lap five. Rachel still wanted me to leave her, so I promised that if we hadn't seen the finish line with 2 minutes to go, I'd sprint off.

Despite being confident all would be fine, I did start to worry towards the end of the lap. It was my imagination, but I'd swear they added some extra bends to the course. Several times we'd run around a corner, certain to see the finish line, but it wasn't there.

With no finish line in sight, we heard three blasts of the whistle. Uh oh! This meant we now had three minutes to get back. Meanwhile at the start line, Sandi and Mark were desperately hoping that we would suddenly appear, yet fearing our races were over.

With strangely renewed enthusiasm, we picked up our pace, desperate to get back in time. Even if we did get back in time, there would be no leisurely resting in my chair, refilling water bladder, grazing on food, or having the group photo we'd taken every break. We now had less than three minutes not just to get back to the finish line, but to also turn 180 degrees and step back out onto the course to begin the sixth lap.

As we rounded the next corner, with great relief, we finally saw the final grassy straight leading to the finish line. The second whistle came, blowing away any chance of complacency. Two minutes to go. I asked Rachel to hand me her backpack so I could fill up her water bladder for her. I didn't want her to have any excuse to stop. If she could just get to the finish line and then restart lap six, even if she didn't finish it in time, our girls would be there to see her run in at the end.

As we came in, I experienced a series of surprises. I knew Sandi and Mark would be waiting nervously for us, wondering whether we would both be out of the race or not. Now when I looked ahead to the starting corral, I saw not just those two, but all the other runners assembled. They'd all finished their lap and their breaks. Ready to start their sixth, they looked with anticipation at us running in and began cheering us on to finish. As we crossed the line, a wave of applause came up for Rachel from our competitors and the nearby spectators. They knew it had been a struggle for her and that she'd triumphed.

Amidst the cheering, we heard the final whistle blow. One minute to go!!!! Then for my next surprise, I saw half a dozen of our Runners Jam friends. We'd invited anyone who wanted to come along and support us, but only knew that Sandi and Cameron were coming. It was a bit overwhelming to see them, given the drama, but it felt great. I started running past them all to fill up Rachel's bladder, when one of the newcomers, Jodie Egan, took it off me. *I can do that; you get ready to go.* That made complete sense. Someone else brought a chair over for me to sit in for a few seconds, and another supporter put some food in my hand and gave me a Coke to drink. A fourth person took our obligatory photo of the hour, then pushed us back towards the start. Just in time, Jodie ran over with the bladder. I stepped out of the corral to avoid the prohibition on receiving aid while on the course, handed the water to Rachel, and the whistle blew to send us on our way for the next lap. We'd made it, and I felt exhausted from the thrill of it all.

By the time Mark and I caught up to Rachel, after our standard walking start, her mind was made up. She knew that after the travails of the previous lap, and the pain that she was still enduring, there was no point in trying to finish in under an hour. All she had to do was finish, no matter the time, and she would have run 40 km, even if the sixth and last lap would not count towards her official Backyard tally. It would still be a magnificent effort, and it seemed like a sensible plan.

The massive advantage to her starting this lap was that, given our girls were coming at 3 pm, by the time she came in they would be there and ready to cheer her in for a worthy finish.

Reluctantly, but understanding, we ran off and left Rachel to enjoy her final, slower, lap. To my surprise, this was one of my most painful hours. My legs hurt and I felt exhausted. Despite my earlier fears about not responding well to breaks between laps, perhaps my body did want me to have a decent rest. Most likely I was also experiencing a lull after the adrenaline and consequent endorphins stemming from the previous lap's excitement.

Every time we ran past Rachel, we saw that she was running well. Each time I would suggest that I'd be happy to run back to her and get her to the finish line again, but she dismissed my offers swiftly. On the way back, I did some rough calculations about how fast she would have to run to get back on time from a certain point. To my surprise, if she picked up her pace just slightly she could still get back on time. When we passed her the final time, again I suggested I run back and push her to finish on time, but she wouldn't risk me dropping out on her behalf.

As we got close to the end, at the start of the final straight, I was thrilled to see five girls cheering. Our daughters had arrived, and they were waving the massive signs they'd made. After an exhausting and emotional couple of laps, to see them there was amazing. It was literally my running fantasy realised.

One of my girls was a decent runner, so I called out to her. *Becky! Aunty Rachel won't finish this lap on time, but she's still out there. Start running along the path we just came from and you'll find her. She'll love it!* She looked puzzled, but off she went, happy for a run, and keen to see how her aunt was doing.

Mark and I finished our last 200 metres, the other girls following along, continuing to give their encouragement. Eventually, Becky found Rachel. With no need to finish on time, she had slowed for a walk. Rachel's daughter Ruby followed along and met up with them both. As we went out on the seventh lap, we saw them all running in, having a great time together.

It had been sad to see Rachel finish, but it was also, for me, the start of the most fun part of the race. My amazing wife, our four girls, Ruby, and Matt, Jodie, Cherith, Hayden and Peter from Runners Jam were all there to support us. Now having around a dozen supporters was electric. Transitions became easier and more helpful, and the buzz as we started and finished each lap was incredible. There's nothing quite like running into a crowd of cheering people—I could get used to this. It almost felt like an unfair advantage for us to have all this support, but other runners mentioned how much they enjoyed all the cheering too. We were happy to share.

Around this time, the beginning of each lap was fun, but felt a bit peculiar. Our friends and family gathered to support us as we went off. The cowbell would ring, they would cheer with enthusiasm, but once again, as everyone else ran off into the distance, Mark and I would calmly walk along, impervious to the calls from the crowd to run. It was a lot of fun for us, but I suspect a tad underwhelming for those watching, and it felt like we were deflating their enthusiasm.

Unfortunately, having all those supporters coincided with an unexpected storm cell that passed over, dropping heavy rain for a few hours. It didn't bother me much while I was running, as it had been quite hot earlier, hitting 29C/84F. I sweat enough that it was nice to have some cooler moisture on me that was less pungent. I was still running along with a big smile on my face, but the downside was that over the next few hours the puddles grew, and we slipped over several times trying to avoid them. We all cooled down, and I was shivering in between laps.

The rain was particularly annoying for our support crew, as keeping our gear dry was now difficult. The Runners Jam gazebo, our pride and joy, only had one side, so the rain and wind affected most of what was underneath it. Consequently, Hayden raced off and brought back another gazebo, doubling the size of our base and adding in walls to keep out the rain and wind.

Our crew numbers dropped as we got into the later evening, but soon Neil and Cameron joined us, and Rachel started helping out too. She was feeling good again, albeit wishing she was still out there. I was amused how quickly her thought *I can't run another step* had disappeared. Our family all stayed longer than they had planned, but went home in time for dinner.

It was fun getting to know the other competitors, or at least those slow enough for us to run with occasionally. We tried to talk to them as much as possible, and there were a few that we got on well with. Some mentioned the various ultramarathons they had previously completed, and we realised there were quite a few runners more experienced than us taking part. Some were by themselves, but a few were in teams. Naturally, we started looking at the various runners, and tried to calculate what might happen in the team competition. Did we have any chance? Mostly, though, Mark and I were just running together. We were used to that from training and were quite happy chatting merrily along hour after hour.

When the storm came through, a bunch of people dropped out, and I suspect the drenching rain had something to do with it. From then on, during most laps we'd notice someone was missing. We'd stand in the starting corral, looking around at the others, and comment: *I'm pretty sure there were more people here last lap, weren't there?*

For each drop-out there was a mixture of emotions. We'd be running along with someone and they'd tell us they were about to stop. I'd always try to persuade them to continue, and I meant it. *I'm happy to run with you for a few laps to keep you going. You can get through this rough patch.* Having others to run with made it easier for me to keep going, and I was still enjoying it all. And helping others somehow gives you more energy too. But there was also some joy, along with the regret, each time we noticed someone wasn't there at the start. *Ooh, we're doing a bit better! Less competition!* By 6 pm we'd done 60 km, nine yards, and were in the top 10, which was exhilarating. Not bad for our first time! I was pretty sure that we were sitting in second or third place in the team competition, which was good news too.

Not long after it got dark, in the dogleg section of the course, we ran into a swarm of insects. For a couple of hours, each time we ran through that area, which was twice per lap, we could feel thousands of tiny creatures flying up against us. We had to keep our mouths closed, otherwise they would get in our throats. We tried turning off our lights in the hope that would stop attracting them, but it didn't seem to make much difference. They were really quite annoying, but we were even more surprised when we found later that one of the more experienced runners had dropped out because of the bugs.

By now, though, I had accumulated a variety of aches and pains. Every now and again, some body part would hurt for an hour or two. Then that ache would dissipate and be replaced by another. Neil's massages were helpful, especially when I started getting bad neck pains.

Even with the occasional discomfort, I was still enjoying myself. At the end of most laps the crew would ask how we were going, and I'd almost always reply positively. *This is so good! I'm having the best fun!* Given that running was something that I loved, it only made sense to me that I'd enjoy a race that allowed me to run for as long as I wanted.

Around 10 pm we'd made the top eight and 87 km, closing in on the longest distance we had ever run. Something, though, went wrong. I finished a lap, but when my crew asked what I wanted, I couldn't answer. My swirling thoughts wouldn't turn into words.

They encouraged me to lie down. I did, and enjoyed some massage, but when I stood up a few minutes later, I felt even more dizzy and disoriented. When the whistles blew, the support team pushed me toward the start and handed me my food, light and backpack.

I started walking, but waves of dizziness and nausea flooded over me. I still had no desire to quit, but I wasn't enjoying the sensation. It felt a bit risky, but as Mark was with me, I thought it was fine to continue.

I told him about it, and it turned out he'd been feeling the same for a while, but was just less of a whinger. The symptoms stayed with me for around three hours, but with each lap, I noticed they decreased slightly, which boosted my hopes.

Around 11 pm, my brother James surprised us with a visit, bringing a Big Mac in case either of us wanted a treat. I'd heard stories of Backyard runners craving all kinds of fatty foods once they'd been going for a while, and in theory it sounded good. But with the nausea, neither of us was tempted. In fact, since the nausea began, whenever I put food into my mouth, my stomach would beg me not to swallow.

My plan, to keep the energy intake flowing, had been to eat at least two portions of food each lap. I tried to eat healthily, with a few lollies and some salty chips for variety, and most laps I'd have a large cup of Coke or an electrolyte drink.

But now that we were feeling so queasy, neither of us could handle solid food, and went for a while with only liquids. Later I tried cherry tomatoes, and they were a lifesaver. As they are almost liquid, they didn't upset my stomach. I could throw three or four in my pocket at the start of each lap and have one every ten minutes. Then when I bit into one — exhaustion presumably enhancing my taste buds — it had a stunning, sharp taste. It felt like there was an explosion of joy inside my mouth. For too many hours those tiny little tomatoes were all that I ate.

At midnight, along with five others, we hit the magical 100 km mark, the furthest we'd ever run. To our surprise, Tamyka had finished a couple of laps earlier. She stayed around and offered the occasional support, with the noodles she offered much appreciated. Three more stopped at midnight, and now there were only four of us left. Nicole Jukes was there, running strongly from the front each lap, Ian Valentine, who we'd chatted to a lot, Mark and myself. It was exciting to be part of such a small group still running in what was now the early morning.

Ian did just the one more lap, and Mark seemed to be fading. We were still running together, and talking occasionally, but much of the frivolity of our earlier conversation was gone, and there were long periods of silence. Both of us were feeling tired, and not having the energy to chat reduced our normal encouragement for one another.

Throughout the day we regularly checked in on each other to see how the other was feeling, and ask how much further we thought we could go. We tried to never get too far ahead of ourselves and predict final totals, but would say things like *I can't imagine quitting in the next three or four hours*. Over the last few hours, though, I'd stopped receiving such reassuring replies from Mark. Instead, I'd hear *I can get through this lap at least*.

In all the lead-up to the event, I'd assumed that Mark would run furthest of the two of us, as did everyone else we knew. But over the last few hours, even though I'd been in pain, I knew I could keep going for a while yet, and I started to suspect that Mark would not last much longer. He'd stopped eating back in the daytime, and I thought that was beginning to make a difference.

When we got about a kilometre from the end of the 17th yard, I asked how much further he thought he could go. His reply was ominous: *I don't want to answer that question*. Soon he elaborated: *This is enough for me*. The disorientation that had started five hours earlier for Mark, that had now subsided for me, was still hitting him hard. Physically he was looking good and running well, but he just didn't want to keep going.

I gently pushed him to continue but knew his mind was made up. Selfishly, I was aware I was still running strongly, and worried that without his companionship I might not get much further. Would I be scared of the dark? Lonely? Bored? We'd agreed that when either of us wanted to quit, the other would push to keep them going, and we would only stop if we absolutely had to. But when it came to it, I didn't want to bully him into continuing, and I could see that he had made his decision. We ran in together, and Mark celebrated as he crossed the line, a new personal record of 114 km in 17 hours.

At 2 am, it was just Nicole and I who began the next lap. I was feeling great, and kept thinking *I can do this all day!* Each lap was a bit strange from then on, with only two of us on the starting line. I had assumed from the start that the rest of the field was playing for second, and had been pleased at the prospect of being part of history with the first female winner. I've got four daughters, so the idea of having a strong woman dominate the field was attractive to me. I also knew that, Nicole having run 30 yards before, and on a more difficult course, I didn't have another 13 or more hours left in me, at least not running alone. If Mark had continued, I could imagine going on indefinitely.

Whenever I saw Nicole out on the course, she was running fast and looked strong. She was in her element, enjoying herself. After the event, I saw some photos of the two of us towards the end, and the contrast was stark. One of us looked strong and able to continue for a long time yet. The other looked like he was just hanging in there and was ready to drop at any moment.

With Mark finished, I asked him to work out what was happening in the team competition. He found that there was another team a few laps ahead of us at the time, but if I got to 6 am, or 21 hours, then we would have an equal score with them. That would be enough for the win, as in the case of a tie, the team with the person going furthest would get the victory. Alun had also mentioned earlier that the lowest winning total in Australia had been 21 yards. It occurred to me that if our race had the first female winner, it would be a shame if we also had the lowest winning total. But if I could get to 21, Rachel, Mark and I would get the team win, and Nicole would be the champion with a healthier winning time. All I needed was four hours running alone.

The next couple of laps were surprisingly good. The temperature fell to 15C/59F, cool enough for pleasant running, but not cold enough to be a problem. I felt strong, even when it rained again. The support crew of Rachel, Cameron, and — after a quick nap — Mark, were magnificent. I enjoyed the solo running, but still expected that I would stop at 6 am. Soon, though, I started wondering, *Why would people ever stop in these races? This is so good!* My first lap alone was the fastest in hours, an exception to my trend.

Since the start of the race, the previous day, I'd noticed that my times had consistently slipped. Some laps I tried to walk less and run faster to get a longer break, but found that I would still finish around the same time. But without that speeding up, the breaks would get too short, and it seemed that the rest time was precious for my recovery.

Then, on my third post-Mark lap, I felt myself slow down massively. It was the only lap where I took my phone with me, and I suspect that it was a distraction. I tried to go faster, but my legs just wouldn't cooperate. If I didn't finish that yard, we'd be two short of winning the team event, and I'd miss seeing the sunrise. Plus, that would mean getting home around 5:30 am, which didn't seem a friendly time to arrive. I figured that if I finished at 6 am, then waited for Nicole to do her victory lap, that would get me home closer to 8 am, and I wouldn't wake my now sleeping girls.

I kept going, but my thoughts took a dark turn, fantasising about what would happen if I tripped over. Although I could run just fine, I wasn't sure that I'd be able to pick myself up from the ground. If it happened after the halfway mark on the course, I pictured myself lying there groaning until Nicole came by an hour later on her next lap.

This was the first lap where I wanted to quit, feared I'd fail, and wanted to not continue. It hurt more than ever, not so much muscular pain, but just the effort to go fast enough to finish on time. I knew that all I had to do was finish this lap, then the next, and I was done. I pushed on and finished with a few minutes' margin.

I told my crew that I'd do just one more, as I'd been planning. I left my phone, hat, hydration bladder and even light behind, hoping that being lighter would make it easier to finish. If I wasn't running after this lap, going an hour without water wouldn't matter too much. The parallel isn't ideal, but I had the image in my mind of Spanish explorer Hernán Cortés, who scuttled his ships to show his men that there was no turning back from their mission.

Surprisingly, yard 21 was my favourite. The sun rose twenty minutes in, and there was a gorgeous orange hue and a stunning fog on the fields. For a moment I thought I saw a small settlement and later, some emus running around. I suspect these weren't hallucinations but rather the creations of an over-active imagination. The mist rising from the river was breathtaking, as was the sound of thousands of birds waking from their slumber. I pitied the runners who had finished earlier, knowing that only two of us were experiencing this.

I finished that lap knowing that I would go no further, but acted as if I was preparing to keep on going. I told my crew to play along and make the normal preparations for the next lap. Partly, I liked the drama, and partly, it occurred to me that if Nicole just happened, by some incredible fluke, to pull out just before me, I would be more than happy to run one more lap.

Then, with one minute left, it was obvious that Nicole was raring to go for the next hour. I walked over to her on the start line: *Hi Nicole, I'm Stephen. You've run so well. Enjoy your last lap.* She was stunned for a moment, then checked: *Are you sure? Are you really sure?* In that moment, I had no doubts, although I'd rethink this moment repeatedly over the next year. *Yeah, definitely.*

She thanked me, we congratulated each other, and she was off. Nicole flew through her final lap, the only one out there in the early morning, earning a well-deserved victory.

For me, it was an honour to have been the assist to a great runner and the first female Backyard winner in Australia.

The next day Alun, the race director, advised that he had made a mistake, and another female runner had previously been awarded a win in an Australian Backyard. Back in 2019, Geordi Maclean had won the Backyard Blister with ten laps. Nicole graciously shared on social media that she was only the second winner, and congratulated Geordi.

Then, as the week went on, more information came to light. Alun discovered that after nine hours of the Backyard Blister, severe weather had forced the final three runners to stop. After a three-hour break, only Geordi continued, although the others could have restarted also. Geordi was — quite rightly — awarded the win. However, according to Backyard rules, any results after the pause would not count toward any records. Alun reverted to his original celebration. Geordi won her event, but Nicole was certainly the first record-eligible Backyard winner in Australia.

As for me, I'd now run my furthest, by a long way — almost 141 km. Second place was as good as a win for me, and winning the team event was the icing on the cake. I was excited about how well I'd done and surprised at how far I'd run. Even more surprisingly, my recurring injuries and cramps hadn't bothered me at all. Afterwards, apart from a few toenails, I felt better than I normally would from a long race, despite the distance.

I suspect there were a few factors at work in handling it as well as I did. The course itself was nice and flat, and the weather suited me more than most. The rain brought the temperatures down and stopped me sweating too much. Most likely, the regular breaks each hour helped my legs, and the regular infusion of nutrition each lap, whether solid food, drinks, or those delightful cherry tomatoes, all had to help. I suspect the biggest impact, though, came from our support crew, with all their practical and emotional assistance. Their encouragement made all the difference on multiple occasions. Even my injuries, much as I detested them, may have helped on the day. Months of slow running had trained me to keep going at a relatively sedate pace.

I'd also found Josh Duff's podcast advice helpful in practice. His warning about waves of problems, each of which would appear fatal at the time, but with each ultimately passing, proved true. Repeatedly throughout the day, I'd hit a difficulty. It would appear insurmountable, then a few hours later was just a memory. Whether it was helping Rachel to finish, the rain, neck pain, nausea and dizziness, losing Mark, or any of numerous leg pains, each issue would be with me for a while, and then it too would eventually disappear. Best of all, when the next problem came, I could remember the previous one, and think *This too shall pass*.

Although I wasn't shattered the next day, it still took a good month for my legs to fully recover from the event, and my pace was slower than ever. A few days later, I went for a short run and thought I'd listen to another podcast about Backyards while I was still excited about it all. I typed in Backyard Ultra in the search engine and found one I hadn't heard before, literally called 'A Backyard Ultra Podcast'. It was brand new; the first episode had only come out a week earlier, and the one I listened to dropped on the day our race finished.

Even better, I found that the podcast was created by an Australian runner, David 'Patto' Patterson. Although at the time he had only run two Backyards himself, he was hooked on the format, and would soon add many more to his resumé. After running sixteen hours for his first, he drove home, went to sleep, and was amazed that when he woke up the other runners were still going. Soon enough he would produce scores of quality interviews with many of the best Backyarders around the world.

I was happy to see that this episode, which was only its second, was about the Backyard Ultra World Satellite Championships due to start the following week.

I started shuffling along for my run, and had quite a shock a minute or two into the podcast. Patto was providing the results from the latest Backyard Ultras:

> *... at the States of Origin Backyard Ultra in Queensland. Now this was an awesome result. Nicole Jukes was the first female in Australia to win a Backyard Ultra. So that's a massive achievement. She did it running*

> *22 yards ... an awesome achievement. And well done to Stephen Parker, the assist.*

I was excited to hear my name and continued to listen to every episode from then on.

I was more disappointed, however, when I heard a common refrain in other episodes. Multiple guests remarked that *No one ever drops out at sunrise, as you get so much energy from the start of the day.* Every time I heard that, I thought *Maybe I should have kept going*.

I was also excited to start following the upcoming Satellite Championships. I hadn't been following the sport for the 2020 version, so didn't know what to expect.

5

International Showdown

TWO WEEKS AFTER our race was finished came the World Backyard Ultra Satellite Championships, starting 15 October 2022. This was the sequel to 2020's Covid-inspired event, and now a regular biennial pattern had begun. One year would be the Satellite Championships, where each country would simultaneously host their own 15-person national championship event. The following year would be Big's Backyard in Tennessee, where the Satellite winners and the best of the rest would gather to compete.

After the success of the 2020 Satellites, Laz had extended his ticket system to more races. In 2019 he had established golden ticket races around the world, each of which guaranteed the winner a start at Big's. Now each country had its own championship event, each of which would effectively have golden tickets. Obtaining a spot in those races became a coveted prize. In countries that had the demand, six races would be allocated silver ticket status, and their six winners would be guaranteed a spot in the national Satellite Championships. The other nine runners would be those with the highest totals. Some countries would also have another level, where the winners of bronze races would then get entry to silver ticket races. As some of the silver ticket races had been selling out within hours, the bronze races provided a way for good runners to secure a spot in the silver events. It all added to the anticipation for the Satellite Championships that were to come, with so many athletes around the world striving to compete.

Although the 2020 event was exciting enough, in reality it was just a preview for what might happen once potential for the Satellite format was unleashed. Whereas 2020 had seen 300 runners in 21 countries, 2022 would have 555 from 37 countries. The stage was set for an amazing race—or series of races. There were multiple competitions to take place — who would win each of 37 national events, which country would win the team competition, and which individual would triumph internationally by winning their event with more laps than any other winner.

This time, the various competitions came with the benefit of some event history, so the theoretical challenges were a lot more personal. Would Harvey Lewis defend his title won at Big's in 2021? Would he regain the world record that he'd set there with 85 yards, now lost to Merijn Geerts with 90? Would the ascendant Belgium again win the team event?

Closer to home, as an Aussie, I was fascinated by the prospect of the local contest. The Australian team was dominated by Western Australia, with the state providing seven of the 15 runners. Pivotal to their chances was Phil Gore, who had previously held the Australian record. Queenslander Chris Murphy had the earlier record of 46 laps from his win in the 2020 Satellites, but Phil had run 48 at Herdy's Frontyard Ultra in March 2021, beating Kevin Matthews. He extended it to 51 over Michael Hooker at Birdy's in August, then again to 54 at Birdy's in 2022, this time over Aaron Young. Just nine days later Ryan Crawford had run 59 yards, with Kevin Muller the assist, at the Clint Eastwood course. The Australian record had returned to the East Coast.

With a 4000 km distance between them, it was little surprise that the West Australian runners hadn't yet raced against the best of the East. In the 2020 edition, Australia's state-based Covid restrictions had prevented the event from being truly national, with Queenslanders dominating the team by necessity. Although Phil Gore had a best of 54, he didn't know how far he could go, having never been pushed by the eastern runners. And although Ryan had done 59, if Phil or others could push him past that, who knew what he could do?

Unfortunately, Australia's runner with the second-highest total was unable to compete. After he won the Clint Eastwood with 42 yards in 2021, Kevin Muller had the year's highest international Backyard total for several months. His 58 in 2022 behind Ryan guaranteed him a spot in the Australian team. However, he also served in the Australian Army, and was on a mandatory field training exercise at Puckapunyal from which he couldn't be excused. Nevertheless, we still had a strong team, and the prospect of seeing many of our best competing was alluring.

I also wondered, with an American team fired up to push each other on, how far could they go? I was predicting Harvey to get both the world record and overall win, the USA to win the team event, and for Ryan Crawford to take out the Australian contest. Fortunately, I didn't put money on my speculations.

In every Backyard Ultra, there is always some fascinating story of endurance, courage and unexpected events. In the 2022 Satellite Championships, these stories were multiplied 37 times over, with each country having their own challenges and surprises.

But beyond the sheer number of races, there was a different element at work here. As well as the 37 individual races and the race to go furthest overall, the 37 teams also took seriously their responsibility to see who could go the furthest collectively.

I asked Laz about the dynamics of these races, and he explained that it is this team element that makes them so amazing. Runners will push themselves harder for their team than they will for themselves. Normally in a Backyard, even the best runners often stop when they start to think they have no realistic prospect of winning. They might know that physically they could go further, but if they become convinced someone else will go a lot further than them, their motivation to continue disappears. It's what makes hope and a positive mindset such a pivotal aspect of the races. It's what knocked me out in the States of Origin, as if I had no realistic prospect of winning, I might as well stop.

In the Satellite Championships, though, that tendency to drop out if you couldn't personally win was gone. Here the motivation was to accumulate as many laps as you could, not just for your own record, but to help your team.

Laz says that it is often the runners ranked 8-12 in these races who make the most difference. They're not going to win, or come last, but if they can keep on going further than they have before, then they can make a massive difference. The way to win, then, was to encourage your team-mates to go as far as they can.

Once it comes down to the final two, though, more often than not the race reverts to a battle between the remaining runners to see who can take the win. By then the team standings are often locked in one way or the other, and whoever takes the national win gets the coveted ticket to Big's the following year. With only a limited number of Big's entries each year, the Satellite win was the safest way to guarantee an entry.

To add even more interest, countries were divided into three divisions, small, medium and large. Some of the categories seemed strange. Iceland, with a population of 370,000, seemed to fit in the small division well, but not Pakistan and Brazil, each with over 200 million residents. Similarly, India's 1.4 billion people appeared an odd fit in the mid-sized country listings, while Ireland and New Zealand's five million wouldn't naturally fit in the large list. The allocation of countries was made, not on the basis of their population, but on how many of their team had completed Backyards of 24 hours or more. As such, it allowed countries with less depth and Backyard experience in their ranks to have a chance to win, perhaps not the overall competition, but against their peers.

The race started at 7 am, 15 October, in Tennessee, and at the equivalent times in 36 other locations worldwide. Many runners dropped out early, mostly from the countries with less experience. Four athletes finished after just three laps, another two after six, and six more at each of laps seven and eight.

Perhaps the most shocking loss of these was John Stocker of the UK team. He was their number one ranked athlete, and rightly so. A three-time winner of the Suffolk Backyard Ultra, his 2021 win there with 81 yards had taken the world record from Belgium's Karel Sabbe. He'd never been beaten in a Backyard. With terrible timing, he had been sick in the lead-up to the Satellite race, but had assumed and hoped he would be able to push through it. He was wrong. Eight laps in, he had to finish due to illness, a massive 73 yards short of his best effort.

The first two countries to finish their races were India and Mauritius. Kartik Joshi and Julien Law Hin Chin both finished with 22 yards, winning their national championships and a ticket to Big's. However, even though Venezuela went further, with 23 yards, and Malaysia 24, the team results were different. India finished higher on 241 total laps than Venezuela with 201, while Mauritius's 173 beat Malaysia's 161. It showed early on that what mattered most was not how far your best runner went, but what your entire team could do together.

By the time all the competitors from those four countries had finished, seven others were yet to drop a single runner. That didn't last long. The next lap, Denmark lost Lars Skaarup Brodsgaard, Canada Mike Huber and the USA Brady Winkles, each their team's first to finish with 25 laps. Harvey Lewis, meanwhile, was looking strong as he ran into a new morning, as if he was only just getting started.

On the following yard, disaster struck the Australian team. Jessica Smith was one of the stronger runners, having run 45 yards for third place at Birdy's Backyard earlier that year. She was hoping to push well past her best for the sake of the team, like so many would do. However, with the Australians having a difficult start time of 11 pm, they had already entered their second night while many others were finishing their first. Around midnight, and still running well, she went for a well-deserved nap after completing her 26th lap. Unfortunately, her crew was similarly feeling the effects of fatigue and inadvertently missed the start of the next loop, having also fallen asleep. Both crew and athlete slept through their alarms, the three-minute whistle, the two-minute whistle, the one-minute whistle and the starting cowbell. The Aussies were down to fourteen.

Afterwards, Jessica shared her experience:
> There were so many feelings and emotions that went through my head in the moment I was woken up by the run director. I heard the knock on the door, looked at my watch and it was 1:04 am. Panic, sadness, relief, disappointment, empathy. Sure, I was disappointed for myself and for the team, but I also knew it's only a run and we would be ok.

By this stage, the 27th hour, only some European countries — Hungary, France and Belgium — still had their full teams of fifteen running. France would lose Charles Payen that lap and end up in eighth place. Hungary wouldn't lose anyone until yard 32, when three finished, with another two on the next, coming sixth place overall. When Belgium lost their first at thirty, Hungary was able to enjoy briefly being on top of the international team table.

Towards the bottom of the field, Pakistan was an outlier. The team itself finished in 32nd place, but their winner, Jamal Said, completed 50 laps, and attained the 17th highest winning total. It was an incredible performance, given his previous best was only 14 hours, and Pakistan's national record just 26.

Ukraine, though, provided much of the early drama. With the event taking place eight months after the Russian invasion, nothing went smoothly. Although Laz does his best to stop politics from intruding on his sport, occasionally circumstances demand an exception. After the Russian invasion of Ukraine, he did not enforce a ban on Russian athletes in Backyards, but they could not enter a team into the Satellite competition. He explained that:
> a lot would have to change before a Russian team would be able to participate in the team championships. … The only war we want is the figurative war of competition, where we compete to the limits of our abilities, and then share the embrace of friendship that comes with shared experience.

The Ukrainian team wanted to participate, and were warmly welcomed, but it would not be easy for them. Alex Holl had kindly invited the Ukrainians to share a course with the German team, even starting a fundraiser to help defray their costs. But with a ban on Ukrainian men leaving their country, for fear of weakening their defence efforts, that proposal had to be abandoned.

With an impressive 46 yards, Viktoriia Nikolaienko-Bryantseva was the Ukrainian record holder. She agreed to take over the responsibilities for organising her country's race and set about recruiting a team, which was harder than usual with many of the best runners on the front line. She pleaded with suppliers to provide Ukrainian flag-inspired blue and yellow shirts for the team. Constant shelling, limited electricity and uncertain deliveries made everything especially difficult, but two days before the event the shirts finally arrived at her house. She also found a hopefully suitable location, though with much of the country under siege, it was not simple to find somewhere with a semblance of safety.

Her words to the Satellite organising team were inspirational for many:

> *There is a terrible murderous war going on in our country, but life goes on for us. Running is an important part of our life – it is what [keeps] the psychological state more or less stable, and participation in competitions, as well as representing Ukraine at the World Championship, is an honor, hope and opportunity to open Ukraine to the world. The Ukrainian Spirit is unbreakable. We continue our lives and move towards our dreams even in times of war.*

Viktoriia had planned to run with the team, but three weeks out had to withdraw. Her parents were living in the occupied town of Oleshky, in the Kherson region. Twice Russian soldiers visited their house, taking her father away at gunpoint the second time. When she injured her Achilles tendon not long before the event, it was the final straw. She realised she could not organise the race and run herself, so devoted herself to team leadership duties.

When the Ukrainians began at 3 pm local time, they had one of the more inexperienced teams, all with far less training than they would like. It turns out that running huge numbers of miles each week is not that easy when missiles are regularly flying overhead. Even where training was possible, there were often far more urgent tasks to focus on. Three of the team's runners were over fifty, one was 66, but their motivation outweighed any effects of aging. Even their equipment was limited, with some of the runners having gifted their best gear earlier to the army. Alex Holl's fund-raising was helpful, with the shirts, generator fuel, transportation costs and food for participants and volunteers all provided for. The leftover food was given to a centre for displaced people, and the remaining money offered to the Armed Forces of Ukraine.

The team knew from the start that this Backyard would have to operate under different procedures than in peacetime, given the curfew that was in place. They managed to secure permission from the Territorial Defence Forces for a course that would run through a forest. The starting tent was covered with camouflage. Instead of the standard cowbell, potentially alerting the enemy to their presence, the starter instead calmly called out *One, two, three, start!*

One hour later, despite all their careful preparations, the police arrived and ordered the organisers to stop the race. For hours they debated, the organisers showing the permits and explaining the safety precautions in place, while the athletes continued lap after lap. Finally, the race was allowed to continue, but only by moving the starting tent further into the forest and covering the time clock, hopefully hiding them better from Russian drones.

Nazarii Hnat won with 28 yards, while the ever-smiling Oleksandr Slipets was the assist with 27. Each only ran two and four laps fewer than they had two years earlier, before the war, but back then they were the team's seventh and ninth-best runners. The war made an impact on them all, but the bravery and perseverance of the team, despite their myriad problems, was an inspiration to many. Their 27th place was a great result for Ukraine given what its people were going through.

South Africa and Finland might not have been at war, but they didn't get much further than the Ukrainians. Their disasters were of the natural kind. In South Africa, before the race began, some hikers lit a fire, and because it was the dry season, the grass began spreading the flames so that a massive fire erupted along the runners' intended route. The organisers went to see if it was possible to still run the original course, but the smoke was too bad for them to even get close. Two alternate routes were tried, but neither proved safe. The organisers would tell the runners to use the new course, then it too would become unsuitable and they would have to change to another. This all wore down the runners physically and mentally, and many of them dropped out as a result of the danger, smoke and constant changes. Eventually, the assist Melikhaya Msizi called it quits. One last out-and-back route was developed so Thembinkosi Sojola could complete the course and take the win with 31 yards. The team also finished in 31st place. There was some relief that they stopped then, as the fire was only getting worse, and soon they all would have been forced to evacuate.

Finland's race was held in Vihti, about 50 km from Helsinki. The route took the runners along a ridge near Nummela airport, exposing them to the breeze. It began with what was, at first, just wind and rain. However, a few hours from the start, the organisers had to remove the finish line arch as the wind had picked up to an incredible degree. There was a cold front off the southeast coast of Finland, and the wind continued to increase its ferocity. It would be recorded elsewhere at 39.2 metres per second, or 88 mph, one of the strongest winds ever recorded in Finland.

And then it got nasty. After Emil Söderlund finished at the end of yard 32, there were three runners left. Visa Kivinen, Juha Jumisko and Anton Aro all began the next yard, running into hurricane-like conditions in the dark. Shortly after they started, the wind knocked down several trees behind the race headquarters. The timing equipment was broken, and loose items were scattered. The runners' support crews expressed concern about their well-being. Meanwhile, the competitors' focus was, as always, just to complete one more lap.

Afterwards, Visa reflected: *I think runners, who have [run] 32 hours are not able to judge safety conditions correctly ... still we really noticed that weather conditions were very extreme and dangerous.*

Race director Juha Seppälä realised he had to intervene, and at yard 33 suspended the race. He couldn't risk the runners' lives. The next day, when he checked the course, he found dozens of fallen trees and power cables lying across the trail. It was a good decision.

Later, Juha wrote to Laz seeking special permission for their team to determine a winner. With the race abandoned, there was no winner, and no recipient of the Golden Ticket to Big's. Laz acquiesced, and in April 2023 Finland organised a special runoff event. It was most likely the smallest Backyard Ultra in history, with only the three competitors who had been forced to stop. Visa ended up winning with 23 laps, earning the right to represent Finland at the World Championships later that year. The low winning number of yards was also evidence that to get higher totals, a broader pool of runners was needed. Despite the ability of each of the three to go much further, the smaller field was not conducive to the runners pushing themselves to their limits, even with Big's as motivation.

Nearby, Norway and Sweden had taken a different approach. Inspired by the UK and Ireland teams sharing a course at the 2020 Satellites, Norway asked if they could run at the Swedish team's venue. Norway had not been able to get a team together for 2020, and this would save the organisers a lot of effort. Sweden agreed, and the combined races added to the atmosphere of both events.

It ended up being a long drive along icy roads for the Norwegian team to get to Älvdalen, a tiny isolated town in the middle of Sweden. The starting corral was adjacent to a hotel in the centre of the town, and most runners set up their support crews in the hotel itself. One runner from Norway booked one of the hotel rooms and would occasionally go to his warm and comfortable bed to relax in between laps.

Jon Asphjell, the Norwegian record holder, and Ekeberg Backyard Ultra race director, took a different approach. For the first 24 hours, he was alone outside the hotel, preferring to stay in the huge tent just by the corral. He explained that the hardest part of any Backyard was when you get up to start the race again for the next lap. His approach was to make this as easy as possible, by never getting too comfortable. He avoided the warmth of the hotel, never laid down, and would sit in his chair as close to the start as he could. After the first day, a few of the other runners joined him.

The course itself was flat with a mix of trails and gravel road. The two teams would start and finish in the same location, but run the course in opposite directions, allowing the athletes to smile, wave and high-five each other as they passed one another.

The conditions were some of the coldest of any Backyard Ultras. The first night it was around 0C/32F, and raining. The runners thought snow was on its way, but it held off. Although it was only October, the nights were already long, with almost thirteen hours of darkness. The second night brought even more rain, a lot of injuries, and a number of physical and mental breakdowns.

Jon ended up winning the Norwegian event with 38 yards; Eivind Svellingen was the assist on 37. Jon was also renowned in Backyard circles for another reason. Under the name Jonny Aspen, he had released a song he had written about Backyards, suitably called Last One Standing, which he occasionally would perform at races.

On the Swedish side, all except one runner made it to the 24-hour mark. When Filip Sodering finished after 41, only two more were left. Branislav Pavic and Tobbe Gyllebring then ran together for another fifteen hours, until Tobbe won with 57 laps. Norway finished in 20th place, while Sweden had the 9th highest team score.

Norway also took the win in the small country division. Their 392 cumulative yards just edged out nearby Iceland with 384 and Finland with 377, putting them in 21st and 22nd places.

In the medium-sized country list, Mexico won with 517 total laps for 10th place, over Italy in 16th place with 454. The winner of Mexico was a surprise to many; Reyes Satevo had a previous best of 30 yards from the 2020 Satellites, and came in as the second bottom-ranked Mexican runner. Now aged 26, one of the youngest runners, he more than doubled his previous best with 66 yards.

Meanwhile, many of the larger teams had dropped out a lot earlier. Repeatedly, there would be a wave of countries finishing at the same time. At 46 hours, only two hours before the 200-mile, two full days mark, three countries finished. Sam Harvey was best for New Zealand, Hendrik Boury was Germany's winner and Patrik Hrotek won for Slovakia. Five hours later another four countries finished on 51 hours. Their winners were Joshua Toh from Singapore, Oriol Antoli from Spain, Jivee Tolentino from Ireland and Christian Mauduit from France.

Now there were only 39 runners left worldwide, spread across 10 countries. Denmark, Sweden, Italy and Hungary had two left each, while Mexico and Canada had three. At the top end of the field, the USA were showing their depth with 10 runners remaining. A long way back was Japan with six, Belgium on five, then Australia with four.

In fifth place overall, with one of the more fascinating races, was Canada, accruing 620 yards on their course in Summerland, British Columbia. Their high-scoring finish came from a strong all-round team performance. None of their runners finished before yard 24. When Mike Huber did finish on 25, he didn't lie down for an extended sleep, as most people would want. Instead, he joined Amanda Nelson's support crew and remained a crucial part of the Canadian team effort.

Even then, the Canadians only dropped off slowly, until finally they finished the 40th lap, which nine of them reached. Suddenly, in the middle of their second night, four decided to call it quits at once. Matt Shepard (the Coffee Shop Guy), Cedric Chavanne, Stewart Wyllie and Marco Poulin all had had enough.

Marco, though, was not finished. Once he concluded his lap, he stayed at the finish line rather than going off to recover at his tent. He waited until his crew chief, and girlfriend, came over to him. The 57-year-old athlete was already regarded as somewhat of an inspiration. Previously he had been a homeless drug addict and dealer who spent time in prison. Now well and truly reformed, he was a social worker and motivational speaker, helping others to avoid his mistakes.

When his girlfriend walked over to him, Marco slowly, awkwardly, lowered himself down to one knee; running 268 km had taken its toll. In front of many of his teammates and a mass of support crew, he proposed marriage to her, and a marvellous day was made even more special.

Brian Bondy finished two laps later, then Michel Leblanc the following, on 43, and the Canadian team was down to their final three. When Australia's Margie Hadley finished on 47, and the USA's Jennifer Russo the next lap on 48, suddenly Canada's Amanda Nelson was the only female left internationally.

Amanda was an accomplished runner, but still relatively new to the scene. She had begun running consistently in 2015, and only made the step up to ultras in 2020. In 2022, just two months earlier, she had competed in — and won — her first Backyard, the Persistence Backyard Ultra, with 33 yards.

Unfortunately, she didn't have an ideal start to the Satellite event. Two days before it began she woke up feeling unwell, so went to the hospital the morning before her flight. The hospital was unable to see her in time, so she decided to just hope it would be okay. Once she was with her team, her coughing woke several of them up as they tried to sleep just hours before the start.

As the race began she still felt awful, and her strategy was to just do however many laps she could and not disadvantage her team too much. For a while, things seemed to just get worse and worse. Early on, a black bear decided to walk across the race path about thirty feet in front of Amanda and the other runners. The bear was even more scared than they were, and quickly ran off into the nearby bush. As she got into the thirties, she felt awful from inhaling dust and wildfire smoke, and started to feel homesick.

She told her team-mates, Eric Deshaies and Ihor Verys: *I won't be in much longer.* They encouraged her to keep going: *No, you will be ok, it's just a tough time right now. You will come out of it.*

She again tried to quit after lap 41. She wanted to see her family back home, was coughing far too much, struggling to breathe and desperate for sleep. She walked into her tent and told her crew chief *I'm done; I am not going back out.* Mike Huber and Leslie Barata walked over to her and pulled her out of her chair, dragging her to the starting corral. *You will regret this if you don't go.* With tears in her eyes, she went back out again, repeating to herself: *This is for the team. It's just one more for the team.*

That lap, things started to improve. She pulled herself together and her fight came back. At the same time, though, the effects of her sleep deprivation were growing. Her hip pain had been so bad that for many hours she found herself unable to sleep. Eventually Easton, a massage therapist, helped her to get to sleep, and he continued to massage her while she slept. At one stage she thought it couldn't hurt to close her eyes, just for a moment, while she was running. It may have been more than a moment, as suddenly she woke up as she felt her right foot go off a cliff edge. She had been having a series of hallucinations, but by the 53rd yard she had stopped knowing what was real and what was not. She wasn't sure if she was awake, asleep, or just confused.

By lap 55, she was coherent enough to know that things were starting to get seriously dangerous. She had heard bears and other wildlife near the course and didn't think she would have the mental capacity to deal with any animal encounters. She couldn't remember where she was on the course. *Did I miss a turn? Did I make it to a certain point yet?* She prayed for help. With the cliffs to navigate every yard, and her tiredness increasing, the risks were only getting greater. Yet she also had great confidence in her two remaining teammates and knew that Eric and Ihor would be able to keep on going. They had encouraged her so much, with their positivity sustaining her, that she knew it would allow them to go a long way themselves. At the end of lap 55 she finally finished, the last female standing worldwide, setting a new Canadian women's record.

At 28, Ihor Verys was one of the youngest in the field, with no one younger than him in the top seventy runners. He had moved from Ukraine seven years earlier to go to college in Canada and had been making a significant mark in the ultrarunning world. His only Backyard result at that stage, though, was a win with 39 yards, and by now he was already sixteen hours past that.

Eric Deshaies had run 50 the previous year at Big's and was most renowned for his triathlon exploits. In 2008 he had won the Double Ironman Triathlon World Championship in Canada, where instead of completing the normal, already extreme, ironman distances, competitors did double the swim, double the ride and double the run. It was a good base for a Backyard athlete, and he was putting it to excellent use now. In his day job, he worked in a sleep lab, and that too may have been useful for this sleep-depriving event.

After Amanda finished, the two ran on for another eleven laps. Eventually, Eric finished after yard 66, leaving Ihor to set a new Canadian record of 67. Both had smashed their previous best efforts. Ihor now had two wins from two Backyards and was excited to see how much further he could go.

At this stage, there were now only thirteen runners left in four countries, and the international competition was getting particularly exciting. On the same lap that Ihor had to finish, Japan's Kurai Quatresous made his last loop, leaving three Japanese runners still going. Belgium lost Frank 'The Tank' Gielen, leaving just two Belgians. Australia had three left, while the United States still had five.

Japan was now coming fourth in the team race, with 697 yards, and had three runners left. Belgium was in third place, on 720, albeit with only two competitors remaining. With every lap that Japan could keep their one-runner advantage, they would take a lap off Belgium's current margin of 23. If everyone held on, Japan would pass Belgium in 24 hours, but if Belgium's assist stopped, the three Japanese runners could catch up in eight hours.

Earlier, Australia had been in second place by a greater margin, but after a wave of dropouts at yards 47, 48, 48, 49, 50, 51, and 56, Belgium had been slowly catching up. From lap 57 on, Belgium had five runners to Australia's three, and were getting closer by two laps per hour. When Belgium lost Kevin Sneyders after 65 yards, they had almost drawn level, being just one lap behind Australia. Next gone was Frank at 67, and now it was Australia with a one-runner lead over Belgium, with no losses since Ben Nichols at 56. Their overall lead, which had almost disappeared, began growing again by one lap per hour.

By now, it did seem that the USA had the team race all to themselves. Their total score was 828 yards, 107 above the Australians. Their five runners remaining meant that the lead would keep on going up, so their position looked secure.

More and more spectators began following the race, perhaps because the sheer complexity of having had so many runners and so many countries had naturally reduced, and now it was easier to follow. Would the American lead be insurmountable? Could the Japanese hold off Belgium, and Australia hold off both countries? Meanwhile, sleeplessness was becoming more evident, not only for the runners, but for spectators staying up all night to follow the races.

For the Australian team, considerable drama had already occurred before the race began. The plan was for their event to be run on the paddocks of Mirrim Wurnit, a farm an hour's north of Melbourne, Victoria. It was a beautiful course with stunning views on mostly dirt trails. It had decent elevation and rugged terrain, so it would not be easy, but interesting for the athletes who went many laps. It was the same venue as the first Backyard in Australia, back in June 2019, where David Giles won with 33 laps.

However, two weeks before the race was due to begin, a torrential downpour made much of the course waterlogged and boggy. Peter Munns and Peter Clarke, the race directors, cut the course back to loops of the parts that would still be runnable.

Four days before the race began, another massive rain event hit. Over the next 48 hours, the Macedon Ranges received more rainfall than in any comparable period in the last fifty years. The farm's creek burst its banks, and water came up above the farm's fences. Peter Clarke explained that *about 25% of our planned course for the Backyard Ultra World Team Championship was under water. We were in trouble.*

Two days before the race began, the athletes began arriving, and many found that their camping plans had been washed away. It looked like the race might be too. Messages began flying between the runners and organisers, and the prospect of the event being relocated or even cancelled was raised. The runners were devastated at the idea of not being able to compete on the world stage after — in some cases — years of preparation. Their consensus was clear: even if they had to just go up and down a driveway or around a hay bale, they wanted to run.

The day before the race, the race directors spent much of their time on the phone to various local councils trying to arrange an alternate venue. The problem, they soon found, lay in the logistics of hosting an event of an indefinite length. Crews, runners, event staff and even spectators each had their own various needs. Soon they realised relocating was not plausible in the limited time they had. Whether they cancelled, relocated or used the existing course, there were no good options.

Phil Gore reported that just before he went to bed the night before the race, the runners were told that the event would go ahead on the original course. The rain had subsided, the creek had receded, and the course itself was no longer — technically — underwater. Large sections were still waterlogged, but everyone would all do their soggy best to make it work. Phil lamented: *It would be messy, it wouldn't be pleasant, we wouldn't be competitive on the world stage.*

The runners woke to what felt like a miracle. The road leading into the farm was still flooded. One section was a metre underwater, and completely impassable, so the local council closed a stretch of it just outside Mirrim Wurnit. Suddenly the event had four kilometres of runnable, and amazingly dry, dirt road that was now closed to traffic, only twenty metres from their starting corral. Could this be the answer to their dilemma?

On the morning the race was due to begin, the dry road was quickly measured, and a 6.7056 km course created. Without the road closure, it would have been untenable to run there amidst the traffic. Now there was a brilliant opportunity for the runners to have a safe, dry, relatively flat and fast course. From the farm they would run straight to the road and up the only hill. At around 400 m there was a slight bend to the right, and from there it was completely straight until the turnaround point, from where they would retrace their steps. It was as simple an out-and-back course as you could design. It had none of the typical features runners would use to break a course up into smaller sections and decide where to walk. It was described later as the most boring course they had ever run on, but it was the best option under the circumstances.

The race directors were still not convinced it was a permanent solution. The paddocks were drying, and by the next day should be a lot more runnable, and it seemed a shame to deprive the runners of their beauty. Also, at any stage the council might re-open the road, forcing a sudden change from the new course. An official announcement was made that the race would go for ten hours on the road, then revert to the paddock for the remainder.

After ten hours, the switch to the paddock was delayed for a while, as although the weather had improved, the course was still wet. The runners' feet would be soaked the entire time, and they weren't keen on that. During the laps, the support crews would talk to the race directors about their latest thinking about the race, then, when the runners came in, the crew would pass on the updates. Over many hours the three-way discussions flew backwards and forwards. Eventually it became clear; the runners would prefer to stay on the road, and the race directors agreed that would be best. The entire race was eventually run on the temporary course, and the council kept the road closed to traffic.

It was a good decision, as the Australian team performed far beyond their expectations. From all the previous Backyard events, only six Australians had ever reached 48 hours. Incredibly, at the start of yard 48 at Mirrim Wurnit, ten were lined up at the start. At this point they were second in the team event, and had the second largest team. Margie Hadley did not finish the lap, but beat her personal best by nine laps and set a new female Australian record of 47. The remaining nine all joined the elite group of 48. It was a great all-round team performance, with the top seven Australians increasing their previous best by at least ten laps.

Most dropped out over the next few hours. By the start of lap 57, the Australians were down to three runners. By lap 68 they still had three, the same as Japan, one more than Belgium and two fewer than the USA. In the team race they were narrowly in second place, just the one point ahead of Belgium.

The final three were Rob Parsons and previous record holders Ryan Crawford and Phil Gore. Rob had a previous best of 44 yards and ended up with the biggest improvement on the team. His 73 yards were a massive 29 more than he had done before. It was performances like that which were the foundation of the over-performing Australian team, each person desperately trying to do their best not for themselves, but for their new mates.

With Rob gone, there were only ten runners left worldwide. An hour later, on lap 74, Tokimasa Hirata and Jon Noll both finished. Now there were four countries left, each with only their winner and assist. Japan was in fourth place with 718 yards, Daiki Shibawaki and Yukinori Yoshida still running. Belgium was in third on 734, Merijn Geerts running along with Ivo Steyaert.

Australia had steadily moved ahead of Belgium at a rate of one lap per hour, until Rob had finished, and were now on 741 yards, seven above third place. Phil Gore and Ryan Crawford were both still going. The USA was far ahead on 857, the team race seemingly decided, Harvey Lewis and Piotr Chadovich their last runners standing.

To the delight of the spectators, the potential of the international competition was being realised. Merijn, the current world record holder, was still running in Belgium, as was its former holder Harvey, in Tennessee. Which one would triumph? Whose assist would allow them to get the furthest? In Belgium, although Merijn had run 90 yards, Ivo's best was only 50, and he was already 24 past that. Similarly, in the USA, although Harvey's best, and former world record, was 85, Piotr's was only 60. The Americans seemed to have the lead. The Japanese both looked like they were out of their depth. Yukinori had only run 54, and Daiki Shibawaki 45.

In Australia, Phil's best of 54 and Ryan's 59 looked a long way away now. The hopes of an epic west versus east battle had paid off. My pick was on the Queenslander, Ryan, not your standard runner. Before discovering the joys of ultramarathons he had been a champion Mua Thai fighter, with 20 wins from 24 bouts. He had never taken running seriously, until one day when he saw a dusk to dawn race advertised. He entered it on a whim and won. Hooked, he began to push his limits on the road and trail just as he learnt to do in the ring. The strong mind that he had developed through fighting was a particularly useful asset for Backyards, as he knew that there was always some way of pulling out a win, even when a situation looked hopeless. Listening to him talk, the topic of pushing perceived limits often comes up; he loves to both push his own and encourage others to push theirs. His training is exhibit A. He regularly woke at 11:30 pm to have 'breakfast', drove to his workplace at 12:30 am then ran four hours before starting his work in construction. It's an arduous schedule, but suitable for someone with a relentless commitment to go as far as he possibly could.

When Ryan hit the seventies he was still looking good, running separately from Rob and Phil. Rob was too slow for Ryan to run comfortably with, and Phil was too fast. Physically, he felt strong, even if the cold temperatures were uncomfortable. He noticed Phil running sideways up a hill to avoid triggering some leg pains and was pleased that he had no injuries to worry about.

Phil had started to have serious leg issues at lap 63. They became so bad at the end of that yard that he'd woken his wife and crew chief Gemma to tell her he was going to stop. She convinced him to do just one more, and as the story typically goes, he kept going after that 'one'.

Soon Phil found that running hurt less than walking, so he dropped his walks and ran more. The pains began to subside. By now his thoughts of being the last one standing had disappeared, and he was simply trying to finish as many laps as he could for the team. Ryan and Rob both looked strong, and now Phil thought that he was there to help them. But when Rob dropped out, the lure of the Golden Ticket to Big's began to give him fresh motivation. Earlier on he had been encouraging all his teammates to keep going. Now, if Ryan wanted to quit, that would be great.

Ryan's mind, normally such an asset, was different now. He had been hallucinating for a while and was sure that someone was trying to trick him into thinking that he was in a race. At the end of a lap he asked his crew: *What am I even doing?* He was so disoriented, so confused, that he was sure the event was all some kind of joke. He realised now that he had not paid enough attention to getting good sleep early on and was paying the price. He'd tried to sleep, but without much success, the deprivation was hitting him hard.

Phil, on the other hand, had taken the matter of sleep more seriously than most. He ran most of the night laps faster than in the day so he would have time for a decent nap in his break. Even more extremely, he had adjusted his sleep patterns in the weeks leading up to the event. He knew that the Australians would start at the uncomfortable time of 11 pm, an hour when he would normally have been asleep. To avoid beginning the race with a sleep debt, he had adjusted the time he went to sleep by one hour each day, synchronising himself with the start time of the event. On the day the race started, after sneaking in a five km parkrun at nearby Sunbury, he went to bed at 2 pm and slept for eight hours, waking at 10 pm, an hour before he began running.

Ryan and Phil both finished lap 75, which was well beyond their previous best results. At the inaugural Satellite Championships two years earlier, Karel Sabbe had won the event and set the new world record with that score. Now eight competitors were still going.

When they began on 76, Ryan didn't start fast like he normally had. He ran slowly, then decided he would walk for a bit. He kept walking. After a while, it occurred to him that he had only been finishing each lap with minutes to spare, and because he had been walking so much, he probably wouldn't make it back on time. He explained *If I'm walking I'll never get back. I might just lie down.* And with that, Ryan was done.

When Phil began his return leg, he was surprised that he did not see Ryan close behind. He started to think that perhaps he might have the win. Eventually, he saw a figure far off in the distance, and finally got to the now surrendered Ryan. There was no point in trying to encourage him further; he would not be able to get back on time. Phil stopped, had a quick chat, checked that he was okay, shook his hand and said he'd send a car back for him. Ryan was grateful. Phil completed the lap and at last could stop; his final solo lap completed.

A similar scenario had played out at the top of the USA field in Tennessee. Early on, the Americans had shown incredible depth in their running ranks. After Brady Winkles had finished on 25 yards, the USA briefly fell from being equal leaders into fifth place. However, no more stopped until Kevin McCabe on 38. By then, 437 of the 555 runners had already finished. Kevin had battled with stomach issues for many hours. When he finally turned back on lap 39, all he wanted to know was whether he had made a difference for their team. Yes indeed, they were now in first place, and would not give up their lead again.

The only country even close to that depth was, fittingly, Belgium. They had lost Karen Clukers at 30 and Filip Germeys at 35. However, although Justin Wright was the USA's next to fall at 44, in that time Belgium lost a series of runners at 36, 37, and two each at 40 and 43.

One of the few Americans to do less well than they hoped was Chris Roberts. As their second-ranked runner, with a best of 84 as assist to Harvey Lewis' former world record, he had high hopes. Ultimately, an awfully timed Achilles tendon injury intervened, and restricted him to a still astonishing 60 yards. For twelve hours he persisted through the pain while his compatriots watched on in awe. Afterwards, several conceded that they only went as far as they did because of his example. *If he could do it, they could too.*

Five Americans reached 70, a mark reached only by two Belgians, three Japanese and three Australians. Then the slide began. Dan Yovichin finished at 70 yards, Steve Slaby at 72 and Jon Noll at 74.

Seemingly in sync with the Australians on the other side of the world, Harvey and Piotr began lap 76. Harvey was the previous winner, with a best result of 85. To the surprise of many, not long afterwards he walked back in, allowing Piotr to take the win. For the Australians, it was unanticipated, and an honour, to bow out at the same time as the top-ranked Americans.

The race had shrunk to a two-country, four-person event. The Japanese team were one of the biggest revelations. In the 2020 Satellites they only had 10 runners, making 291 yards in total. Their race had stopped at 43 laps, putting them in 18th place.

This time, nine Japanese went further than their 2020 winner, and for much of the race they sat firmly in fourth place. At lap 74 they closed to within 16 of Belgium, and 23 behind Australia. It was with the loss of the third-last Japanese runner, and the last two Australians, that the race dynamics changed.

With only two runners from each of Belgium and Japan running, the 16-lap margin would remain constant until one of the teams stumbled. Australia's lead over Japan, though, would shrink by two every lap. For Australians like me watching from home, interest in the race had never been higher, even with our stars finished. At lap 80 the Belgians had taken second place off Australia. If now one of the Japanese could get to 88, just shy of the current world record of 90, they would take third place from the Australians.

The Japanese event was organised by Tomokazu Ihara. A talented ultrarunner himself; he has attempted the arduous Barkley Marathon four times. On one of his visits there, Laz suggested that perhaps Japanese runners were crazy enough to enjoy a Backyard. Tomo, as he is more often known, sprang into action. In 2020 he began one, then multiple, Backyards across Japan. One of his innovations was to develop the

Satellite concept across Japan in a Last Samurai Standing Backyard Ultra. Across a half dozen venues, runners would race in separate but simultaneous races, with Tomo watching them all via a live stream and delivering a regular commentary.

People began to refer to him as the Japanese Laz, and Tomo was happy to play along. He would often dress in a red checked flannelette shirt, and a matching red beanie emblazoned with the word Geezer across it, both matching the clothing that Laz himself would often be seen wearing at races.

Now at the 2022 Satellite Championships, Tomo was looking after his runners well. He hired a chef to ensure they had a constant supply of food, buffet style; Japanese favourites like rice, noodles, rice balls and miso soup happen to be the type of foods that others worldwide include in their Backyard diets too.

When Hisayuki Tateno and Minoru Tanaka ran into the fifties, they both were ready to quit. Tomo attempted to prod them on for the proverbial one more lap. *Shut up! Don't tell me to do one more loop!* was their reply, before going on to finish after 52.

Next to fall, at yard 67, was Kurai Quatresous. According to Drew Damron in the Japan Times, Kurai had a curious approach to hydration. At the end of each lap he would sit down and drink a beer while enjoying a massage from his crew. Then he would get into a nearby car, close the door and nap while his crew watched on.

Just before the last Australians and Americans stopped, Tokimasa Hirata finished with 74. He had been virtually running in his sleep since lap 60, and at the end of his final yard collapsed over some chairs. When he would not respond, Tomo was tempted to call an ambulance, but Tokimasa eventually replied that he was just sleeping. They covered him with a blanket and let him stay where he was.

With each lap, the final two came closer to the Australian total. Although both were over 30 yards past their previous best, they were looking strong, and it appeared inevitable that they would keep going and take third place. Then, a fraction too early, sleep deprivation got the better of Yukinori Yoshida, and he stopped at 85. Daiki Shibawaki ran his final lap of 86, and the team fell an agonising three yards short of the Australians. Yukinori and Daiki would later explain that although Tomo and the crew all knew how close they were to the Australians, their exhaustion and focus on pushing themselves to finish meant the runners themselves weren't aware. Afterwards, they were devastated at just missing out. Their final placing, while off the podium, was a fantastic improvement. They had improved from 18th and 291 yards in 2020 to fourth place and 741 yards in 2022, and the Japanese team committed themselves to improving even more in future years.

And then there were two. In Belgium, Ivo and Merijn kept on running, lap after lap after lap.

When Australia and the USA finished at the end of yard 76, the top three countries were clear. The USA were far in front on 860, Australia was second on 744, and Belgium was third on 738. Belgium moving into first place seemed farcical, as they would need to get to 137 yards for a tie, or 138 for a win. Given that Merijn held the current world record of 90, he knew better than anyone how far off 138 was.

Australia, though, was easier pickings. At lap 79, with the Australian score stuck on 744, Belgium drew even, and at 80 they were in second place. Nevertheless, they still had to look over their shoulder, over an ocean or two, at Japan, stubbornly 16 yards behind. If Belgium stopped, it would only take eight hours for them to be caught.

From the start, though, this had been an amazing Belgium team. Their incredible results in the 2020 Satellites, with Karel Sabbe going the furthest with 75, and them taking the overall team win, had been met with great celebrations. Now they were hungry for more.

The 2022 team was stronger still, with no weak links, but the rest of the world had improved too. One advantage they had was the friendship between the runners. The strong ultra community in Belgium and the Netherlands had over many years led to healthy relationships amongst the Backyarders. The team members all knew each other well, having raced each other multiple times and volunteered in the same ultras together.

Having a team of friends brought immediate benefits. Many of them would run together, encouraging one another along. When one would have a weak moment, the others would be there, gently supporting and prodding them on.

Bart Stes, one of the Belgium race directors, elaborated:

> *That way every runner from Team Belgium managed to pull out a couple of extra laps — after they were completely spent. And if every runner in your team does that, that amounts to a lot of extra laps at the end.*

Their team was also optimistic that they had a course that would help them. They had used it in 2020 and found it ideal. It was very flat, half concrete, half trail, and if it rained it would not get muddy. They did get heavy rain for two laps, but otherwise had perfect weather, and the course dried off swiftly. The runners also had a useful building adjacent to the start, with a kitchen and enough space for all the competitors to shelter in their breaks. For most runners it was an ideal situation.

After a brilliant start, then a steady wave of losses in the thirties and forties, Belgium had moved their way up the field. Much earlier, at lap 65, they had come to within one point of Australia, but two losses at 65 and 67 slowed their attack.

Their third place runner was Frank 'The Tank' Gielen, one of the more colourful characters in Backyard circles. In the 2022 Belgium Legends he had won in 42 yards, and as part of his victory celebrations he completed the last lap wearing a full-length beer suit, allowing what looked like a bottle of beer to cross the line in first place.

Towards the end of the Satellite Championships, he started having hallucinations, something he always looked forward to, finding they would keep him entertained as he went deeper into races. He explained to me:

> *I was pretty tired and started to see different things in the shapes of the trees. But it was not top of my mind. When I came back on a loop I saw people applauding, and behind them the famous statues of Easter Island! And then it crossed my mind. Wow, they build those statues so fast, in just one round. A moment later I saw I mistook trees for statues.*

Earlier, during the third night, he was able to see Ivo have his own experience of hallucinations:

> *Ivo told me that he hears odd stuff when he gets really, really tired, as if people whisper or run behind his back. We stop talking and run half a mile. There suddenly is a school of children cheering and shouting to support the runners. And I ask Ivo, do you like this? And he is a bit surprised and responds to me: Oh, is this real?*

For all the runners, having spectators come along to watch and cheer was a new experience. They were used to having friends, family and crew cheering them on, but having the broader community turn up, particularly as the race went on longer, was a pleasant surprise.

By lap 67, Frank was in trouble. His focus had stopped being on the competition, and he missed being able to run along with his friends. Sure, Merijn and Ivo were also running buddies, but they went faster than him, so much of the time he was alone. Now he couldn't see any reason to continue.

At the start of 68, the team thought they'd secured a commitment from Frank for just one more lap, with the standard hope of many more after that one. He started, along with Ivo and Merijn, and the three went around the first building. To the support crew's surprise, several minutes later Frank turned up back at the start. Rather than running one more lap of the course, he'd done a much smaller lap around just the one building, and he was now finished.

Not long later, at lap 76, the Americans and Australians ended. Then at 86, the Japanese were gone, and it was just Merijn and Ivo left. Second place was now guaranteed, and the Americans were far enough in front that first place wasn't worth considering. The only question left was, how far could they go?

Bart Stes was watching it all unfold:

Meanwhile in Belgium we started realizing that with how good Merijn and Ivo looked, it was very well possible that we would be witnessing history.

Years earlier, Merijn had read an article in which Maggie Guterl had predicted that one day someone would get to 100 yards in a Backyard. To some that felt like the four-minute mile or two-hour marathon, an almost impossible test of human limits. Would it be more like the former, with many runners now beating the mark each year, or more the latter, which unassisted humans have to date been unable to achieve? Back in 2014, Johan Steene and Jeremy Ebel had set the world record in tying for the Big's win. Their record had lasted for just over three years. At the time it seemed unbeatable, yet they had run only 49 yards. In this race, exactly 50 athletes ran for 50 yards or more. It was an incredible progression, and it looked like another advance was impending.

Ever since reading that article, Merijn had assumed that Maggie was right; before too long someone would get to 100. Once he and Ivo hit 90, equalling Merijn's world record, it started to become a real possibility that perhaps it would be one of them who would do it. Although there had been the standard joking and boasting before the race, they had not seriously considered getting to 100 themselves until they were running in the nineties.

Merijn understandably had mixed feelings about getting to 90. He hadn't thought the world record would be broken in this event; it was far more about the overall team total than getting high individual scores. But while there was no chance he'd voluntarily stop before then, he was the sole existing record holder. He thought *going past that point could mean I would lose it.*

The organisers and crews started to get excited. They bought a birthday cake so Merijn could celebrate his birthday while out on the course. They extended their booking of the venue in case the runners went further than expected. And without telling them, they rushed through an order of special T-shirts for them all to wear. They were emblazoned with a picture of the two champions, Ivo kissing Merijn on the cheek during one of their earlier breaks. Underneath was the hashtag #breaking100. No pressure boys, but a lot of shirts are going to look silly if you don't make history. Fortunately, the two of them were completely oblivious to all the plans unfolding behind the scenes.

It was around then that the media began to turn up. Backyard Ultras have always been a niche sport. Articles get written about them, as they are incredible feats of human accomplishment, and the occasional news item will feature a local win. Here, though, was history in the making. The Belgium team had vanquished the rest of the world and was approaching a seemingly impossible mark. Camera crews arrived, spectator numbers grew, and there was a growing sense of excitement and anticipation. Little did the runners know that overseas interest was greater still, with bleary-eyed fans following the various discussions and feeds online at all times of the day and night.

As they moved into the late nineties, the atmosphere in the crowd began to change. The runners looked good, with no major physical issues, and it started to become obvious that they would get to 100. But what would happen after that? Was there a chance they could just keep going indefinitely? With no injury reports, spirits were high. Were the 137 yards needed to beat the American team not as farcical as they had seemed earlier? How much further would they go? How much further could they go? How hard would these two friends fight one another to get the win?

The stakes were high. Although prize money is rare in the Backyard Ultra scene, the winner of this race would receive 1,000 euros to help towards their travel to Tennessee for Big's 2023. Earning one of the Golden Tickets to Big's was itself a massive incentive for the win. While some in other countries would get their Gold Ticket by running for less than a day, these titans had already run for four full days, and still one of them would miss out. The winner would also be the holder of the world record, with all the attention and acclaim that would bring. The assist, despite smashing the previous world record, would receive a DNF, theoretically a failure, despite the accomplishment.

The organisers and crews tried talking to the runners as they approached 100 yards, looking for some insight into their intentions. They were left none the wiser. Around lap 98, Ivo and Merijn came up with a plan: they would aim for 100 together, then keep going until there was only one winner.

When they began their 100th yard, the organisers sprang into action. Out came the hidden T-shirts which had been designed, printed and delivered within half a day. The crews and organisers put them on, and they waited excitedly for their endurance warriors to return.

Just before the final turn, someone handed the runners flares, which created a cloud of coloured smoke following them as they ran the last short section around some benches. They put the flares down, wrapped their arms around each other's shoulders, and walked around the final corner together. They saw the now much larger crowd, many adorned with the new T-shirts. They laughed when they realised they were pictured on the front. The crowd erupted in cheers. Bart said *The moment we 'broke' the clock is a moment none of whom were there will ever forget, I imagine.* Between the T-shirts, fireworks, media presence, sleep-deprivation and the adrenaline rush shared by both athletes and crowd, it was certainly memorable.

Nine minutes later, it was time for Ivo and Merijn to head out again, the crowds still wondering what would happen. If you watch the video of the official race timer at the start of their 101st yard, instead of showing 100 hours, it moves from 99:59:58 to 99:59:59, then, as the two runners disappear around the corner, the clock remained stuck there. Although the organisers knew it was coming, the technology was not yet ready for this great progression by the runners. Fortunately, some hasty resetting fixed everything for the subsequent lap's finish.

Ivo and Merijn ran together for yard 101. The two were friends, and enjoyed chatting. They had run together regularly throughout the last four days but, more often than not, would keep to their own pace. Ivo would go faster so he could sleep; Merijn was happy to run more slowly and sleep less.

Earlier both had been generous towards their teammates, helping wherever they could. Ivo had supported several runners to complete their one more loop. Merijn would share his wealth of Backyard wisdom. Both encouraged and motivated their team throughout. Sportsmanship and friendship were ideals for both men, and this race was a strong example of that commitment.

They finished lap 101, rested, and lined up again at the start for 102. The cowbell rang sending them out once again. They stood there for a minute, then Ivo waved to those inside the building, presumably gesturing farewell before the next lap. Instead, he moved over to Merijn and the two embraced. Tim De Vriendt, one of the race directors, walked over and they explained to him that they were stopping. Now.

There would be no winner. Both would receive DNFs. Neither would receive the Golden Ticket to Big's. Neither had discovered what their limits would be. Both would always be left to ponder *I wonder how much further I could have gone that day? I wonder which of us would have triumphed?* It would become the question that could never be answered, but repeatedly asked by Backyarders around the world. Both were looking strong and feeling well and had an incredibly supportive environment surrounding them. We will never know what could have been.

I asked Merijn for his story, and he explained:

Although Ivo and I spoke about it (somewhere around loop 98) and decided to go on after 100 until there would be one winner, the atmosphere after breaking 100 was so special that it made us reconsider. It didn't feel right anymore to go on like nothing happened. So, as my wife suggested, we ran 101 together to have a chat about it and decide what we would do. We both felt this moment was too perfect to go on, so we decided to stop after that round.

This was, once again, sportsmanship and friendship at their finest. Why should one of the two receive the glory, and the other defeat? Why should two friends, who had worked so hard together, as a team, in a team event, suddenly turn on each other to resolve who was the best between them?

Soon the online world would be debating these and other questions. Was what they had done against the spirit of the Backyard? What would Laz think? Wasn't it cheating? Weren't both quitters who should have tried harder? Or was their action more in tune with the spirit of the sport than those who fought to the end?

Laz's summary showed clearly where he stood on the issue:

maybe meryjn and ivo summed up the championships best in their final act.
when they walked off the course together.
ending their greatest [performance] with a positive message.
Together Everyone Achieves More.
amid the avalanche of negative stories we hear today, there is this.
two men worked together to reach the pinnacle of their sport.
and then walked away from personal victory at the expense of the other.
they had already achieved all there was to achieve on this day

Later he would add - *This is the first time the runners defeated me.*

The decision to tie the race had gone backwards and forwards for a while. In the mid-nineties, Ivo and Merijn had come up with the idea: *Why don't we stop together?* Johan Steene and Jeremy Ebel had done so back in 2014.

The two Belgians kept it quiet at first, then eventually mentioned the strategy to the organisers. There was a mixed reaction. Bart explains *We wanted them to go on as long as possible, but we also hated the idea that one would be the new world record holder and the other would be left empty-handed.* Soon a consensus was reached, and the runners were told: *It's entirely up to you, but if you decide to go through with this plan, we will split the money and give you each half of the 1,000 euros.*

At lap 98, as Merijn explained, they decided no, they would keep going until they had a solo winner. Then at 100, they changed their minds.

All this time, the organisers were left in the dark. When the 100th yard was over, they still wondered how much further the two would go. When the 101st yard was done they had no more clarity. When Ivo and Merijn walked out to begin 102, they were surprised once the runners called it a draw. The friends had successfully kept everyone in suspense.

Finally, the race was over worldwide. Of the 555 starters, 358 ran for at least one day, 58 for at least two days. Twelve ran at least three, but only two managed to run for four days. To be precise, four days and five hours, an extraordinary performance, well above the average of 29.4 laps of their peers in the global event. With a few exceptions, due to unique circumstances like the wind in Finland and war in Ukraine, almost every team went substantially further in 2022 than 2020. Belgium improved from 574 yards to 788, while the USA went from 517 to 860.

Now the great clean-up began. After running for 101 hours and entertaining countless followers, Merijn and Ivo stayed to help tidy up. That shows character. It may also be further proof that they hadn't spent all their energy, that they could have kept going.

When the dust settled, each was given their share of the prize money. Neither would receive a Golden Ticket to Big's 2023, but there were spots open to runners around the world who had gone the furthest, what Laz called the 'at large' list. There were no guarantees, but as the two competitors with the best results in Backyard history, they would be safe to book their flights. Unless a wave of athletes suddenly started running past 101 yards, they would be at Big's in twelve months' time.

Now that the bar had been raised to a new level, the questions became: would others rise to meet that challenge? Or would Belgium 2022 be a one-off result, an unrepeated outlier? And if it would be beaten, how soon would that happen?

On the other side of the world, in Australia, Tim Walsh thought he'd give it a crack.

6

Dead Cow Gully

TIM WALSH DOESN'T describe himself as a runner. He runs a bit, but when you're rubbing shoulders with people who run for days on end, he knows that's not him. He is, though, one of the growing breed of Backyard Ultra race directors. Between Shaun Collins in New Zealand, Alex Holl in Germany, Lindley Chambers in the UK, and Tomo Ihara in Japan, to say nothing of Laz himself in the USA, they're people cut from a different cloth. Combine some eccentricity, innovation and a preparedness to push runners to suffer, and you've got a successful Backyard race director. Tim fits in well. Since 2021, he's been organising Dead Cow Gully in regional Australia on his family's cattle property in Nanango, Queensland, a few hours west of Brisbane.

Tim had been a teacher, then he moved into caring for people with disabilities. That's still his main occupation; his race directing a labour of love rather than a career. That's a good thing, as he's lost a lot of money on some races, and from those that are profitable, he pours the money back into future events.

Going back a few years, in a familiar story for those getting serious about running, Tim decided to give up alcohol. Once he did that, he was inspired to do other things that would improve his life. He began going to parkrun, running several dozen of the five km events, and volunteering at twice as many. He dipped his toes into some Run Queensland events, another group that organises trail and ultramarathon events, and he realised that he liked the people and was attracted to their lifestyle and overall vibe.

It was around this point that he heard about Backyards, and he joined a group from Brisbane Trail Runners who were doing a training run on the Clint Eastwood course to see what all the fuss was about. As he ran lap after lap, he started to wonder whether this could be the kind of thing that would attract people out to the bush. He loved the rural lifestyle himself, and often thought it would be great to help those in the city experience its delights for themselves.

He started looking around his family's land on Walsh Road. The 1600-acre property has been with his family for six generations and 150 years. To his surprise, he discovered that where he lived was ideal for a Backyard Ultra. He was able to design a simple single-loop course taking runners from his 110-year-old Iona homestead across a gully and back to the start. It didn't need any out-and-back sections to add distance, or the multiple loops that runners dread.

One area the competitors would run through was known as Dead Cow Gully, after one of the Walsh's cattle that had lost its footing and tripped by the creek's edge. As the main feature of the course, with the only significant elevation, it seemed the ideal name for the race itself. And soon enough, the Dead Cow Gully Backyard Ultra was born.

From the beginning, Tim threw himself into the task of preparing for the race. He spent hours clearing the property to create a safe and clear track, nearly destroying a lawnmower in the process.

Tim knew that only an hour away lived one of the living legends of Australian distance running, Ron Grant, who was more than familiar with the idea of running laps; in 1983 he had run a single lap around Australia itself, the first to complete the feat. In 217 days he had run 13,383 km, an average of 61.67 km per day. In 1992 he set the new world record for the longest distance run every hour for 1,000 hours. His hourly three kilometres might be less than half of what Backyarders do each hour, but to keep doing them for 1,000 hours was phenomenal. As a race director himself back in the day, he'd established a series of ultra-marathon events, also in the Nanango region.

Appreciating the value of having someone involved who knew all about running and organising events, Tim arranged for Ron to act as his mentor, and later an official Dead Cow Gully Ambassador. Ron started the first event, and would walk the course in reverse direction so he could encourage each runner as they came towards him.

Now Tim had a mentor and a course, the next thing he needed was some runners. He found a few friends who were happy to come for a test run, and they all ran two laps of the new course. He arranged for a photographer to take some high-quality photos, then began sharing the images on social media. Next, he offered some free training runs on the course. For Tim it was all win-win — more people were discovering the beauty of regional Queensland and going back home to tell how spectacular the course was. Even better, the photos from the training sessions looked stunning, and more and more people began to follow what was happening.

Tim went to the second Clint Eastwood in August 2020 to try running a proper event himself. He had the privilege of making some more history when an unexpected injury forced him out after only three laps, the first finisher. The experience was worthwhile though, as he was able to tell more people about his new race.

It looked like all his efforts were proving worthwhile, as when Tim opened up registrations for the inaugural event the response was rapid. Almost 200 people signed up and were excited to try the strange new format on 3 April 2021. It looked like this new Backyard was going to be a stunning success.

Then, five days before the race was due to start, Covid once again proved a problem. The Queensland Government announced a three-day lockdown for the greater Brisbane area. The lockdown would end over two days before Dead Cow Gully would begin, and the race venue was not inside the affected area, but like countless other situations at that time, it was not clear what would or should happen next. Would the lockdown be extended? Given the Covid outbreak was in Brisbane, would it be responsible to invite hundreds of people from that city to come to the so-far unaffected Nanango area? Would the local community want all these potential disease-carriers?

Given all this uncertainty, Tim initially cancelled, then postponed the event to 2 May. It meant that the runners could reschedule their Easter plans, and hopefully the race could still go ahead. Fortunately, it did, with Ryan Crawford taking the win with 44 yards.

After more success in 2022, Tim began to set his eyes on broader pastures and further innovation. Dead Cow Gully was a success again in 2023, and for the 2024 event, Tim wanted to introduce drug testing, offer a $10,000 prize for the overall winner, and have live streaming with commentary by David 'Patto' Patterson from the Backyard Ultra Podcast. For the icing on the entertainment cake, he would add a Chilli Dog eating competition at the end of lap 6. The competitors would have three minutes to eat as many as they could, with a $1,000 prize for the winner. When I first read that, I assumed it was an early April Fools' joke, but it was later clarified that the competition was only for the spectators, not the runners. Although the drug testing plans were abandoned, each of these ideas were innovations in the Backyard world.

With his capacity to innovate, entertain, attract big-name stars and draw crowds, Tim had the vibe of a Backyard P.T. Barnum. He'd attract similar debate and criticism, but he'd also bring runners and spectators into the Backyard scene.

Back in 2022, his big plan was for a new event on his farm in which the best of the best would come to compete. He was trying to address a problem that had existed for years. With the exception of the Satellite Championships, the best Backyard runners in Australia normally only raced against those in their own region. The occasional athlete would fly elsewhere, but the biggest races in different states had times that would clash, so that didn't happen much. Given the format of winners being limited by how far the assist would go, without having a stronger level of competition, it was difficult to discover how good our runners could be.

And so, Tim came up with another big idea. Convincing people to drive a few hours from Brisbane wasn't enough. Could he get the best of Australia to come by creating an event where the titans of the Australian Backyard scene could clash?

On 18 May 2022 he announced, in addition to the now-regular event, the birth of the Australian Backyard Masters, to take place on 24 June 2023. It would be held, naturally, in Dead Cow Gully, and invite the best runners from Australia and the rest of the world to take part. The time was chosen with care, avoiding clashes with other Backyards, and giving athletes time to recover before the individual world championships, scheduled for October later that year in Tennessee. As a carrot to encourage the best to come, he set the standards high, initially restricting the field to those who had previously run 35 yards or more. Even better, entry was free. Now Australia's best runners were interested. A free event, where they could expect to have serious competition, and be able to test their mettle against the best in the world. It was a concept that had worked well with Masters events in Europe, and it looked to be a success in Australia too.

In his launch, Tim lamented the fact that, at the time, the Australian record was only 51 laps, while the world record was 90. His pitch was *Let's CLOSE THE GAP by bringing Australia's best LOS [Last One Standing] runners to DEAD COW GULLY, alongside international representatives.*

Two days later Tim opened the doors to the international field, extending an open invitation for runners who had achieved at least 60 yards, one more than the current Australian record. Not only would their entry be free, but Tim would pay for their return flights.

Then in September, Tim made another announcement. After multiple negotiations with runners around the world, he had landed one of the biggest names in the sport. The American Harvey Lewis would be joining Phil Gore, Ryan Crawford and a host of other elite runners at the Australian Backyard Masters.

In this young sport, Harvey was a superstar. He'd been the assist at Big's three times, to Guillaume in 2017, to Courtney in 2020 and to Piotr in 2022. In 2021 he'd won both Ohio's Backyard Ultra and Big's. His personal best was 85 yards, which was a world record at the time. That was now well below the new record of 101, but he was still extremely well-regarded and a massive drawcard.

Part of his growing success was his consistency as a runner. Around 2013 he showed the students in his government class a film about climate change. He promised them that he would stop driving his car to work, and started running instead. For the last decade he'd done that, running to Cincinnati's School for Creative and Performing Arts in the morning, then back home each afternoon. The commute only takes a few miles if he goes straight to work, but often he will vary the route and make it more of a substantial training session.

He'd also had a long running streak; until the 24-hour World Championships in France, October 2019, Harvey ran at least one mile every day for five years. He had hurt his Achilles towards the end of the race and was frustrated to have to take five days off running.

His streak re-started, sometimes going to extremes. After he won Big's in 2021, he stayed around for a while, then drove home, getting to Cincinnati at 11 pm. He had finished running the day before, so when he got home, he went for a short run just before midnight, despite having just set a world record by running for 85 hours.

While running the trail loop on the fourth day he'd fallen over on some rocks and broken the fourth metacarpal bone on his hand. He had been able to keep running and had not realised that it was broken. But now, after completing–of course–the one-mile run needed to maintain his streak, he realised that he needed to go to hospital. He jumped in the car and drove to the emergency room, where he was relieved to find the injury was a clean break and didn't need surgery. He came home, grabbed a few hours of sleep, then was up again at 7 am for his usual run to work.

One of the secrets to Harvey's success, at least according to him, was his diet. He had become a vegetarian over 25 years ago, after seeing his mother's ill health when he was young. He adjusted his diet and found it suited him well. He subsequently had fewer injuries, recovered from those he did have more quickly, and had more energy, all of which he attributed to his new diet. In 2016 he took the next step and became vegan, and his results only improved.

Harvey believes that his eating gives him an advantage over other runners, particularly as he can eat more during a race without it upsetting his stomach. Some of his mid-race favourites include watermelon, vegan muffins, dried fruit, noodle dishes, BBQ chips, avocado and hummus wraps, pea soup, mangoes, chia seeds, coconut yoghurt with blueberries, and lentil soup. The irony with the new event was that the special guest, a vegan, was to be hosted on a working cattle farm.

Tim also managed to entice some other internationals to attend, including Johan Botha, who had represented South Africa for many years in cricket, and who had now moved to Australia and taken up ultrarunning. New Zealand sent a strong team of seven, all with matching shirts showing a kiwi bird shooting a laser at a fallen Australian cow. Shaun Collins was their most renowned, having organised ultra races in New Zealand for over 25 years. Sam Harvey had the strongest record of the crew, with a best of 46 achieved while winning the New Zealand Satellite Championships the previous year.

Although Sam already had his entry to Big's in October, for most of the other runners, this was their big chance. Hopefully, the quality of the field overall would encourage some high yards. Given that there were only limited number of 'at large' spots open for the world championships, the entrants were all chasing the largest total they could. Of all the Backyards run worldwide in the year leading to Big's, only those who had gone the furthest would be added to the list. No one knew how many laps would be required, but guesses were that it would be in the 55-65 range. If you could get toward the upper end of that, you could feel confident of making it to Big's.

Of the Australians, Erchana Murray-Bartlett was making her first attempt at a Backyard. Her running credentials, though, put her ahead of most others in the field. Earlier that year she had completed a special endurance mission to raise awareness of the risks of extinction facing some Australian plants and animals. She set a new Guinness World Record of 150 marathons in 150 days, running 6,333 km from Cape York at the top of Australia, all the way to Melbourne at the bottom of the mainland. Despite that, the Australian Backyard Masters would be the first time she would attempt to run more than 50 km in a single day.

Many of Australia's Backyard best were there too. A few came up from Victoria: Tim Kacprzak was there, along with his 15-year-old son, Ollie. David 'Patto' Patterson, of Backyard Ultra podcast fame, had driven for two days to be present. Ryan Crawford, as always, was one of the favourites, and the best of the Queenslanders. Aaron Young and Phil Gore flew over from Western Australia, adding to the excitement about the various battles that might unfold.

Would this be round two of the Ryan versus Phil show? The Satellite Championships had been the only time they had raced, with Phil winning 76 to 75. Would Ryan reverse his loss?

No one knew what the Kiwis were capable of either, particularly the thirty-year-old Sam Harvey. He had six Backyards under his belt, with no one going further than him since his first, two years earlier. Although his best was 'only' 46 laps, he had no idea of how far he could run with stronger competition.

The last key contender was the other Harvey, the American Harvey Lewis. Perhaps he would drag the rest of the field up towards his best of 85. But that mark had been set almost two years previously, and one year later he had 'only' managed 75 yards as the assist. I can recall describing him as an *older gentleman*, until I discovered that I was three years his senior, which was when I realised that he was entering the prime of his life.

But still, at 47, Harvey Lewis was one of the oldest in the field. Was it possible that his best efforts were behind him, and that the jetlag resulting from flying from Ohio to Brisbane would take too much out of him? Everyone knew that he had Big's coming up in October, and presumably that would be his main focus. Then he happened to mention that he would be running his twelfth Badwater, 135 miles, only two weeks after the Australian Backyard started, back in the States. Perhaps he was just here to see the sights and clock up some frequent flyer miles.

When the runners stood in the starting corral just before 7 am that Saturday morning, Tim had what he wanted, an exciting race with limitless possibilities. He had some of the best runners in the world, a spectacular course, and all the time in the world for them to run as far as they could.

The course itself was ideal for the runners. Patto told me he was surprised that the previous course record was only 44 yards, as it was flat, with soft dirt trails and the occasional grass. The fields, trees and ridges combined for beautiful scenery. It was the photos of these picturesque scenes that had enticed so many to drive out for previous races.

They began from the homestead and headed out on a two km flat section along a farm road. The runners would go along dirt track and slashed grass, through the cattle yards towards the top paddock. Then, they would descend a steep incline into the gully that the course was named after and go along the dry creek bed for 700-750 metres. This was the trickiest part of the course, and although it was mostly runnable, it became the place where most would choose to walk due to its technical nature. There were logs and tree roots to jump over, uneven terrain and occasional sandy sections. Once they came up the hill out of the gully, they followed the boundary fence on a track, looping around a dam. Then they would run another two kilometres along the edge of a creek through trees. They would go past a waterhole, cross a creek, go around another dam, and head back to the finish line. Once the runners saw an open field of purple flowers, they knew they were almost back. Apart from the gully, it was a relatively fast course, and that feature added just enough interest that most runners saw it as a positive.

Although they all knew it was fast, no one was expecting what happened on the first lap. In most Backyards, the faster runners will do laps of around 40-50 minutes. Sometimes they might manage an exceptionally fast lap around 35 minutes. Sam Harvey thought he'd throw down a challenge to the field from the start and ran 26 minutes for his first. This was reported as the fastest Backyard Ultra lap run anywhere in the world that year. The other runners were amazed. *This guy is serious!*

But this also raised questions. Had he spent too much energy too quickly? In a race where you can't build a lead, where every runner starts in equal first place every yard, was there any benefit to running such a fast lap? Yet Sam had accomplished what he wanted—now everyone knew he was a force to be reckoned with.

Sam was fascinating to watch. If the event was fiction and you were writing a script for the race, he would be one of the characters that you'd want in from the start. He was the young, rebellious upstart who acted as if he didn't care what anyone else said or thought. He was brash, cocky, and assertive.

Running the first lap fast wasn't a case of a young runner getting overexcited at the beginning and forgetting to pace himself. No, this was deliberate strategy. He was trying to mess with the other competitors, to throw down a challenge early on, to show that he was there. Running a 'hot lap' at the start was just one of his plays.

Before the race began, he told anyone who would listen that he was going to beat the world record. That's not the way most of the runners talk. If you listen to the interviews before races, they're generally reluctant to make predictions. More often, you'd hear things like *I'm here to run as far as I possibly can. Of course I'd love to win, but it's such a great field. I don't like setting goals.*

But that wasn't Sam. He was happy for others to know that he was there to smash the world record of 101 yards, something which made his fellow competitors look at him twice. *Who's this bloke shooting his mouth off like that? He can talk the talk, but can he walk the walk?*

Despite his bravado, he was new to the ultra and Backyard scenes. As a kid, running had not been a big part of his life. He stayed fit by riding his bike a lot. Living, as he says, in the middle of nowhere, he would often cycle ten kilometres to rent a movie from the video shop, back before streaming was a thing. If he wanted to go to town, he'd ride the 40 km. He attended Lincoln High School, just outside of Christchurch,

New Zealand, and participated in their cross country each year. His capacity for improvement was evident, going from not finishing in the first year, to 41st, 17th, 11th and finally second.

As he grew up, he got into boxing, and like most good Kiwis, Rugby Union. Running was a good way to stay fit for both of those sports, and he began to realise that he was not bad at it.

In 2016, he came up with the bold idea of moving to Nashville, Tennessee, to help kick-start a rugby program there, just an hour from the home of Backyard Ultras. He spent his time playing, coaching, and helping to develop the sport in an NFL-obsessed country. While in Tennessee his fitness peaked, and he participated in as many sports as he could. He kept up the boxing and rugby, but added in mountain biking, triathlons and anything else he could find. He entered his first five km running race and came fourth.

During some time back in New Zealand in 2018, he thought he'd try an ultramarathon, the Krayzie Kaypers 50 near Christchurch. He took off like a rocket, and other runners kept suggesting that he might need to slow down. He ignored them all, won the race, and set a new course record. It was then that he started taking ultrarunning seriously, and over the next two years was never out of the top ten in races from 50 km to 100 miles in the USA, New Zealand and Australia.

It wasn't until 2021 that he turned his attention to Backyards, and even then, he didn't have the standard origin story. While he was in Tennessee coaching rugby, he'd met his now-wife, Anna. But then he returned to New Zealand, and the couple entered the hell of a long-distance relationship, with 14,438 km between them. In 2020, Covid made the geographical gulf even more difficult to navigate.

He managed to get to the USA to see Anna again in November 2020 and took her to Frozen Head State Park. By then, he'd become enthralled with the Barkley Marathons and wanted to visit the venue where it all happened. While they were there, he asked her to marry him. She accepted the proposal, and he took home two pebbles from the Barkley trail as a memento of their engagement.

Sam travelled back to New Zealand and endured two weeks of Covid quarantine. It was worth it to have seen his girl again, but now he knew it would be some time before he would be able to get back to her. Travel restrictions were strict, and it would be difficult for either of them to visit the other.

Five months later, in April 2021, Sam heard about the new running concept that had reached New Zealand, the Backyard Ultra. He was intrigued that it had been started by the Barkley's creator, and that its home was in the same state as Anna. He was even more interested when he discovered that a race in Auckland, to take place just over a week away, would grant the winner a Golden Ticket to attend the world championships that October in Tennessee.

Sam made contact with Shaun Collins, the Riverhead Backyard ReLaps Ultra race director, and begged for a late entry. Shaun explained that it was Sam's lucky day, as someone had just pulled out, and he could take that spot. Now all Sam had to do was beat some of the best runners in New Zealand, in a format he had never attempted, and he could be reunited with his fiancée.

In a race that is all about determination and grit, Sam had all the incentive he needed. On each lap he carried the pebbles from Frozen Head with him, reminding him of the stakes. Occasionally he would look at a photo of Anna on his phone.

After 30 hours, the longest run of his life, it was just Sam and Chris Bisley left. Chris was coming off a streak of six successive traditional ultramarathon wins, and was keen to reverse a loss in his only Backyard to date. For seven hours, the two competitors ran along together. There was no conversation, no banter, no mutual encouragement. Sam said *you could cut the tension with a knife*. Both just wanted to win.

At the end of yard 37, Chris was struggling, and knew he only had a lap or two left in him. His wife gave him a strong boost of caffeine to keep him going, but—surprisingly—it was not necessary. When Sam came in, he approached his crew and told them that he was done. He hadn't slept and had hallucinated about seeing Baby Yoda and an alligator on the course. One of his legs was ready to give way. He couldn't go any further.

At 12:59 am the one-minute whistle blew, and Sam stumbled into the starting corral. He fist-bumped Chris and wished him luck. The dream was over, and Chris completed his fastest lap of the event.

Despite the loss, Sam had now discovered something that he excelled at. He went on a winning rampage, undefeated for five successive Backyards. In one, though, things did not go to plan.

In the 2022 edition of the Riverhead Backyard ReLaps Ultra, Sam was keen to take the win, even though Anna was now in New Zealand with him. In a replay of the previous year, after lap 30 it was just Sam and one other, this time Craig Torr, running his first Backyard. The final two spent a lot of time running together, and Sam noticed that whenever he stopped for a walk, Craig would too. He also observed that Craig didn't even have a watch, so had no way of judging how fast he needed to go to get back on time.

After they started their 36th yard together, Sam hatched a cunning scheme. He knew he was faster than most ultrarunners, with a half marathon best of 73 minutes. He should be able to outsprint almost anyone at the end. So, his plan was to walk much more than usual, and if Craig kept his pattern of matching Sam's pace, then, when Sam sprinted off for the last section, Craig wouldn't have the speed to finish the lap on time. Instead of the two running together for another ten hours or so, Sam was trying to hurry things up. With his wedding to Anna set for only six days after the race began, perhaps he was keen to get it over with so he could concentrate on choosing the table decorations.

The problem with his scheme was that after having run for 35 hours, with limited sleep, his mind wasn't working at its best. Although Sam is a bright guy, and he calculated the distances and pace needed correctly, his sleep-deprived brain overlooked something crucial. Earlier in the day he had stopped his watch for a few minutes, and the numbers he was looking at were based on the watch's running time, not the actual time of the day. So off Sam sprinted, running as fast as he could with fatigued legs, almost to schedule, but not knowing that he had fewer minutes to complete the lap than his watch was telling him.

At the finish line, Shaun Collins stands in the dark wondering where his two runners are. He rings the 36-hour cowbell, and the race is officially over. Then off in the distance, a light appears in the darkness, moving rapidly. It's Sam, hoping against hope that he can still get back in time. He sprints the final section, crosses the line, two minutes late, and laments his own stupidity. And perhaps for the first time in Backyard history, every runner received an involuntary DNF.

Here was an unconventional guy who liked doing things his own way. His crash-or-crash-though approach might ruffle some feathers, but it would at least be interesting. Now at Dead Cow Gully, he was ready for action. Later he would remark that *I was the strongest, fittest and most confident I could have been going into a race.* And after his first lap, it looked that way.

Now Sam, Phil, Ryan, Harvey and a host of other great runners were in Nanango. Although the race was targeted at the superstars, later Tim had opened the race to others for general entry, runners who were not planning to go quite as far. It added atmosphere to the event, and eased some of the potential boredom early on for those hoping to get three or four days. For the best runners, the real challenge would come once they were exhausted, when each lap would be a challenge.

Overall, the first day atmosphere was a lot of fun, as the runners took time to get to know each other. For those planning to go for a few days, there was not much else to do than chat with other competitors.

Phil Gore said that his favourite moments that first day came each time he got to the 5.7 km mark, which was a spot where spectators would gather to cheer on the athletes. One of the runners, Mark Owen, would stop there each lap and tell a joke to whoever happened to be there. Phil, and a growing number of others, would time their loops to be there to listen to the latest from 'Dad Joke Guy'.

Harvey Lewis seemed to be having a great time, thoroughly enjoying his Australian adventure. He would run with groups, learning their names and encouraging them all. Afterwards, many would report what a pleasure he was to run with, with his positive attitude uplifting them.

On the other hand, Harvey would mention later that he found the pace many were going at the start too fast. He suggested that perhaps they should slow down, but no one was receptive.

While it was still daylight the first nine dropped out, mostly children and locals. At 6 pm the race switched to the night course, an innovation for the Australian Backyard Masters. For the three previous Dead Cow Gully races, every lap was run on the same course. However, when Tim invited Harvey to compete, the American suggested that it would be helpful if they had two courses, like Big's in the USA.

Since 2012, Big's had used two different loops, one more technically complex on trails for the day, and an easier and faster one on the road for the night. At first, runners spent twelve hours on each loop, but later Laz changed it to thirteen hours on the night and eleven on the day course. The change of courses came to be something that they would all look forward to.

After running all day on the trickier course, it would be a welcome relief to switch to the faster night course, where the competitors could run more freely with less concentration. Best of all, they could finish a lot quicker and be able to bank some valuable sleep in the dark. Then, towards the end of the night course, the runners would be desperate for the light to return, when they could run more slowly on a softer surface. Many would think *I just need to last a few more hours to get to the day and I'll be fine*. Then half a day later, *I just need to last a few more hours to get to the night course and I'll be fine*.

The variation was perceived as a helpful tool that encouraged the runners to be able to continue for longer, so Harvey was keen to incorporate it into the Australian race. Tim could see how that made sense and went out to measure a second course.

For the night they would use the same starting corral but begin from the other end and go in the opposite direction. Runners would head out towards the road, then follow an out-and-back, T-shaped loop. The first and last 800 m was dirt road, with about five km of bitumen in the middle. It was flat and boring, and soon the runners would complain about how much they hated the night course. But the turns broke the monotony, and the change from the day course was helpful. It was nice to see the other runners coming toward you at the two turnaround points, which you did not get in the daytime single-loop course.

The one difficult section came 300 m from the corral, where runners had to traverse a cattle grid, designed to prevent cows from leaving the property. If they didn't watch their feet carefully, they could easily step into the gaps between the metal bars and twist an ankle, or worse. Even if you haven't been running for days, and it's broad daylight, cattle grids can be tricky. When I saw photos of the course I started wondering how many people would curse the hazard as they finished their races. At a minimum, it would tax their concentration each time they crossed it, twice each lap. Tim made sure there was a warning sign and multiple lights illuminating them, but I still feared a catastrophe.

The nights were long, with the event held at the winter solstice, giving the runners the longest night and shortest day of the year. Although the days were warm, as is expected in Queensland even in June, the nights were a surprise to many. The winter temperatures plunged to -2C/28F, and people wore multiple shirts, jackets and buffs. As some complained about frostbite, more dropped out through the first night.

As usual, there were many who finished at the 100 km mark. Tim Kacprzak's fifteen-year-old son, Ollie, did an incredible run, stopping at lap 15. Erchana Murray-Bartlett had begun the race intending to stop there, and was true to her word. There would be no 150 days of running from her this time, unlike her previous solo effort. She had previously agreed to run 63.3 km as an ambassador for the Gold Coast half and full Marathons just six days later, and knew she had to save her legs for that.

At 5 am, while it was still dark, those who were watching the start line had a surprise; half a dozen of the runners turned up wearing not just their normal running gear, but brightly coloured tutus. It was a tradition that had begun in Western Australia and was starting to spread. Phil had noticed that at some parkruns, when the event fell on the 22nd of the month, participants would wear a tutu, or two-two. He suggested it to some Backyard friends, so when they got to lap 22 they would wear the tutus for the entire yard. It added a lot of fun to the proceedings.

Early on day two, Mark Owen's joke-telling came to an end when he timed out after completing lap 25. He stayed around to follow the action until lap 54, and wished Phil all the best at the corral before the start. Phil looked over at Mark and said *Do you have a joke for me*? He replied, *I have a lot of jokes about umbrellas, but they all go over people's heads*. Phil chuckled, *That was one of your best, mate*.

There was a wave of Kiwis concluding the same time as Mark. Helen Waterworth completed the miler with 24, Angus Ward stopped at 25,

Adam Keen and Shaun Collins at 28, and Fiona Hayvice at 30, leaving just John Bayne and Sam Harvey from their team. At this stage, it still looked like the cattle grid hadn't taken anyone out.

Future Backyard race directors Rowan Cassidy and Brett Standring finished at 32 and 36. Ryan Crawford, one of the top contenders with a personal best of 75, was a shock loss at 40. I'd expected that he would be pushing the others to a big total, and started wondering if perhaps the overall finish might be quicker than hoped. Soon Johan Botha stopped with 43, John Bayne was the second-last New Zealander with 51, and Ollie's Dad finished with 55.

When Tim Kacprzak stopped due to an ankle issue, he looked fine at first, but after talking for a while he began to turn white, and there were serious concerns for his health. An ambulance came out to check on him. As it was explained that Tim had just run 368 km in 55 hours, you could see the incredulity wash over the paramedic's face. His reply captured the attitude of many outside the ultra scene: *Whatever you're into I suppose. Better than meth.*

Although it is a rare Backyard that has multiple runners going after 55, it still felt discouraging that there were now only four left: Harvey, Phil, Sam and Aaron Young. Aaron was already past his best of 53 and Sam was well beyond his previous record of 46. If Harvey was holding back for Badwater, then Phil might be the only real contender left.

Eight hours later, Aaron made it three, improving his best to a formidable 63, and virtually locking in his entry to Big's later in the year. He was looking and feeling great, but had picked up an injury. Harvey Lewis was looking strong, and was often seen running along with the other Harvey, Sam.

The other competitor still going was Phil, which made sense. One of the jokes made by the West Australians was that the definition of a Backyard Ultra was an event where everybody runs around in circles and then Phil wins. After his success the previous year, Phil was at the pinnacle of the sport in Australia. He was a true gentleman, generous with his time, encouraging to other runners, and keen to help promote the sport. When I asked to talk to him for this book, he was more than happy to chat for as long as I wanted.

Phil also had a familiar story from high school days; he was never particularly good at team sports, and found that running was something that he could do on his own without worrying about fitting in with others. He wasn't great when he started, but was one of the top few by the end of school. Then came the also standard decline in exercise following his school years, as work took more of his available time.

Then in 2014, the year he turned 28, he started a new career as a firefighter. Shift work gave him time to run, and that helped to keep him fit for the job. In September that year he discovered parkrun and enjoyed running the five km each Saturday morning. He decided he wanted to get better, so in 2015 he opened an Instagram account where he publicly committed himself to running five km each day, hoping the accountability would encourage greater consistency and improve his times. He kept this up for three years, and soon tried some half and full marathons. In 2015 and 2016 he ran the 46 km Six Inch Trail Marathon, held about 80 km south of Perth.

In 2019 he was offered a free entry to the Lighthorse Ultra, where there were options for running three, six and twelve hours. The format was simple, just run as many 2.5 km loops as you can in the designated time. Given that his entry was free, but the longer events were more expensive, he figured he might as well choose the longest race and get the most value. Then, even if he stopped at three or six hours, he lost nothing, but had the chance of running the most expensive option for free. He ended up running 124 km and placing second. Although he assumed the monotony of the endless loops would be frustrating, he discovered that the consistency suited him.

In August 2020 he drove three hours south of his home in Perth to attempt the first of what would become his specialty, Birdy's Backyard Ultra. He had no real plan coming into the event, apart from to stay awake for as long as he could and eat whenever he was hungry. He managed to run for 39 hours as the assist. The winner, Michael Hooker, would provide the answer for Backyard trivia nights for years to come: *Who is the only person to ever beat Phil Gore in a Backyard Ultra?* Phil reflected afterwards that:

> *I had pushed myself beyond what I thought I was capable of, and found new limits. I had absolutely destroyed myself and had to literally be carried away from the start line.*

Despite the pain, despite the loss, Phil had found his sweet spot. Doing so well, but not quite winning, ignited a fire in him to do whatever he could to go further. He's often reflected in interviews that if he had happened to win that first race, his subsequent pursuit of improvement might not have happened.

In March 2021, he began his winning streak at Herdy's Frontyard Ultra. This time he developed a comprehensive plan for each hour. He recorded on a spreadsheet how long he would take to run each lap, when he would take meals, and when he would sleep. The plan worked, and he ran for 48 hours, setting the Australian record.

Later that year he would win Birdy's with 51 yards, and Hysterical Carnage with 38. In 2022 he'd win Herdy's with 50, Birdy's with 54 and the Satellite champs with 76, the last two Australian records. Now in 2023, he had won Herdy's with 57 but skipped Birdy's. He had no idea of how far he could go. Since coming second to Michael Hooker, he had never been beaten, so didn't know what was possible. Here now at Dead Cow Gully, he was keen to find out.

By now, Phil had further refined the plans that he'd begun at Herdy's into a fine art, believing that the more prepared he could be, the better he would go.

For training, in a quiet week, he would run 80-100 km, building up to 160-180 at peak. He began to work with a running coach, nutritionist, physiotherapist and mindfulness coach, all to help optimise his performance. One of his key regular crew members was Nathan, a doctor who also practiced hypnotherapy. Sometimes, if Nathan could not be present, Phil would phone him during a race, and he would help the runner get to sleep.

Phil's preparations would begin well before the race. Just as he prepared for the Satellites by adjusting his sleep time, now he knew the nights would be nearly freezing, and he didn't like the cold. For months he prepared by having cold showers to get used to the sensation.

Phil's spreadsheets were another of his key tools. Since he began creating them, they had become more and more detailed. He would calculate the calories needed for each lap, and record what he should eat each time. He gave a score out of five for each yard showing how he felt, which could then be cross-referenced to what he ate, enabling him to look for patterns and correlations.

His pace calculations also became very specific, showing how long it should take for each lap. The details would vary for each event, but he had three main paces that he would aim for; a 50-minute slower lap, a 45-minute lap when he wanted to eat more, and a 40-minute lap when he wanted a shower or to sleep.

Over the years, he had refined his pacing and sleep strategy even further. Of the runners who aim to sleep between laps, most will focus on the night-time laps, when the darkness will naturally encourage sleep, so they will aim for faster laps at night, giving more time for rest. Courses like Big's, and now Dead Cow Gully, were conducive to this approach, with their faster and flatter night courses.

However, Phil had discovered that simply aiming for faster laps all night long could get exhausting. He developed a pattern in which he would run three night yards quickly, with good sleep in the break after each, then run the next lap slower, skip the sleep and eat a larger meal.

For twelve hours of the night course, this then created a pattern of three sets of four hours. He would run fast and sleep three times, run slower and eat a larger meal once, repeat this cycle twice and then the night would be almost over. For his final night yard he would have a shower, which appeared to have amazing recuperative effects. When he emerged from the shower, clean and with fresh clothes on, he felt like a new man. Overall, the night routine helped his nutrition, maximised his sleep, recharged his energy levels, and broke up the dark hours nicely. It was that kind of meticulous, predictable approach that would be the hallmark of his racing.

With Phil's West Australian teammate Aaron Young now gone at lap 63, it was a formidable trio that remained. Adam Keen summarised it well: *we were down to 3 runners: the legendary American Harvey Lewis, the clinical Aussie Phil Gore and the cocky Kiwi Sam Harvey.*

By now, they were well past the venue record of 44 yards, although the faster night track admittedly made this easier than the previous trail-only courses. Fourteen hours later the trio hit 77 hours, the three of them now holding the record for the furthest gone on Australian soil. Phil had beaten his old record of 76, as had Harvey and Sam.

Strangely, around this time Phil started to feel better on this third night than the previous two. After his shower at the end of the third night, he felt like it could have been day one. Afterwards, he shared with Patto on the Backyard Ultra Podcast:

> As I'm running, I'm just thinking, this could go on forever. Are they going to have to bring in a cap? Are they going to have to say you can't have Backyards go past five days anymore? You get to five days – that's enough, we call it quits. Because the way I feel now, I feel like I could keep going and going … If I get through the fourth night and go and have my shower and feel refreshed again, am I still going to feel like it's back on day one and I'm going to keep going again? Everything else I feel like I can keep going. But if there's an injury or some sort of medical emergency, that'll be what stops me.

Only hours later, on the fourth day, he achieved a kind of flow state, where running stopped being monotonous. He felt a deep connection to his movements and surroundings. He explained later:

> Everything felt balanced, from my sleep and nutrition to my physical and mental well-being. My performance felt effortless, and my endurance maximised. In simple terms, I was like I had reached a point where I could run indefinitely. This was my life now – run, rest, rinse and repeat.

Nine hours later the runners hit 86 yards. This took them past Harvey's best and gave him a new USA record. By now, though, they were all in uncharted territory. Although Phil's spreadsheets covered this contingency, he was ten hours past his previous best. Harvey was just the one hour past what he achieved at Big's two years before. And Sam? He was a monstrous 40 hours past his 46-yard best. Yet still they kept going, none giving quarter.

At this stage, most of the other competitors had travelled back home, their normal lives waiting for them. By now, many had slept two or three nights in their own warm beds, while the final three runners just kept on going.

Four laps later, after an incredible 27 hours with just the three runners, it was down to just two. For the last few laps, Harvey had started to show signs of exhaustion. The sleep deprivation, and perhaps the jet lag, were kicking in. At the same time, Sam was feeling stronger and faster than before, so the two were no longer running together. Harvey only narrowly finished lap 90, but they all set out again for 91. When Sam finished about 47 minutes later, he told Samuel Hartman, his new friend's crew chief, that someone needed to go back for Harvey, who was hallucinating badly. As Sam had run in, he'd seen Harvey out there, and knew he would not be able to get back on time and would appreciate the help back.

He might not have got the win, but it turned out Harvey wasn't there for a holiday. He wasn't holding back for Badwater. Despite the distance travelled to get there, despite the unfamiliar territory, despite his arduous racing schedule that year, he'd gone further than he ever had before. He'd gone further than any American too, his 90 yards a new USA record. He'd also gone further than almost anyone else in Backyard history, the only exceptions Merijn and Ivo hitting 101 the previous year. At the moment he finished 90, Harvey was sitting in equal third place for potentially the longest Backyard ever, along with Phil and Sam. And then, as they finished their 91st yard, those two pushed him back into fifth place on the all-time ladder.

One of the common lines you will hear in Backyard circles is, *It's easy until it's not*. Sam was now firmly in his *It's easy* phase. He'd outrun Harvey, and he was looking strong. Whenever I saw him around this time, I thought, *this could go a long way*.

The other thing I noticed about Sam was what he wore. He sported a black shirt, not great for the heat during the day, with a large white circle on the front. Inside the circle, in huge letters, were the words I AM HOPE. At first, I assumed that it was a Jesus thing—the hope of the world. But a quick google later and I discovered that *I am Hope* was a New Zealand charity with the goal of promoting positive societal change around mental health.

For Sam, it wasn't just a shirt either. This was a cause close to his heart, and he often would talk about the issues involved in interviews, as he knew societal trends weren't helpful. Afterwards, he explained that *quite central in our culture is the idea that everything will be sweet as. It's like a cover, we say everything's ok, and we have a pathological fear of admitting how we are actually going.*

I loved that Sam was promoting such a great cause, and that his actions were living out his message; he combined a strong positive self-belief, with the crucial ability to share his weaknesses, doubts and failures. If you listen to him in interviews, he's sure he can beat the world, but also admits his mistakes and fears.

And to see him running lap after lap proclaiming hope, that was gold. Hope is also perhaps the one essential ingredient for Backyard success. The best runners rarely drop out because they physically have to. They stop running when they get to a point where they think they have no hope of winning, improving their best, or doing anything worth continuing for. When you look over in the starting corral and see your opponent jumping out of his or her skin with excitement, ready for the next lap, you can lose hope, and drop out. Sam's I AM HOPE was a great message to be shouting for days on end.

The New Zealand team started to get excited about their champion's prospects. Sam's growing support team cancelled their flights home, as it seemed like they were going to be needed for a while longer. Adam Keen joked that perhaps they might need to start living at the gully permanently, as both athletes might keep running indefinitely.

Phil noticed how strong Sam looked too, and for the first time started to have his own negative thoughts. How much further would they have to go? He began to fall into a pessimistic cycle, breaking his usual rules: *don't worry about what anyone else is doing or how they look, and don't think too far ahead.* Eventually his crew were able to encourage him along, and he started thinking more positively.

Around the end of lap 93, in the early hours of the Wednesday morning, Sam started feeling the second part of *It's easy until it's not*. Without Harvey, he was struggling being out on the track alone. Even worse, the cold had got to him, and he had what appeared to be a chest infection. He had been putting on a brave face on the course but practiced some of the I AM HOPE vulnerability with his crew, admitting that he was in trouble and might need assistance to get through the night. His crew approached Phil's and suggested that it would be best if the two ran together, just for the next few hours, to get Sam through to the sunrise.

Phil wasn't enthusiastic about the proposal. He had his plan for what speed to go at for each lap, particularly during the night. Accepting the proposal would mean that he would run at a slower pace that was uncomfortable for him. It would also mean he would not get any sleep for the next few hours, which his race strategy depended on. And frankly, if he said no, then Sam would drop out and Phil would get the win. It was a competition, after all, and the race would be over when one of them stopped.

But then Phil remembered what he was there for. He tried to avoid specific goals in Backyards. He wasn't there for the win or a particular number of yards, as he found that having a set goal made it harder to keep going. Instead, each time his goal was the same: to run as far as he could. And given that was his goal, the best way to achieve going as far as he could, was to help Sam to keep going. He needed Sam, and Sam needed him. As with all Backyards, there was a delicate balance of rivalry and teamwork, of competition and cooperation. They were only three hours from the next massive milestone, 96 hours. That would be four full days and four hundred miles, an epic accomplishment.

After a few hours of running together, the sun rose, and their emotions seemed to swap. Sam started to feel a lot better and went back to running by himself. Phil noticed Sam's improvement, felt his own exhaustion, and dwelt too much on the sleep that he had just lost. A few hours ago, it felt like the win would be his, and now that appeared to be slipping away. An insidious thought crept into his weary brain: *were the crew messing with him to disrupt his sleep strategy*? Perhaps it was just a trick. Given Phil's detailed plan had worked so well for him for in many races, his departure from it threw him into an irrational spin. He began to reinterpret small niggles as major problems, and he came to his lowest point of the race.

It didn't last long. Sam had improved, but his chest infection hadn't gone away. The Kiwi crew had tried to play down how unwell Sam was to avoid any chance of him being pulled from the race; but early in the morning Tim Walsh went out to capture some photos of the warriors still on the course for lap 97. He saw Sam coming toward him, who cried out *I can't breathe, I can't breathe!* To Tim, it sounded like a cry for help, so as soon as he got back, he told Sam's crew. To his shock, they admitted the runner had been suffering like that all night.

Tim started talking about a possible medical withdrawal. He couldn't stomach the thought of someone suffering permanent damage on his watch; he had an ethical and legal duty as race director to care for his athletes, and Sam looked like he was in serious trouble. The crew begged for Sam to be allowed to go out again, and Tim relented.

At the end of lap 98, Phil was sitting back in his chair with his crew. As usual his wife, Gemma, was encouraging him. Nathan, his friend, doctor and hypnotherapist was helping him put his shoes back on. Suddenly, they heard Sam come into his tent and collapse. This time Phil and his crew could hear Sam cry *I can't breathe!* Phil told Nathan not to bother with his shoes; he was needed more next door.

This put Nathan in a quandary. If he encouraged Sam to continue, he might contribute to his own runner losing. If he encouraged him to stop, it might be seen as bias favouring his friend, Phil. And if he didn't stop Sam from going on, worst of all, as a doctor, he might be allowing harm. But as a professional, he just had to do what was right and call it as he saw it. He advised that there was a likely chest infection, possibly pneumonia, and that Sam should stop running.

Hearing this, Tim was keen to stop the race. Sam listened to the discussions, lying on his lounge. Having run for 98 hours, he had no doubt; he wanted to keep on going. They were only three hours from the world record and felt too close to stop now. Sam explained afterwards *I was desperate to get the job done that I came here to do. Break that … record.*

The debate raged throughout the break. The crews, the potentially-hospitalised runner, the doctor and the race director all sharing their thoughts. Eventually, a compromise was reached. Tim would allow Sam to keep on running, but he had to either run with, or at least stay in sight of, Phil. Tim and Nathan would both follow Sam, watching from a distance as a medical tail, ready to pull him out if he deteriorated further.

And there would be a limit to this special arrangement, three laps only. The most Sam would be allowed to do was laps 99, 100 and 101. That would allow both runners to become equal world record holders, assuming, of course, they could survive three more hours. Phil, as the healthy runner, would then be allowed to do one more, if he could, to take the win.

Laps 99 and 100 mostly went without incident, both finishing with plenty of time for rest. However, each time Sam came up the incline to exit the gully, the exertion, combined with his diminished lung capacity, forced him to stop for about thirty seconds to recover. Despite his body clearly failing him, Sam's persistence, and unwavering belief that he could get the job done, kept him going. It was as if his body had given up and was begging him to stop, but his mind willed the broken body to keep on moving.

Then it came down to the final yard. They had already completed 100, more than anyone in history outside a small town in Belgium. The champion Harvey Lewis, with his new USA record and personal best, had finished ten hours earlier. Now all the trans-Tasman rivals had to do was finish this lap and they would equal the world record.

Unfortunately, Sam wasn't any better. Running doesn't help chest infections improve. He had to keep stopping to catch his breath. If you see the videos of him there you can understand the desire to pull him out. He looked absolutely beaten, physically destroyed, almost incoherent.

By now it was the middle of the day. Sam was sweating unhealthily, and he didn't have any water with him. With almost four kilometres to go, Phil had almost run out of water himself, but feared Sam was on the point of not making it back. Without Sam finishing this lap, Phil could not run the next, and he would fall one short of a new world record. He offered the last of his water to Sam, and they both kept going.

As they approached the finish line, Phil let Sam go ahead so he could enjoy his moment. He ran strongly, shouting for joy, arms stretched out behind him in celebration. He explained later:

> I came across the line doing the eagle dance, a tradition of victory in Mongolia known as devekh, it symbolizes grace, strength, bravery and invincibility. It is a tradition carried out by Mongolian wrestlers to show off their physical prowess and to imitate a victorious bird of prey.

And yes, this was a magnificent victory for Sam. He had indeed shown off his physical prowess—and mental strength. He may have been the assist, not the winner, but what he endured was incredible. In that moment, he was the third person to run 101 yards, the new equal world record holder. He had increased his best by 55 hours, an almost unimaginable feat. Or at least unimaginable by anyone except for Sam, who had predicted he would do exactly this. And it was a triumph too, over the critics, for those who said he was foolish for shooting his mouth off. It was a win that justified his decision to keep on going when so many others had wanted him to be withdrawn.

There's a great photo of Harvey hugging Sam at the finish line; the older champion congratulating the younger, the new friends who had run for so many days together. Now the student had surpassed the master, and the master was beaming with pleasure.

Sam's finish was an act of service too. By finishing second, he exemplified the Backyard's tradition of the noble assist who allows the winner to do far more than they otherwise could. Now Phil was on the verge of becoming the sole world record holder.

Phil sped through the last lap, enjoying every moment of it. Now there was no planning to be done, recovery to maximise, people to defeat. He could just enjoy the scenery.

As he ran in, the small crowd erupted with applause. He ran past the spectators accepting the high fives of all who offered them. He had a massive smile and was running well. It was hard to imagine that he had run further in a Backyard than anyone else ever. He looked so good that it made those watching wonder *How far can this guy go?* He showed no hint of discomfort, no signs that he was anywhere near his limits. Gemma waited on the finish line to offer a well-deserved hug. She sobbed with relief and joy that together they had succeeded.

Tim, meanwhile, had achieved all he had dreamed of and more. He hadn't thought a world record was likely but had hoped to push the Australians to new levels, and that was done. He hoped to encourage more people to enjoy rural Queensland, and he would be amazed in the coming months to discover how many people had been watching around the world. The little town of Nanango was now on the international map, and for a time at least was the centre of the Backyard universe. Although he had been concerned for Sam's health, he'd enabled the world record to be broken, and everyone had survived.

Afterwards, Sam was flooded with a range of emotions. Mostly he felt joy for what he'd done, and relief at dodging a medical withdrawal. He felt even more relief at not damaging his health badly — and proved it by running 43 hours less than two weeks later to win at the Krayzie Midwinter Backyard Ultra. But he also felt massive regret. He wished he had not been pushed to stop. Wished that he hadn't agreed to finish at 101. Wished that he could have kept going for another day or two.

He knew, though, that he'd made a statement. He soon elaborated:

> *… your playing small does not serve the world. There is nothing enlightened about shrinking so that others will not feel small around you. In a society that would have you be less in order to satiate the narrow and tiny existence of the masses, I stand tall. I make statements of great things that I will achieve and then I pursue them relentlessly until they are made real in this world.*

Quickly enough, Sam was predicting that he would win at Big's, and run 150 hours if he needed to. It was clear that he'd pursue that goal relentlessly too.

For those watching, both in Nanango and around the world, there was one thing they all agreed on; in four months' time, October's World Championships were going to be epic. We had two freshly minted champions in the form of their lives, ready to go up against each other again, along with the best runners from the rest of the world.

For now, it seemed that Phil's approach was dominant. His extensive preparations, sleep-maximisation strategy, and scientific approach to all details was a winning formula. Countless athletes would be studying his videos and copying his plans, all while plotting to dethrone the new King of Backyard Ultras.

7

Big Dog's Backyard

FOR TWO YEARS, the best Backyard athletes from around the world had 21 October 2023 pencilled into their calendars. It would be their chance, if only they could qualify, to run the race of their lives, against arguably the most outstanding collection of elite ultrarunners the world had ever seen. For many of them, the race had been on their agenda for even longer, given that many internationals had been unable to get to the 2021 edition due to Covid travel constraints.

This year would be the first unrestricted world championships for the sport since 2019, when Maggie Guterl had won with 60 yards. For 2023, 45 of the 75 entrants had qualified with more laps than Maggie had run to win. An astounding seven had more than the 85 that Harvey Lewis had won with in 2021.

There were various reasons for the higher totals the runners were completing. Partly the sport itself was moving out of its infancy, and people were discovering what they were capable of. The biennial Satellite Championships had stimulated competition in more and more countries, each helping runners to get closer to their potential. But the biggest carrot for runners everywhere was that the longer they ran, the better chance they had of acquiring an increasingly rare and desirable ticket to Big Dog's Backyard Ultra Individual World Championships.

For the Barkley Marathons, the entry process was shrouded in mystery. The best runner in the world could want desperately to compete, but might not get in. It all came down to the runner working out how to apply, crafting a suitable application, then waiting for Laz to exercise his discretion.

For Big's, the process was clear. The 37 national winners of the 2022 Satellites would each get an entry, leaving 38 spots for those others who had the highest finishing numbers, for a total of 75 runners. This led to people from around the world competing furiously to get in. As with the Australian Backyard Masters, many would fly to races overseas to seek a competition that would push them to a sufficiently high number. With each race giving new results, there was no single number of laps which would allow them to feel completely secure.

However, of the 37 Satellite countries, only 36 had entrants who qualified by winning. Although Belgium's Merijn and Ivo did not 'win' their event, they both easily earned entry to Big's with their tied 101 yards, despite their DNFs.

Another five winners could not make it to the race in Tennessee. Nazarii Hnat from Ukraine had the most unfortunate reason. Not only had the Ukrainian government prevented men from travelling abroad during the ongoing war, but in April, six months before Big's, he had decided to join the army to defend his land from the Russians. Also missing were Julien Law Hin Chin from Mauritius, Moises Lopez from Venezuela, Jamal Said from Pakistan, and Hugo Alves from Portugal. This left 31 qualifying entrants based on their Satellite wins, allowing 44 others to enter based on their best performances.

In May Alex Holl had held The Race of the Champions Backyard Masters. This invitation-only event in Germany was renowned for impressive performances. In 2022, Merijn had set the world record there with 90 yards, Ireland's Keith Russell the assist with 89. In 2023, the totals weren't quite so daunting, but Italian Antonio Di Manno's 74 to win and David Stoltenberg's 73 as assist, a Nordic record, were both still worthy. The following week, Laz announced that anyone who had scores of 70 or more would be wise to book their tickets, as even five months out, it was unlikely that they would not get an invitation.

In the end, anyone who ran 54 yards or more qualified, but it took them some time before their entry was confirmed. Tim Kacprzak ran for 55 laps at Dead Cow Gully in May, but for most of the next five months he was just below what was required. It looked like he would not get to Big's. Still, he continued to train, but tried not to get his hopes up too much. For three months he sat at position 76, an unpleasant location given the 75 entry slots available. If just one person would drop out, he was in. Coincidentally, for the 2022 Satellite Championships he had been the last Australian to make the team. At the time his best of 34 was just enough to scrape into representing his country. Now history appeared to be repeating itself.

Eleven days before Big's began, Tim was sound asleep in bed, when fellow Aussie Ben Nichols texted him. Although Ben had only done one lap more than Tim, he was already confirmed with a place at Big's. When Tim's bleary eyes could read the text, he saw the words *Wake up, you're going to Big's!!* He accepted the last-minute invitation, convinced a good friend, Joel, to join him as crew, and booked their flights.

Markus Schieder of Austria was the last to be invited. Sitting at 77 on the list with 54 yards, he assumed he would not be going, and booked himself into the Austria Backyard Ultra. Then, due to another withdrawal, a week and a half before Big's he received the last invitation. He accepted with glee, but still thought he'd have a go at the Austrian event. After 25 yards, he was convinced to stop, but even then, 167 km was not a standard pre-race taper, one week from the start of Big's.

One notable absence was Big Dog himself, the event's namesake. He'd died earlier in the year, so Little would have to take over the athlete-welcoming duties.

Finally, the best 75 Backyarders who could assemble were finalised, and attention could turn to speculating about who would win the contest. Although Maggie Guterl and Courtney Dauwalter had both won previously, neither were present this year. Despite the race having twice been won by women, only had four qualified this time. Angelika Huemer-Toff from Austria had a best of 44 yards. Amanda Nelson from Canada had run 56. France's Claire Bannwarth had a best of 61, while top was Jennifer Russo, who recently had taken Courtney's female world record at the Capital Backyard Ultra in May. Her 74 as the assist behind Scott Snell made her the qualifier with the 20th highest record.

Thirteen of the runners had run 80 yards or more. The Japanese looked particularly strong. Terumichi Morishita had qualified two years earlier with his 81 at Big's in 2021. He was the one who fell on his last lap, narrowly missed the cutoff, and finished third. With two more years of training, he wanted to show what he could do now. Meanwhile, Yukinori Yoshida and Daiki Shibawaki were the assist and winner at the 2022 Satellites, with 85 and 86 respectively.

England's John Stocker, and Matt Blackburn had bests of 81 and 80 from their win and assist at the 2021 Suffolk Backyard Ultra. The two had raced together for 44 hours, to this day the longest one-on-one battle in Backyard history. National news outlets had picked up the story as the runners passed European and International records. Andrew Smith, a previous winner and assist at Suffolk, had retired from his own race with a knee injury and joined Matt's crew. Locals heard about the race from the news reports and came to support the runners with homemade food and offers to pick up extra supplies. In the end, Matt turned back on loop 81, as sleep deprivation won the battle over his loosening grip on reality, no longer sure whether he was in a race or an endless nightmare. John finished loop 81 and was crowned the new British and world record holder. It would take Matt another 3 years to settle an old rivalry and regain the British record at Suffolk 2024 with 87 yards.

Hendrik Boury represented Germany, but lived in London, and he had a best of 81 from his assist at Suffolk earlier in 2023. He was crewed there, as usual, by his wife Hélène. She was joined by Matt Blackburn, and by Andrew after his race ended. This year at Big's, being close friends, Hendrik and Matt would be sharing gazebo #24. They were crewed by Andrew and Vedrana, Matt's wife, who helped Matt to the 80 yards in 2021.

Catalan Oriol Antolí Sarrau had one lap more, with 82 from his win over Hendrik at Suffolk. Keith Russell represented Ireland, his assist of 89 from the Race of the Champions putting him in the top echelon.

One lap further, and fifth on the overall ranking, was perennial competitor Harvey Lewis. His best was 90 at Dead Cow Gully, but he was the defending champion from the individual world championships in 2021, where he had run 85. Since then, though, he had only managed the assist behind Piotr Chadovich at the 2022 USA Satellites with 75, and a third place in Australia. There was a line of reasoning that he was a good assist, having finished second at Big's three times, his win in 2021 an aberration. That Covid-restricted event only had 34 starters, and it was assumed that this year, with 75, it would be a lot harder to win. Perhaps his best days were behind him, and his racing schedule too hectic. Big's would be his sixth successive month competing in an ultramarathon. These were no training runs either, with even his worst result being an excellent fifth at Badwater, and that less than two weeks after Australia. Would he have the legs for another win, or even another assist? Harvey understood the doubts, explaining in his pre-race video, *I think I come in as a bit of an underdog*. However, he added *I plan to be there through the duration. I have some new manoeuvres I plan to implement*. He was ready to give it everything he had.

From Harvey on 90 there was a massive jump in qualifying distances, to 101 yards, with three runners. Sam Harvey provoked a lot of speculation. His Australian result was incredible, but he seemed to have hit his physical limits. After the jump he had already made from his previous best of 46, was it too much to expect much more? He didn't think so. In his pre-race interview, he predicted that he would win overall, and that it might take 150 hours to clinch it. If it had been anyone else making such claims, they could have been easily dismissed. But after his dominating performance in Australia, equalling the world record, just as he had predicted, it would be foolish to rule him out from doing just what he said.

Then there were the two top Belgians, Merijn and Ivo. Although Phil Gore had beaten their world record of 101, they had stopped voluntarily in the 2022 Satellites. Both were still feeling strong when they finished; neither looking on the verge of pulling out. After a year wondering how much further they could have run, now they had the chance to find out. They and the other four Belgians also had a point to prove. Because their course had been designed to be as helpful as possible for their runners, there was conjecture that they had an easier run, and perhaps their score wasn't as formidable as one on a more difficult course. This armed the six from Belgium with even more determination to show they were indeed a force to be reckoned with.

Phil Gore started as the clear favourite. His 102 yards was the official world record, and he had never been beaten since the assist at his first race. To those who had watched him run into the corral at the end of his final lap at Dead Cow Gully, it was clear that he still had the potential to do a lot more. He looked smooth, comfortable and filled with energy. But this would be his first time running at Big's, and it was difficult to know how much impact the effort five months earlier would have on his performance. He played down his chances, acknowledging that he was the favourite, but freely admitted that the field had numerous other plausible winners.

I saw the favourites as Phil, Merijn, Ivo and Sam. In reality, though, there were a lot more threats. The rest of the top thirteen, who had run 80 yards or more, were all top contenders. Just outside that group, though, were a pack of American runners who all had bests in the seventies: Dan Yovichin, 70, Jennifer Russo and Jon Noll, 74, Scott Snell, 75, and Piotr Chadovich — the USA team winner from 2022 — with 76. All of these runners had two important advantages. As well as competing in their home country, with less travel required, each had run at Big's before. With its difficulty greater than many other courses, those with some experience of what to expect might well be considered to have a better chance.

Even so, some of those with less experience were also serious potential threats. Given that how far a runner goes is limited by the competition they face, or when their assist stops, there were many runners who did not yet know what their limits might be. Was it possible that some obscure runner had the ability for an incredible breakout, but that their latent potential had so far been held back by a lack of competition?

In total, there were nine Big's competitors who were undefeated in Backyards. With his best of 29, David Christopher might not have looked likely to win, but across four races, three of them in his home country of Malaysia, he had never been beaten. Bui Van Da had won two in Vietnam, Abderrahmane Ait Haddou three in Morocco, both with a top of 32. Kartik Joshi, with a best of 41, had five wins in India. Nima Javaheri had won six in Switzerland with a best of 51. Fabrice Puaud had qualified with just the one Backyard, for 60 yards in France. Bartosz Fudali had two wins from two races in Poland with a best of 64, while Ihor Verys had two from two in Canada with 67 as his strongest performance. Top of the class was Daiki Shibawaki. He had two wins from two races, his best winning the 2022 Satellites with 86 yards.

Tobbe Gyllebring looked like a similar threat. He was not undefeated, but since coming fifth at Big's in 2019, he had won five Backyards in Sweden with a best of 57. No one knew what the limits were for all these runners. Was a huge result lurking somewhere there? Or would the lack of overseas competition limit their progress?

There was also some friendly rivalry between the various events that produced qualified runners. Although there were qualifiers from each of the 37 nations in the 2022 Satellites, there were six events that contributed substantially more, only two of them part of the Satellites. Lindley Chambers' Suffolk Backyard Ultra had produced two who were eligible for Big's due to their runs there. The Australian Backyard Masters, at Dead Cow Gully, technically only qualified Aaron Young and Tim Kacprzak, as Phil, Harvey and Sam had already secured their entries. From the 2022 Satellites, Tomo Ihara had put in three from Japan, while Bart Stes and Tim De Vriendt managed four runners from Belgium. Laz's home course of Big's naturally brought a good number, with five. However, Alex Holl's Race of the Champions lived up to its name, with six competitors from that event earning their ticket to Big's.

Of these six major races, all except Japan had also recorded a world record at some point. From Backyard Ultra's inception at Big's in 2011, every record had been set there until Karel Sabbe's 75 in Belgium in 2020. Since then, the record had gone to Suffolk, back to Big's, to Germany, back to Belgium, and now to Australia.

Given that so many great runners were now at Big's, many assumed that the record would be coming home. One of the things that Laz was heard saying repeatedly throughout the event was *That was the greatest field of multi-day runners ever assembled, and you were one of them.* Although the claim was subjective, it had merit.

The qualifying process for the event had brought performances to a new level. In the first six years of Backyards, no one had ever gone further than 49 yards. It wasn't until 2017 that the mark was surpassed, and even then, only by two runners. Now, another six years later, 64 of the 75 competitors at Big's had run 50 or more. In the previous individual world championships in 2021, only five runners had got to 60. This time

48 had qualified with 60 or more. One year earlier, the best mark had been Merijn's 90. Now four runners had done more than 100 yards.

What would it take to win this year? Most would not put a number on it, but many said the winner would need a new world record. Jennifer Russo estimated it would take 125, while the highest guess was Sam Harvey's 150.

In the lead-up to the event, Scott Snell conducted an informal poll of the Backyard community to see their expectations. The vast majority, 90.5%, thought that a new Big's course record would be set, beating Harvey's 85 in 2021. Only 56.2%, but still a majority, thought Phil's world record of 102 would be beaten. When asked who they thought would win, Phil was the favourite with 29.2%, Merijn second on 16.1%, and Sam third on 13.1%.

When the competitors assembled just before the 7 am start there was a mood of excitement, expectancy and nervousness in the air.

Laz added to the nerves, greeting the crowds in the starting corral, saying *This is the best of the best. I stand in awe of what you've done.* He acknowledged, with regret, that politics had prevented Nazarii from Ukraine, Moises from Venezuela and Jamal from Pakistan from participating. He explained some of the rules, begging everyone not to break them. He focused initially on the crews; they were banned from supporting athletes once they were on the course, including inside the corral. *If they try to hand you something, slap it down.* Then he got even more serious: *Every race, we have to disqualify someone, and it breaks my damn heart.* This got the athlete's attention. Every race? Which one of them would it be this time?

After some instructions from Mike Melton, Laz blew his first whistle blasts for the week. Three for three minutes to go. Two for two minutes to go. One for one minute to go. The levels of anticipation skyrocketed, particularly amongst the first timers. When Laz counted down the final seconds, *Ten, nine, eight* the crowd roared the numbers along with him. *Seven, six, five, four, three, two, one*! At zero, as he would do for every subsequent lap, he rang the cowbell and called out *Happy Time*! And off they went, some running strongly, others jogging gently, some shuffling along, on to the first of many laps on the day course.

Sam Harvey stuck with the strategy that had worked so well for him before, winning the first lap with a dominant 37:43, Daiki Shibawaki two and a half minutes behind in second. Last place, as she would be for the first five loops, and many more, was France's Claire Bannwarth.

After he blew the first whistle for lap two, Laz wryly noted to his assistants that some of the athletes were already lining up, three minutes before they needed to set out. *Rookies,* was Mike Melton's assessment. They were wasting valuable minutes of rest, important even at that stage.

When the laggards arrived, they were greeted by another of the peculiar features of Big's, the 'jeerleaders'. Since 2018, the start of many laps would begin with several women performing a variant of a typical American cheerleading routine; but instead of trying to boost the athlete's morale, the jeerleaders would chant defeatist ditties at the Backyarders.

Their first effort was uncharacteristically positive: *Just go big, or just go home! Who will be the one who will take the throne?* By lap four, they were on typically negative form: *You better not trip, you better not fall, Laz will never hear your call.* A day later, they began lap 27 with *Two, four, six, eight, in three more days we'll start the race.*

A favourite from previous years was a twist on a famous tune: *If you're happy and you know it, clap your hands.* Instead, they jeered *If you're hurting and you know it just drop out. If you're hurting and you know it just drop out. If you're hurting and you know it, then you're probably gonna blow it, If you're hurting and you know it just drop out.* Throughout the days of the race they would regularly remind the runners that they were in pain and had a lot more to endure. Their words were discouraging, but their humour and energy often brought a smile to the runners' faces as they headed out.

Although the jeerleaders provided entertainment, and the race was all about what the runners could do, Laz would regularly steal the show. Just before the start of lap three, Malaysia's David Christopher acknowledged this reality: *It's an honour to be here. It's like the only race where the race director is the biggest superstar. The runners are secondary.* On cue, just before they headed off, Laz addressed them all: *Thirty Seconds! And hey! Don't throw trash on the ground! I'm too old to bend over and pick it up!*

The athletes were also excited to meet their peers. Many had followed each other on various social media platforms, observing their training, race results and overall approach. This was finally their chance to talk. Some were star-struck as they got to meet those who they regarded as the greats of the sport. Some ran more or less by themselves, but most would engage in conversations now and then. Although almost all spoke English, even if as a third or fourth language, there were those who could not speak it well enough to be understood. Fortunately, the multi-lingual competitors could occasionally offer translation services. With days of running ahead of them, now was the time to get to know the course and each other, and the athletes made the most of it in these early laps.

Many had the same goal: to run as far as they could. They all came with dreams of winning, but most knew that while a win was unlikely, this was a golden opportunity to be pushed further than they ever had before. Those with lower expectations of victory all shared a secondary goal; no matter what, they didn't want to be the first person to drop out. No one wanted that on their resumé.

After nine hours, 74 runners could breathe a sigh of relief, as the second youngest of them suffered the fate they all feared. The undefeated 22-year-old, Kartik Joshi, finished the lap with almost six minutes to spare. The problem was that during the lap he had fallen hard on the trail. This wasn't a rare occurrence; most runners would fall at least once, and in the early hours, with more competitors and unfamiliar terrain, there were falls every hour. On the first lap, James Blanton tripped on one of the many tree roots on the course and fell hard on his left knee, removing some skin and causing swelling. Sooner or later, all the runners had scratches and blood from their falls. Kartik's fall, though, was worse than most, injuring a rib on the rocky trail. After returning to his tent, he knew the right thing was to not start the next lap; rib injuries aren't to be ignored. Although the runners may have been relieved it was not them, Kartik's peers could feel his pain. It was an unfortunate fate to be out so early, particularly when he'd run 41 previously.

In a ritual that would occur another 74 times, Laz handed Kartik a silver coin to celebrate the runner's accomplishment. On one side of the coin were the words *Big Dog's Individual Backyard Ultra 2023*, and the letters DNF encircled. On the other side, where a president or monarch's image might be on a traditional coin, was an engraving of the event's late namesake, Big Dog himself. Surrounding his image was a series of phrases associated with the race: *One more loop. Never give up. Be your own hero. It's easy until it's not.*

By now, all of the newcomers to the Big's course were discovering what the veterans already knew: this was a difficult track. The first half mile was simple enough, out and back on a driveway with a slight incline out to the road. But even on this easier section, the driveway itself was made of rocks that would punish the runners' feet as the days dragged on. The competitors then came back through the starting area again, allowing for another wave of cheering. This enabled them to sort themselves into the order they would mostly run in for the rest of the lap. From there they would proceed into the forest, where they would stick to a narrow single-track trail. Although overtaking was possible in this section, more often than not runners would stick with their current position once they began the trail.

Early on, before the parade of runners dislodged much of it, the trail was covered with leaves and other debris from the Autumn foliage. However, even late in the race they would find that there were still many rocks, roots and sticks on the course. All of this made it easy to fall, and many did. It was also dusty. Jon Noll noted that this was especially problematic on the first day, as the runners kicked up loose dirt. Many were heard coughing and seen with blood noses, presumably from the dust in the air.

The Belgian team arrived early enough that they could walk over the course the day before it began, checking out the infamous terrain. On one level, they were all relieved, as everything they saw was familiar from trails in Belgium. However, even though they would often run on similar surfaces in training and trail races, they were not used to this kind of landscape in their Backyard courses. Later Merijn reported that it was: *The most difficult backyard course we ever walked*. After he'd finished the event, he noted: *The technicality of the terrain makes a huge difference ... I fell over a treacherous obstacle a hundred times*. That might sound like an exaggeration, but given he would run for 100 hours, perhaps not.

It was also hillier than many other courses. The Australians recorded the elevation gain and loss each lap as 170 metres, or 558 feet. None of the hills were severe, but Phil noted that after a few days they started to look a lot bigger.

The course also had the occasional different section to break up the monotony. The two boardwalk sections, where planks of wood provided easier footing for the fatigued runners, were a favourite. Less popular were the rocks that had to be clambered over. Worst of all was a bizarre element where the course literally went through the boughs of a tree. Because one of the Backyard rules insists that runners may not depart from the event course, this meant that runners needed to climb through the tree itself, every single lap.

Although none of the course features were too difficult by themselves, their cumulative effect was immense. After days of dodging roots, climbing through trees and kicking toes on loose rocks, the peril to the runners only increased. The hazards meant that they had to keep looking down at the ground, focusing on their next step the entire time, rather than enjoy the scenery or turn their heads toward those they were running near. The terrain required their full attention.

The second loss came on the next hour. Fabrice Puaud from France had started the race with a pre-existing injury, and he was not able to run through it like he hoped. His ten laps were far short of his only previous score of 60.

At 6 pm, after yard 11, the runners were moved onto the night loop. This was flatter, smoother and wider than the day track. They could run along together chatting in a group, relax instead of focusing on what was coming up under their feet, and stretch their legs out by running faster. Many, like Phil, would use this as the opportunity to skip the walks, finish earlier, and enjoy a longer sleep in the breaks between laps.

The night course was out and back, all on the road, beginning once again on the rocky driveway. The loop only had two proper corners. This created three relatively defined sections up to each of the corners and to the halfway turnaround point, then offered the same on the return. It was a lot flatter, with only 33 m of elevation. There was a small hill in the middle and one at the end. There was not much variation in the course, but enough that the runners could know where they were at any point.

Although Amanda Nelson was renowned as a road runner, and this section required less concentration, afterwards she noted that it was the most mentally draining. Despite her success, she'd never enjoyed the roads, and loved the trail loop at Big's. Whereas the day course demanded more attention, and only lasted for eleven hours, the night route was more monotonous and went for thirteen hours, all while the runners' bodies were reminding them that normal people were asleep at this time.

Towards the end of the first night, there was a strange scene at the start of lap 22. Most of the Australians had brought along tutus, and the rest of the Backyard world was introduced to the tradition of wearing the bright skirts for the 22nd lap. It brought confused looks and smirks from the other runners and spectators. Not long afterwards, tutus were spotted at an Icelandic event.

On the following lap, Laz went for his own sleep. It was his first of the race, and like the athletes, he had a strict regimen that he would aim to stick to. If he could occasionally sneak a sleep in between his race directing duties, he would retain his cognitive faculties enough to keep things on track; with the weight of the Backyard world on his shoulders, it was crucial that he be alert. What was most startling was that his plan included only thirty minutes of sleep for the whole night, yet it seemed to work.

That was also the last lap for Rene Romualdo Cunha from Brazil, the third person to finish. Rene had been vomiting for hours, and eventually reached his limit. He was devastated, and the video cameras streamed his agony to the tens of thousands watching the live YouTube stream.

Much earlier in the night, though, it had looked like Patryk Swietochowski of Poland was going to be the next to fall. At eighteen he was the youngest runner, but came with a formidable best of 63 hours. He had run strongly in the day loops, and the first two of the night, then dramatically slowed down. He began the night with laps of 47:10 and 43:18, putting him towards the middle of the pack. Unfortunately, he started suffering major stomach problems and abdominal pain. He couldn't eat much, and the discomfort prevented him from running at a good pace. He ran each lap from 14-17 more slowly each time, in 56:08, 56:47, 58:07 and 58:40. It appeared that he had entered the infamous 'death spiral' that Backyarders fear.

This phenomenon is when a runner slows down so much that they lose the ability to rest sufficiently and recover between laps. Given that fatigue only increases with each passing hour, it is expected that it will get progressively harder to complete the next yard than the previous one. As such, once a trend of progressively slower laps emerged, it was logical to assume that the trend would continue, and the runner would have less and less time to rest. Before too long, this would become a self-reinforcing problem, as the lack of rest would exhaust them further, leading to even slower running times, and even less rest. Eventually, this would all compound and they would not be able to complete the next lap on time.

For Patryk, with only eighty seconds between yards 17 and 18, he was in real trouble. Somehow, though, he managed to reverse the death spiral, suddenly running the much faster times of 43:04 and 47:26. Back home in Poland, he'd found that when he was struggling, running some faster yards would clear his head. He slowed again for laps 20 and 21, before speeding up once more for yards 22-24. It was a valiant effort, and gave hope that the death spiral could be fought and beaten.

He made the switch back to the physically harder day loop for yard 25, completing that with five minutes to spare. On lap 26 though, he failed to get back in time. The death spiral had eventually done its work, and his race was over. Frenchman Phillipe Pollesel also finished with 25, choosing not to start on 26 when he ended his last lap with only 29 seconds to spare, the death spiral claiming another casualty.

By then, another of the undefeated runners had finished. Bui Van Da from Vietnam had not slowed down at all, but after completing 100 miles in 24 hours, he suddenly failed to complete the next lap in time.

Slowly the perils of the course were claiming their victims. Many who had got through the night now struggled on the day loop. Thor Thorleifsson, from Iceland, had come into the race with limited training due to injuries, and now he was paying the price. As he entered the second day, the death spiral that had already begun for him on the night course went up a notch. On lap 25 he finished with 2:07 to spare. On lap 26 he had just 1:10. Then on lap 27, he made things even more exciting.

Whereas the night course was an out-and-back loop, the day sent runners out in one direction, then they returned coming in behind the corral. It meant that to complete one yard and start the next, runners must run up to and through the starting corral and cross the start/finish line before the cowbell sounded. However, as they had to also leave the corral as soon as the bell rang, they also had to reverse direction twice; a last-second runner would cross the line, come back into the corral, then cross the line again to start the next lap.

At the start of yard 28, most of the runners were ready for action in the corral when they were warned that Thor had not yet returned, and they should be ready in case he did. As Laz called out *Thirty Seconds*, one of the runners saw Thor coming in hard and cried *Runner, runner, clear a path!* The runners moved to either side and, as Laz counted down from ten, began shouting their encouragement to the Icelandic champion. With three seconds on the clock he stepped over the line, stepped back into the corral, heard the cowbell ring, then stepped back onto the course with his peers. However, before he hit the first corner, he realised he wasn't going to touch his best of 50, so turned back and accepted a valiant defeat. He hadn't gone his furthest, but he'd put everything into the final lap and created a special moment for the event.

The start of the second day seemed to have ignited a wave of premature race departures; although only two stopped on the first eleven-hour day loop, fifteen finished on the second day. Many were massive surprises. Denmark's Søren Møller's 29 yards was 37 fewer than his best of 66. Ryan Crawford was the first Aussie to stop, after 30 laps, due to medical issues. For us watching back home in Australia, this helped us to realise how people in India, Iceland, France, Denmark and many other countries were feeling. Here was one of our best runners finishing far too early, well short of his heroic 75 yards in the 2022 Satellites. I was gutted, and Ryan was devastated to stop so soon.

The first local finished not much later; Kevin McCabe stopping after 33 laps, well shy of his previous 57. Denmark's other runner, David Stoltenborg, did 34 laps, 39 short of his best of 73.

As the finest Backyarders in the world threw their best at the arduous course, it seemed that, at this stage at least, the course was winning. As each person finished, the calculations would show the same story, time and time again. Runner from 'insert country here' would stop because of 'difficulty X', surprisingly well short of his previous total. And yes, each of the earlier finishers were men; the women appeared to handle the early days well.

By the end of lap 37, all 23 finishers were short of their previous bests, many significantly so. Despite having Big's as their focus for so long, training, tapering and preparing for it as their number one goal for the year, not one of them could even equal their previous best.

This pattern continued throughout the race. By the end of lap 42, out of the 27 finishers, only one had managed an improvement, Andres Villagran from Ecuador increasing his best distance from 38 to 39 yards. For Andres, this was special. It was his fourth visit to Big's, and twice before he had finished on 38, so finally beating his 2018 mark was a worthy achievement.

After Andres, another series of runners ending on lower totals began. By the end of lap 65, 49 had finished, almost two-thirds of the field, yet only eight had set new personal records. Most of those were small increases too, with just a few notable exceptions. Niki Micallef from Malta, the qualifier with the lowest total, went from 27 to 48 yards. David Christopher improved his best from 29 to 48, and South Africa's Thembinkosi Sojola from 37 to 55.

I started to question if perhaps home field advantage was playing too big a role. Was it simply the case that the untested runners from overseas, many used to their easier courses, just could not handle the rigours of Big's? That probably was the case for most, but the locals weren't doing any better. The two-thirds who finished by lap 65 included eight of the ten in the USA team, so maybe home-grown experience was not the pivotal factor.

As the runners began the day loop for the third time on lap 49, there was a new buzz in the crowd, a sense of excitement in the air. By now only 35 were running, and as they entered their third day the spectators showed these elites the honour they deserved. As each runner completed their lap, an extended wave of applause would continue well after they finished. Then as the next lap started, and again when they returned after the first half mile loop, the spectators attempted to encourage them onto that one more lap. It felt like the quality of the field demanded respect.

A few hours later, the first female finished. In 52 hours, 33 people had stopped, all of them male. Eight hours later, all the women were gone. Angelika Huemer-Toff from Austria, the first of the four women, ended her journey failing to complete lap 53. Given her previous best was 44, her 52 was a rare strong increase. American Jennifer Russo, the female world record holder with 74, completed a still outstanding 53.

Canada's Amanda Nelson was the next female finisher, and she provided one of the most heart-wrenching scenes of the event. The race had been going for three days, and back home in Brisbane I was trying to watch as much as I could on the live stream. While finishing off my breakfast, my iPad in front of me, I saw Amanda cross the finish line for yard 57 with over four minutes to spare.

At the start, Laz had explained that whenever a runner beat their previous record, they should ring the bell in celebration. He had wanted all 75 competitors to do so, but the vast majority had been unable. Amanda had run 56 before, so at the completion of her 57th yard, she rang the bell in triumph.

She immediately sat down, right under the bell, a few metres in front of the starting corral. Her crew rushed over. Thor from Iceland, now finished, was assisting Amanda's sister, Melissa, with crewing duties.

For most of the race, Amanda had run strongly. Her average loop time of 44:13 was the third fastest in the field. She'd finished four of the yards first. However, for hours she had been suffering. On loop 47 she had fallen asleep multiple times while running, then again as soon as she had sat in her chair. She'd had hallucinations of massive, uprooted trees, and of a car hanging from another tree. Early on, her lungs had struggled with the dust in the air; she had coughing attacks, and her breathing had become difficult. She tried breathing through her nose to keep the dust out of her mouth, but found she couldn't consistently get enough oxygen. Over the last few laps, her times had started to slow, her body not keeping up the way it had before.

As she sits under the bell, Melissa encourages her. *You've got this.* Amanda is less optimistic. *I think we're done.* Her sister gives her an ice block to eat, massages her legs, puts an ice flask on her legs to cool her down. Both her crew offer words of encouragement. None of it has the desired result, she still wants to stop. *I can't, I can't do that. It's been bad for so long.* You can hear the understanding and pain in Melissa and Thor's voices, but they both do what they're supposed to do, suggesting: *One more lap.* Amanda replies *I can't even stand. No, I can't. My legs won't work.* They suggest *Well Try!* Seemingly resigned, she says OK, but stays seated. Thor patiently feeds an energy gel directly into her mouth. Amanda looks pale, wide eyed, empty, as the other runners take their spots near her for their next lap.

With 45 seconds to go, the crew try to pull her up so she can start yard 58, but her legs refuse to cooperate. After running for nearly two and a half days, they have nothing left. *I can't stand, I can't. I can't stand, I can't stand, I can't stand, I can't! My legs don't work, I can't do it.* They try one more time. *I can't.*

I can hear the countdown from ten to one. The cowbell rings, and the other runners start jogging past, careful to avoid Amanda on their path. Once they have gone through, she is still seated in front of the start. Her crew come over, carefully pick her up, carry her away to their tent, lie her down. Their care is touching.

Only two minutes later she's chatting happily with Melissa and Thor. She is smiling, laughing, the life in her eyes back. Soon, Laz comes to offer his condolences, one of the few times that he comes over to the athlete instead of making them come to him to receive their silver coin for a DNF. He jokes that the video crew need her to get off her bed and re-enact the finish.

The entire episode felt like a tragedy, but for Amanda, it was a definite win. On a difficult course she had gone her furthest ever, pushing her body to its limits. She had done what every Backyarder said they wanted to do, keep on going until they had no choice but to stop.

The last woman to finish was Claire Bannwarth, and by then she had been adopted by many as a fan favourite. She finished with 60 yards, one short of her best. It was the manner of her assault on the course, though, that drew so much attention. For many laps she was the last one into the corral, and was happy that way. Her fastest was 52:08, the slowest 'fastest' lap of them all. By comparison, Brazil's Rene Romualdo Cunha never went slower than 48:27. On average, Claire's laps took 55:16, the slowest of the 75 runners. Fourteen times she was the last person to finish her lap, but mostly she was not far in front of anyone.

For many of the other runners, this was death spiral territory, but for Claire it was the steady pace that worked for her. Amazingly, she had only a minimal variation in speed between day and night. Her day laps averaged only sixteen seconds fewer than the night. Her variation in times between yards was also astounding. Until lap 55, almost all her laps had been in a narrow band, between 53:02 and 56:44. This gave only 3:42 between her fastest and slowest, with two exceptions. Yard 14 was when she ran her 52:08, and in lap 23, she ran a more sedate 57:22. Eventually, though, her pace, already the slowest, began to get slower still. Her last six yards, from 55-60, were all between 57:02 and 57:50. They were only a few minutes slower than her average until then, but it was a sign that the end was coming. The toll of the road running had impacted her knee. The pain was intense, and the massages in her breaks were too brief. She began lap 61 walking carefully, but did not finish within the hour. She ended her race with a smile on her face and a host of new supporters.

As the four women disappeared from the scene, many of the favoured males were stopping too. Englishman John Stocker finished after 50 yards, a stomach upset causing him serious trouble. His teammate Matt Blackburn stopped at 56, both well short of their bests of 81 and 80. Jon Asphjell from Norway ran 56, not much off his record of 62. The USA's Scott Snell and Levi Yoder both finished earlier than they had hoped, but were pleased with their finish. Running together with two miles to go on lap 57, they realised they were probably going to time out. They decided they'd rather give it their best shot, and sprinted back until they made it to the corral, just before the second whistle. For them it was an epic finish, and their race was over.

Hendrik Boury provided one of the more interesting stories of the race. The 32-year-old German had heard about the events from his interest in the Barkley Marathons, and had been loving his Backyard adventures so far. He enjoyed the social aspects, being able to run with people of all kinds of abilities and backgrounds. In contrast to the solitary nature of more conventional running, he loved that here competitors wanted to help one another.

He came to Big's in the form of his life, and with a best of 81 yards was keen to go deep in the race. By the end of hour 60, he was averaging 48:54 per lap, and looking good with no concerns.

The start of the third night loop went well, Hendrik finishing it with plenty of time, 50:40. As he entered the tent he looked at Andrew, his crew member, and smiled, *I think I'll have one of those jam sandwiches now*. Andrew and Ved—who was previously crewing for Matt Blackburn in the same tent—gave each other a quizzical look, knowing that they had eaten those sandwiches several loops ago. These had never been part of Hendrik's nutrition plan, and this surprised them both. As Ved quickly buttered a few slices of bread and heaped on the strawberry jam, Hendrik decided that now would be a good time to change his socks and pop some blisters. To do that, he had to remove the timing chip that all the runners wore on their ankles. The chips, held in place with a band, allowed each runner to have their lap times measured electronically.

With dry socks and blisters tended to, Hendrik began lap 61 as usual. After a few minutes of running, he realised that he had left the timing chip back in his tent. He didn't want to get in trouble for not having the chip, so ran back to the start and went to his tent.

With so many runners, support crew and event staff, the small number of video cameras ensured that only some incidents would be captured. On this occasion, though, a cameraman happened to stumble on Hendrik, allowing the YouTube stream to show it all.

Now, as he emerges from his tent, the surprised cameraman sees him, and Hendrik explains the situation: *So, what happened is that I forgot my timing chip and that gentlemen said it was not a problem. So I lost 8 minutes.* And off he runs to complete his 61st yard.

On his return, he thinks it might be prudent to make sure that everything was fine with his chip, so he walks over to the admin tent. Again, the camera invites us into the conversation. *I just wanted to check that everything's OK.*

Mike Dobies answers *You have to talk to Laz. Sorry*, Hendrik replies. Again, Mike says: *You have to talk to Laz.* Hendrik appears unsure: *Yeah OK. Uhm, what did he say for?* Once again, Mike keeps it brief: *You got to talk to Laz. Oh, OK, thank you*, the polite German replies.

Hendrik walks over to Laz, keen to resolve the issue before the start of lap 62. He sees him talking to Naresh Kumar, another of Laz's key lieutenants, and tries, hesitantly, to interrupt. *I need to talk to Laz. Sorry, Laz. Laz, sorry.* Laz turns his attention to Hendrik. *Yes?*

And then ensues a conversation both will remember for some time. Back home, by now it was lunchtime, and I was transfixed as I watched the two talk. It was like watching a car crash in slow motion. It was awful, it was tragic, but I couldn't turn away.

Hendrik began: *Hey, how are you doing? Uhm. The Mikes told me I should talk to you about the timing chip.* Laz replied: *Yeah. You can't. Remember the first instruction at the start? Get Nothing.*

Yeah, I'd forgotten my timing chip in the tent and I ….

You can't go back. You can't go back. It wouldn't matter what it was, it still happened.

Yeah, I know. There's nothing?

Because otherwise there's an endless series of 'well, but'. Because it happens. It happened last … it happened two years ago and the guy went back to get headphones. 'It was just headphones. I started, and then I went back'.

There's nothing I can do? I got like an eight-minute time penalty. I ran there and back just to make sure I'm compliant.

Because otherwise there would become endless discussion. Not with you. I mean, I am, I am beyond … I feel so bad you can't imagine. Laz pauses. *Well, you can imagine.*

Maybe, can we ask the other runners how they feel about it?

Because then this becomes a protest committee, endless. I don't know what to say.

Hendrik rubs his face slowly, and you can see it slowly dawning on him that it's over. His dream of winning at Big's, or being pushed to a new level of achievement, gone. All his training, all his hopes, all his plans, dashed on the rocks of Backyard rules.

For the rules were clear. It's stated in the guidelines for every official event: *Except for restroom breaks a competitor cannot leave the course until the Yard is complete.* It was simple, Hendrik had left the course, and it wasn't to use the bathroom. Perhaps if he'd lied, and said he'd run back to use the restroom, he might have got away with it. But his sense of integrity, that demanded he explain what he had done at the start of the lap, and at the end, just to make sure everything was done correctly, would not allow it. It was now game over for one of the brightest young Backyard stars.

Laz put his hand on Hendriks' shoulder and grieved with him. He'd done what he needed to do as race director. He'd enforced the rules, and explained them clearly. Now he could feel the runner's pain. *I'm so sorry. You were doing so … good. I can't go back in time.*

The whistle blew; the continuing runners had three minutes to go, and the conversation paused. After they went off, again Laz sought to comfort Hendrik. *I hope in two years that we get to see you again.*

Around the world, respect for the young German only grew. When he talked about what happened afterwards, he was gracious, understanding, and apologetic. He admitted he knew the rules, knew he should not have gone back for the chip. But he also realised that it was a simple mistake, made due to severe sleep deprivation.

The worst part, to an outsider at least, was that it just didn't need to happen. The rules did not insist on the timing chip being carried. If Hendrik had just run his lap without it, explained the situation and put it back on for lap 62, there would have been no disqualification. But in seeking to do the right—although unnecessary—thing, he broke an inviolable rule. It was a tragedy.

Five months later, when the competitor list for the 2024 Barkley Marathons was unveiled, there was one unexpected name there: Hendrik Boury. It might not have been a win at Big's, but as far as consolation prizes go, a coveted entry to the Barkley was as good as it gets.

After lap 60 there were 28 runners left on the night loop. By comparison, at the equivalent event in 2021, only four were running at that point. This was a true exponential increase in the number of top performances.

These high achievers, though, were having it tough. Harvey Lewis, in particular, was struggling. He had come into the race with less than ideal preparation. Keen to keep his word, he'd travelled to a previous speaking commitment, then on the day before the race he arrived late and only managed three hours of sleep before the event began.

Normally, he excelled at the psychological side of racing and could calm himself down well. For this race, though, he was too excited, perhaps having had too many caffeinated drinks. He found that during the first three nights, despite starting with a sleep deficit, he just could not snooze. Afterwards, he described the first day as the toughest Backyard he had experienced.

Eventually, he managed to get some two-minute naps, the kind that he had been practising beforehand. In his lunch breaks at school, Harvey would disappear for a few minutes into a cupboard. After a micronap, he would come out and be ready to teach for the rest of the day.

Occasionally, while running, he would see a park bench, lie down on it and again practice napping. Now that skill was needed.

By the sixties, though, many of the other runners were suffering too, and the constant parade of race exits led the remaining competitors to wonder how soon the end would come for them. The monotony of the night loop, the lure of their beds and their sheer exhaustion were all enticing the runners to stop.

One of Harvey's gifts, though, is his ability to encourage others. His positive energy, friendly demeanour and generosity of spirit are a key part of his approach to running. For the first couple of days, he had appeared to be more focused on his own race, at least more so than in previous events. Now he turned his attention to those around him. And perhaps he knew that by encouraging them, he would also be carried along. It's a strange dynamic, where helping others gives you the energy boost. But mostly, Harvey sprang into helping mode because that is what he naturally did.

Soon a group of runners gathered around him, and they began running together in what some called Harvey's bus or train. When Harvey saw someone struggling, he would tell them to get on the end of the train and hang on. Afterwards, Ivo would be grateful that he went as far as he did because Harvey had shown him compassion and brought him on the bus. Sometimes they would run in silence, but often Harvey would shout out encouragement to keep them all moving.

Meanwhile, the seven-strong Australian team was doing well, although Ryan Crawford had finished earlier at 30, and Ben Nichols at 50, both short of their best. Tim Kacprzak managed to increase his best by five, with 60 yards.

Tim Walsh, the Dead Cow Gully race director, had come to Tennessee to crew James Blanton. Laz had introduced a rule for Big's that limited runners to a single support crew member, an attempt to restrict the almost overwhelming numbers of people on his property. For many of the competitors, used to teams of support rather than a single person, it was quite the change. Days before the championships began, Laz eased the rule slightly, allowing a crew swap later in the race. The more helpful provision, though, was that once runners had finished, they could then support anyone else. This was how Thor had been able to help Amanda so well.

Now the Australians were able to use that exception too. Once Ryan had finished, and recovered sufficiently, he jumped in and helped look after James. The two of them had finished first and second at the standard Dead Cow Gully event earlier that year. Then, at Clint Eastwood, they had run together for 22 hours after the rest of the field finished.

Once they hit 60 hours, securing a Big's entry for James, they had both stopped with DNFs, neither wanting to be declared the outright winner at the expense of the other, and to save themselves for the main event of the year. Now the partnership was back together for the third time in 2023, Ryan helping James to get to a massive 72 yards.

Aaron Young also increased his best by 12, finishing with 75. Unfortunately, he had lost his running glasses not long before his flight from Australia, and consequently suffered dizziness throughout the race. Once he stopped, Rob Parsons and Phil Gore were the only Aussies left still running.

Another success story came from the tiny island of Singapore. Joshua Toh had entered the event ranked 61 out of the 75 competitors, with a best of 51. He managed an incredible increase of 21 yards, setting a new Singaporean record of 72. He began lap 73, but was unable to get back on time. Eventually, but far too late, he got to the final straight, with the finish line, and an end to his suffering, in sight. At that very moment, the leading runner on lap 74 had returned from the out-and-back section and was now running toward Joshua. Knowing there would be a stream of runners coming through, Joshua delayed his finish to allow them to pass through first. He graciously and humbly stood to the side, hardly able to stand, as he cheered and hi-fived the continuing champions.

Amidst that beautiful scene, Frank Gielen runs along, obviously still full of energy, despite his 73 yards. He sees the photographer a few metres in front of Joshua, leaps into the air, clicks his heels together, lands, and continues on his merry way. As someone who cannot manage heel-clicking when fully rested, I was astounded at his athleticism after more than three days of running.

Further afield, more of the pre-race favourites kept finishing. Ireland's Keith Russell stopped at 74, unable to improve on his best of 89. Japan's Daiki Shibawaki reached 81, his first loss ever, just short of his previous 86.

One lap earlier, one of the event favourites had to stop. Ivo Steyaert, the Belgian who had voluntarily finished at 101 with Merijn, this time only completed 80 yards. Even getting to 80, though, was a huge accomplishment. He'd come into the event with a hip injury and had relied on regular massage throughout to keep going. Even by the second hour he was hobbling, and spent too much energy fighting the injury. Still he went on, lap after lap, occasionally with the assistance of Harvey's 'bus'.

Eventually, his finish was gripping. As the runners wait for the start of lap 81, the final whistle already blown, Ivo is nowhere to be seen. With twenty seconds to go, he appears on the final straight. He's running swiftly, a pace at odds with the 333 miles he's already completed.

Applause and cheers break out through the camp. With ten seconds remaining, he crosses the finish line, steps back into the corral, is handed a fresh backpack, and almost immediately begins the loop again. The speed of his finish must have exhausted him, as his start is a shuffle.

As the other runners complete the next lap, Ivo is conspicuously missing, and the Belgian camp grows nervous. Keith van Graafeiland of the USA and Niklas Sjoblom of Sweden both go out to search for him. When they do find him, he is disoriented, unsure of what he is doing or who these people are. As the others head out on lap 82, they see Ivo sitting calmly beside the trail. Each one offers him their condolences as they run past, Frank Gielen reaching out for a fist-bump, but Ivo is not sure who these people are.

When Keith and Niklas finally bring him back to camp, the concerned Belgian team erupts with joy. *Ivo! Ivo! Ivo!* they chant. Their hero has returned from battle. As they approach, he starts to get glimpses of recognition. *I remember you*, he says to one. *Yes, I remember you.* Another champion has gone, finishing with 21 fewer yards than his best.

Now there were just fourteen runners left, many accumulating higher totals than ever. Jivee Tolentino, living in Ireland but representing the Philippines, increased his best from 62 to 81. Japan's Akihiro Maeda improved from 67 to 83. The second-last Aussie, Rob Parsons, finished with 84, well up on his 73 laps. Despite finishing last eleven times, the Catalan Oriol Antolí Sarrau went from 82 to 89 yards.

During lap 82, the same yard when Ivo was greeting the unfamiliar faces running past him, Jivee collapsed from dehydration. Phil saw him and stopped for about five minutes mid-lap until a spectator could arrive to help. Merijn ran up and poured his water into Jivee's empty bottle, continuing only at Phil's urging. Finally, Phil left, but he had to run much harder than usual to get back on time.

Phil was already in trouble by this stage. For the first three days, he had gone as well as he could have hoped for, the best of any race to date. He had stuck effectively to his detailed pre-race plan; the only revision a move of his sponge bath from 10 am to the end of the night loop. This meant his bath was not as warm as his planned mid-morning wash, but having it on the faster night loop allowed him more time.

However, by the seventies in day four, he began to experience severe lower left leg pain. At lap 74 he asked his wife Gemma to start giving him Paracetamol. The astounding thing is that he had run for more than three days before asking for pain relief.

By lap 88, he was complaining more about his legs. On camera, he's heard arguing with Gemma. She remains patient, reminding him that this is a time when he just needs to do what she says. Throughout the nineties, perhaps sensing his weakness, the feed shows more of Phil in his tent than any of the other competitors.

At the end of lap 91, those watching can see that Phil's cognitive faculties are suffering. He starts to question Gemma as to why he is there: *So you just run out on the road, then run back? It doesn't make sense, why?* She replied *Because this is the stuff that you like to do.* It still didn't make sense to Phil. *This transponder thing on our ankle, so basically you're just carrying this out to there, then carrying it back.* Gemma chuckles. *I dunno, you're the one who likes this.*

About ten minutes before that conversation, another of the Dead Cow Gully heroes, New Zealander Sam Harvey, had run in at 49:03, looking strong. Two seconds later, Polish Bartosz Fudali crossed the line and the two embrace. It appeared that Bartosz noticed something different about Sam, and questioned him: *You quit?* Sam replies confidently, definitely, *No*, and heads off to his tent.

After winning the first yard, he'd left others to take the lead for most hours. Occasionally he'd blast out a faster effort, running laps 15 and 16 in 36:06 and 36:05, the latter his fastest. His average yard took 46:28, the eighth fastest overall, only beaten by Phil in the final twelve. He finished 16 of his laps before anyone else. Once he began day four, the faster yards became more frequent, winning four of them in the seventies.

At the end of lap 91, he came in fourth out of the nine runners remaining. It was still fast, but it was also the first time in eight yards that he had not crossed the line first.

Now at the start of hour 92, they all begin slowly. It's been a long time for them all. Sam trails towards the back, walking unsteadily, a limp that wasn't noticed when he finished eleven minutes earlier. At 37 seconds, his leg seizes briefly, then he continues in what is a more pronounced hobble. The video switches over to showing, once again, Harvey's pre-race interview. Right after he tells us, again, that running a Backyard Ultra is like playing a game of Risk with your body, the replay is abruptly interrupted with live images of Sam being hugged. It is 7:20 into the yard, and it's clear that for Sam, the race is over.

Sam sees Laz, and as so many finishers do, expresses his gratitude to the event founder. *Thank you, brother.* Laz is surprised: *I can't believe it came to the end.*

Especially that way.

What happened? You ran just short of 400 miles. Laz chuckles. *What happened? What could possibly go wrong?*

Ahh, I think I've just had enough Backyards for a while. The last two and a half years have just basically been Backyard, Backyard, Backyard, and there comes a time for other projects, I think.

I can understand that.
I appreciate it though. Thank you for the opportunity.
I recommend to anyone if you have access to a shower ... be sure to get some sleep.
I've been so impressed the last 2 and a half years, especially the last 18 months of Backyards where I've really gotten good at it. What I can will this [body] to do. As soon as it's game over, win or a finish or a DNF, and I turn off race mode, all of that shuts down. Brain shuts down, body shuts down, it's like, you've done your job, have at it.
I had the same experience walking across the country. Five minutes later, you can't walk across the street.
What a couple of days. I did not like the course to start with, and then I fell in love with it, and then I fell out of love with it. Actually, what day is it today? Tuesday, I was starting to get an appreciation for the day, then the sun came out, kicked everyone's ass and then I stopped enjoying the trails.

Sam goes into his tent, lies down, and acknowledges his crew: *Thanks for helping me do this stupid thing. It was big and stupid, but now it's done and we can move on with our lives. What a day.*

The cameraman who has given us access to this all now speaks: *Can I ask you one question? This is unexpected – you looked so strong at the start of the night.*

Sam tries to elaborate: *Ahh, I think ...* (long pause) *Every ultramarathon I run, I run with passion and love and art and, I felt like that race was starting to lose the art, it was just repetition, out on the road, yeah, yeah. It was, there was no beauty. What's life without beauty and art?*

He shrugs. And so, a poet laureate of the Backyard was born; not many waxing lyrically after four days of running, not many share their philosophical musings, yet somehow, despite the trauma, Sam managed to sound eloquent, poetic, rational.

At Dead Cow Gully, it had been Sam's body that seemed broken, his strong mind willing him to keep going. At Big's his body was still strong, but he had lost the will to continue. After 91 hours of arduous running, who could blame him?

When I watched the conversation, I hoped that Sam would not stick with his idea of having a break from Backyards. How long would it take before he returned to the world that he thrived in? Not long, as it turned out. Just as he did after his 101 yards at Dead Cow Gully, he followed up with another race in New Zealand, the Arrowtown Backyard Ultra. This time the interval was two and a half weeks, and he managed to run 34 hours before his efforts at Big's caught up with him. It was not a win, but a promising sign that a great talent had not been lost to the sport.

Back in Tennessee, a few hours later, Laz commented on Sam's departure in the event on Facebook.

there is one common thread between the drops of russell, steyaert, and harvey…
there was no warning.
no death spiral.
they were simply there one lap and gone the next.

It was an ominous reminder that anyone could be next. For the next six hours, the remaining eight managed to avoid being that next person.

In reaching 91, Sam had beaten Harvey Lewis's former best time, and only four others in history had ever gone past that mark. He was one of them, and two of the others were still out there, Merijn and Phil. Harvey, and the other five still competing, were moving into unknown territory, all achieving personal bests each hour that they completed. The comparison with previous totals was even more stark when results on this particular course were considered. No one had ever run past Harvey's 2021 mark of 85 hours at Big's, now eight of the athletes were still going.

Phil finished lap 96 in 45:18. It would be the last time that he would cross first. The next lap, the competitors entered their fifth day of running. Phil was suffering badly, but still running fast. His night loops in the nineties were between 46:59 and 50:31, so he was still getting through them with plenty of time to spare.

A few runners, though, looked like they were in real trouble. Frank 'The Tank' Gielen, Jon Noll and Harvey Lewis all were running a lot slower than the others. For most laps of the nineties, they were the last three to finish. Harvey came in last for yards 91, 93, 94, 95. He'd also fallen asleep many times while running, something which he hadn't experienced before. On this fourth night he found that his foot would hit the ground at an unusual angle, and the impact would wake him up. It was only then he would discover he'd been running while asleep.

Frank came in last on laps 96 and 97, then became the first of the three slower runners to finish. A day and a half earlier, it had looked like he was about to finish. Throughout hours 54-59, at the end of day three, he'd run every lap above 57 minutes, traditional death spiral territory. But then he'd well and truly pulled out of that. He'd run laps 81, 86 and now 97 above 58 minutes. During the fourth night, it seemed like he'd hit his limit when he had to ask his crew what he was supposed to do with his chair. *Sit in it.* Things weren't looking good.

The Tank begins lap 98 but stops midway. He's had enough. Now, seeing the camera, even exhausted, he expresses his typical gratitude and humour: *Thanks Laz. This is empty tank.* He waits beside the track for a while to cheer and hi-five the other runners. When he returns to the finish, Mike Dobies varies his normal shtick. After most finishes, he or one of the other event staff would tell the defeated runner *I regret that you couldn't suffer longer.* Now he can't help but praise the Belgian who has increased his best by 30: *An incredible performance. An incredible performance. Thank you so much for being here. I would say that we regret that you couldn't suffer longer, but you suffered a long, long time.* Frank replies with a voice that is almost gone: *Longer than I expected, at least.* Afterwards, he explains that even when it didn't look like it, he had fun the entire time.

Jon Noll was the next of the three to stop, on the following yard. He and Harvey had been just scraping in on far too many laps. On the third and fourth nights, they had begun running together. During yards 62-72, then again from 85-96, each time they finished within seconds of each other, often bringing along other runners with them.

From hour 50 onwards, every yard Harvey ran was 51:49 or slower, and in many of the day loops, Jon was several minutes behind, falling off further towards the end. From hour 63 onwards, more than half their laps would be above 55 minutes. This was slow, far too slow for any serious rest back at camp. During the night loops, when others were enjoying ten to fifteen minutes of rest, Harvey and Jon were coming in with less than five minutes to eat, drink, tend to the issue of the hour, and get back out. The difference between them and their peers was stark. Toward the end of the third night, on lap 69, they came in more than eighteen minutes after the first runner. Eventually Jon hit his limit and stopped with 98, two agonising hours short of the 100, but 24 over his previous best.

Of the remaining six to approach the 100-yard mark, two of them had been there before. Merijn was the first to break the barrier, with 101. Phil now had the record with 102. Harvey, seemingly only just hanging on, had done 90. Terumichi Morishita from Japan had a best of 80. Ihor Verys had done 67, and Bartosz Fudali 64. There was a massive difference in the resumés of this final half dozen.

All six ran through lap 99.

All six ran through lap 100, but only just.

During the hundredth lap, Phil fell over, landing hard and splitting his chin. When he stood up, he had no fresh scratches on his hands or knees. His reflexes had not sprung into action as they would have fifty hours earlier; his chest and face had absorbed all the impact. Stunned, he slowly continued his way around the course.

Meanwhile, his leg pain that began in the seventies was still causing problems. It didn't stop him from running, but every step was agonising. After hour 82, when he'd had to speed in after assisting Jivee, it had only got worse. He'd been on the verge of pulling out multiple times, but Gemma's care had kept him going.

Now it looked like he was at breaking point. With ninety seconds to go on yard 100, he finally came in sight. As Phil ran in, crossing at 58:45, he looked worse than I'd ever seen him before, and this was his slowest yard of the race by far. He was told to lie down, but didn't have time to get to his chair. Gemma, crying at the sight of her husband, was reprimanded for being in the corral. As she left, she told him just to start walking. Phil did just as he was told, but looked — uncharacteristically — unsteady on his feet.

Slowly he walked, and occasionally ran, around lap 101. Eventually, he looked at his watch and saw it said 37 minutes. He wasn't quite at the halfway mark. He did the maths and calculated that he would not be able to run the remaining 3.5 km of the day course in the 23 minutes remaining. Reluctantly, and for the first time since his inaugural race back in 2019, he gave up, and veered off the course to try to get help. Phil had reached his limit in a Backyard and would receive a DNF. Now the Michael Hooker trivia question would need to be tweaked: *Who is the only Australian to ever beat Phil Gore in a Backyard Ultra?*

As fate would have it, one of his chief pre-race rivals, Merijn, pulled out on the same lap. He'd been looking good, but feeling tired, for many hours. As he attempted to complete lap 101, he felt more exhaustion than usual and decided he would ease off his pace, hoping to catch his breath enough to come home hard at the lap's end. At the halfway point he realised he might not get back in time. When he heard a whistle while still in the forest, he knew he was in trouble. He attempted the closest thing he could to a sprint, until with about thirty seconds to run, he heard the bell starting lap 102. He was done, only seconds short of equalling his record-breaking best. If he had completed three more yards on time, he would have broken the world record for the fourth time.

Terumichi was next to finish, on the following lap, his 101 a 21-yard increase. Language issues had prevented him from having much interaction with the other competitors, but he had been looking good for days, and his finish appeared sudden.

And then there were three.

Bartosz, Ihor and Harvey all finished lap 102, Harvey coming in last. The trio had very different backgrounds. Ihor was the youngest, aged 29. Bartosz was 35, still well under the event's average age of 41. Harvey was the classic elder statesman at 47, although at the beginning there had been eighteen runners older than him. The Backyard was not a young person's sport.

This was Harvey's eighth such event, and his sixth at Big's. He'd won once here, and had three assists, but his best was the 90 in Australia. Both Bartosz and Ihor were running their third Backyards, and not only their first at Big's, but their first outside their home countries. Although the two younger men were undefeated, their wins had been in smaller competition pools of Poland and Canada. Ihor had won both of his Backyards in 2022, Bartosz did his two earlier in 2023. As one of the last qualifiers, running his 64 in July, not much was known about Bartosz.

Ihor and Harvey had at least run together before. Just two months earlier, they had competed in the Canadian Death Race. Renowned as one of the hardest ultra-trail races, Ihor had won it on his first attempt. He'd not only beaten Harvey in the 118 km race, but he'd finished an hour and a half ahead of second place, and two hours ahead of Harvey, who was fourth. In an interview with The Ultrarunning Guys before Big's, Harvey had pointed to Ihor's performance in the Death Race as a sign of what he might be able to do in the Backyard.

Now Ihor and Bartosz were both looking much stronger than the veteran. Watching them run, they seemed flawless and untouched by the last four days. Even so, weariness was making its impact. The two had spent much time running and chatting together. Towards the end, though, although he spoke fluent English, Bartosz was too fatigued to use his second language and kept speaking in Polish. Repeatedly, Ihor tried to get him to switch to English, but with no luck. Eventually, Ihor said to him *Feel free to talk, but know I can't understand you.*

At the end of lap 102, cracks started to appear in Bartosz's armour. He told his crew, *I want to go home*, and was given the standard encouragement: *One more lap.* He lay down for a one-minute rest, ice on his body, and then he was off again.

He finished 103 in 53:25, thirty seconds faster than his previous lap, nearly a minute ahead of Harvey. However, although he and Ihor ran 102 together, Ihor had now sped up, finishing three minutes ahead.

As usual, Bartosz's crew prepares him for the next lap, and slowly he walks to the line with the other two. It's a chaotic start. The jeerleaders are chanting, and then suddenly, Gemma Gore appears just outside the corral and shakes the hands of the three remaining runners. *Phil says to say congratulations, he can't get out of his chair. Congratulations for beating his record.* She's right. In completing the previous lap 103, those left are now the joint holders of the new Backyard Ultra world record.

As Laz counts down from ten to one, the three stand at the line. Ihor's face is blank, staring forward. Bartosz is talking. Harvey listens, smiles, and with five seconds to go, says in reply, *I will never stop.* The cowbell rings, and Harvey backs up his words by speeding off. He'd been doing that occasionally throughout the race, sprinting off at the start, showing his competition that he still had what it took, most likely demoralising many of them. What effect it had at this moment is less certain, but as Harvey runs off into the distance, Bartosz tells Ihor that he is going to stop. The two embrace. As the crowd cries *No!* Bartosz tells his new friend *Chase him,* and gestures toward the disappearing Harvey.

And then there were two.

The established veteran versus the newcomer. One just managing to finish most laps, versus the other sitting around casually with time to spare. Harvey, who had dedicated much of the last decade to this sport, versus Ihor, who wasn't sure he even liked Backyards, and only signed up at his girlfriend's urging.

Ihor had turned up planning to follow Harvey's strategy of running 53 minutes for day loops, but faster at night. In the end, the student followed the strategy better than the teacher, with Harvey's night laps not that much faster than those he ran in daytime. On lap 37 Harvey had finished first in 37:51, his only winning lap so far, but his times since then had been significantly slower. As Ihor watched Harvey, several times he had thought that the veteran was about to finish.

Earlier, Ihor himself had been in trouble. His feet, not used to running so far, had become swollen. Ordinarily he would take size 12.5 shoes; now they had swollen enough that he needed a size 14. Fortunately, Tim Kacprzak's support crew, Joel, was wearing a pair of size 14s. As soon as he heard of Ihor's plight, he whipped them off and handed them over. For the next twenty hours, Ihor ran with the Australian shoes into a new world record.

At lap 93, he'd become delusional. Like many others who had gone that far, he wasn't sure why was there or what he was doing. When Gemma told him ten hours later that they'd broken the world record, it came as a complete surprise.

Once Bartosz had stopped, things got worse for Ihor, having lost his running companion. Marina Schroevers-Striker, an accomplished ultrarunner from Canada, was there as his support crew, and now she had to go into a higher gear. She had already recognised that Ihor was losing his will to continue, so for a few laps she arranged for other Canadian champions to phone him to lift his spirits and focus his mind. At the end of yard 102, Gary Robbins, who also happened to be Ihor's neighbour, had phoned. Listening on the video stream, you could hear the energy in his voice, the inspiration he was offering. It was uplifting, targeted, everything you could hope for in late-race encouragement. But Ihor didn't look convinced, listening, but with an empty gaze.

At the end of yard 104, Ihor appeared unsure what was happening, surprised the race was still ongoing. He asked, *Will all these people stay here until race is over? Will Laz?* Marina replied *Just another lap or two*. For too long she'd been prodding him along with *One More lap*. Towards the end she pushed harder: *I didn't come here to Lose.* At one stage, Ihor thought that he and Harvey were on the same team and that the two of them had already won. Yet competitors they were.

A stark contrast started to emerge between the runners. To those watching there could be little doubt who would win. Ihor ran quickly, smoothly, looking untroubled by injuries or cramps, but Harvey's gait had altered, and now he was leaning forward more often as he ran. Although he kept on bursting off at the start of laps, within a few minutes, Ihor would catch up with him and then go past. With all of Ukraine and Canada behind him, it looked like the younger man would easily have the victory. I was sure Ihor would win.

However, it was a different story watching them between laps. Ihor looked confused, his vacant stare broken only by occasional comments. It appeared that his body could go on forever, but his mind was not convinced that he wanted to. In his tent, Harvey was a different person, smiling, laughing, in complete control of what he was doing. He chatted with Judd Poindexter, his ever-faithful support crew, asked for specific things, made suggestions, and clearly knew exactly what was happening in the race.

Seeing them in their tents, I changed my prediction as to who would win. If it became a battle of mind versus body, I'd always put my money on the mind.

For lap 104, Ihor increased his speed again, finishing in 48:39. Harvey was a long way back with 54:05.

Now with a minute to go before 105 starts, Bartosz is assisted over to see Ihor. He can walk, but needs a person on either side of him to get there. He carefully bends down, shakes the Canadian's hand and adds his words of encouragement: *Thank you very much, I wish you the best.*

Lap 105 was similar to 104, both runners going a tad slower. Ihor ran 49:19, Harvey 54:26. For 106, Ihor slowed down by two minutes, while Harvey increased his speed. Ihor still had a substantial lead, 51:29 to 53:02, but the gap was shrinking.

Now at 107, the last of the day loops, things change. The jeerleaders can be heard: *Just give up. Just give up. Three more days. Three more days.*

Harvey shoots out into the lead again, and Ihor is content to walk for a while. As the two return from the first short loop, Harvey has a big lead. Ihor, on the other hand, stops when he comes back to the starting corral. He begins a conversation with Laz and some others who quickly gather. A cameraman sprints over to capture Ihor sharing more of the uncertainty that he'd displayed in the tent. He talks for a while to an attentive audience, who appear astounded that he's addressing them instead of running. Is this a concession speech? He doesn't seem happy. *Everyone knows how it all went down. I don't want to race again.* Merijn comforts him. *Someone's going to fall asleep in the end. Could be him, could be you.* Ihor tries to keep making his point, but the crowd breaks out in applause and cheering. He gets their point and starts running along, looking strong again.

By now, though, Harvey has his lead, and he's not giving it up. For the first time, the American beats Ihor in a lap. Ihor was another minute slower, while Harvey went three minutes faster than the previous yard.

It's the first lap since 101 where Harvey did not come last. It's the first time he'd beaten Ihor when it was just the two of them running. And it was only the second time in 107 hours that he had crossed the line first. The first, in lap 37, was a long time ago. Ihor, by comparison, had enjoyed eleven lap wins.

Now on his return, Ihor looks slower than ever. His legs move as if he's carrying some hidden weight. By now Thor has joined Marina in supporting him, and they start getting him ready for the next lap.

Again, Ihor doesn't seem convinced he should continue. *This is ridiculous ... So, you want me run to the turnaround and back every hour?* A supporter replies: *The whole world wants you to do that. You have a fifty-fifty chance.* Ihor is dismissive: *What, until one of us collapses?* Later, he complains, gesturing at his foot: *it's really hurting ... I can't believe what we're doing.* Thor throws out another incentive: *Remember, if you win, you've got your ticket to Barkley's.* At this stage, the last thing Ihor cares about is entering another race. *It doesn't matter.*

The two titans walk to the start line for the 108th time, the first of night five, and both begin the yard by walking. After a minute, Harvey starts to run ahead. Ihor follows, trailing behind. He reaches the road's turn after nine minutes. Every step had hurt, but now it was so bad that he could no longer even feel his foot. Wanting to check it, he stops, sits down and removes his shoe. A drone captures the footage for the video stream, and for what feels like an eternity, but is only two minutes, Ihor sits there, unmoving.

Finally, he stands up, and starts to run again. He's looking the best he has for a while. However, while seated, he'd decided that he'd had enough. He isn't running to the turnaround; he's on his way back to the start. Without Marina there to prod him on, he can see no reason to continue. His momentum is gone. Soon he reverts to a walk, and a neighbour drives past, offering encouragement to someone he assumes is still in the race. Ihor doesn't have the energy to dispute the neighbour's assumption and explain that his race is over, so politely says thank you.

After 26 minutes he comes back to the finish. When the crew and spectators see him, the applause is uplifting. Ihor puts his arm around Marina and begins speaking to the assembled crowd. You would hardly recognise him as the person sitting on the chair between yards. It was as if one person started the lap, and another had returned. As he walked back to the start, the pressure on him began to relieve. He no longer had to make decisions, and his mind started to clear. By the time he was back to the finish line he knew what was happening and spoke eloquently, kindly and with clarity.

He thanks Marina for her incredible support, and you can see he feels the need to explain his finish. He knows the crowd wanted him to continue and are disappointed that he stopped. He acknowledges knowing that was what they wanted but provides some context. He hadn't come planning or hoping to win or set a world record. This is only his third Backyard, and third year of running ultras. To finish with an assist of 107 wasn't bad at all, especially for a 29-year-old. *I don't want to jeopardise my health by doing something I didn't plan and didn't want to do.* He is proud of what he's done and hopes the others will not be too disappointed.

As finisher after finisher has done, he repeatedly thanks Laz: *Thank you, Mr Cantrell, for your hospitality, I had quite the adventure ... You've created something truly magical.* Laz in turn is warm with his praise. He offers the silver DNF coin. *It's a DNF, but it's a hell of a good DNF. There's been no better DNF in the history of Backyards.*

And then there was one.

While Ihor was celebrating, Harvey was out in the early evening still running along the road. Midway through lap 108, when he failed to see Ihor running towards him after the turn, he realised that all he had to do was get back on time and he would become the world champion. He would reclaim the world record he'd lost three years earlier. He offered a prayer of gratitude and increased his pace; there was no reason to conserve his energy.

Over the last few laps of the day course, he'd fallen multiple times. After one incident, while lying on the ground, he'd thought: *I'm not going to let the race stop here with my face in the dirt.* And no, his race had not finished with his face down, but with his head held high, running with joy as he approached the line.

Now as he runs in, he hi-fives Laz and some of the spectators, then pulls up one step before the finish line, pausing to savour the moment and add to the drama. The crowd plays along, a chorus of voices exhorting him on: *A little further. One more! One more step!*

He takes the step that puts him into history, completing the lap in 47:31, his fastest time since day two. It was only the third yard he had won. After taking the step he pauses, turns and smiles at the crowd, then says what any sensible person would say after such a long run: *I want to grab my chair.* It's brought over and he enjoys some proper rest.

He spots Ihor and calls out to him. *Ihor, are you all right?* Even in victory, the race over, he remains the same caring, compassionate person. They share a beautiful conversation, two champions honouring each other. As Harvey chats with Ihor, then Laz, then with the crowd, he is focused, full of energy and keen to rejoice in his win. The king of optimism and positive thinking, he admitted that even he had found it harder than usual to stay upbeat: *To be honest, I felt the most tired I've ever felt on day one.*

For hours people had been predicting Harvey would stop. Too old, too slow, not getting enough rest between laps. Even before the event, only 9.5% of Scott Snell's poll had predicted he would win, only 15.3% thought he might be the assist. When he started the race having had only three hours of sleep the previous night, that would have been sufficient reason for him to not run well. When he failed to sleep the next two nights, the writing was on the wall. When he kept falling asleep while running, falling into the dirt, running close to the cut-off in what looked to be a death spiral, his chances of another win seemed minuscule. Laz himself said to Harvey as they celebrated: *We counted you out at thirty hours. You were one of the least likely to win. But as long as you're still there, you can win, it's the Backyard.*

But with all of those weaknesses came a wealth of advantages. He'd run enough laps of the course that he could claim home advantage. He'd flown to Australia and seen the best of their best, and New Zealand's too. He'd practiced his naps, so even running slower loops he was still able to recharge himself enough to continue. And he played the psychological game harder than most. Who knows what impact his repeated charges through the field had made? He looked invincible as he sprinted past others. He was aware that all he had to do was convince his opponents that they had no hope of winning against him, and they would give up.

Even the fact that he took so long each yard had its advantages. His body was taxed less by the slower pace. And more strategically, lap after lap, Ihor, or Bartosz, or almost any other runner, would finish well before Harvey did. They would sit in their chairs, time and time again, and wonder whether he would ever come back in. If he didn't, their chances of winning were so much higher. Yet lap after lap, he dashed their hopes as he sauntered in, had a quick rest, then was once again ready for the next yard. To spoil their hopes, hour after hour, was a form of soul-destroying psychological warfare.

What Harvey never surrendered was his unwavering belief that he could, and would, win. His physical performance went up and down, but his mind stayed strong. A solid support crew, good race preparation and a top mental game; it all paid off for Harvey.

Laz summarised it well:
> *the race was won by*
> *not the fastest*
> *not strongest*
> *not the youngest…*
> *but by the one with the most sheer will to win*

As with every other finisher, Harvey was given a coin that he would cherish. His coin was slightly different to the others. Whereas the other 74 received a silver coin with DNF inscribed on it, his was the winner's gold, and the letters DNF replaced now by LOS. For he was, indeed, the Last One Standing.

The world record was now 108 yards, exactly four and a half days. Harvey and the other 74 had started at 7 am on Saturday morning. When he crossed the line alone on Wednesday it was just before 7 pm. With each day 100 miles, he'd now run exactly 450 miles, which just happened to be the length of the course in Stephen King's The Long Walk. He'd not only improved Phil's world record by six hours, he'd done it on a course that had destroyed most competitors. Almost two-thirds had done less than their previous best, the course proving to be so much harder than they were used to. The record at Big's had increased much more, a massive 23 hours. Harvey had gone almost a full day more than he had winning it two years earlier.

Harvey was now the world record holder, and the worthy winner of a magnificent event. Laz had attracted the best Backyard runners in the world and extracted from them performances that would be remembered for years.

Although the majority of runners had failed to live up to their hopes, falling short of previous peaks, 28 of them had still managed to achieve personal best distances. It was mostly a new wave of stars who had begun to shine; of the top twelve runners before the event, other than Harvey, only Oriol managed a new personal best, seven yards further than before. Of the top twelve results from the race, all except three achieved new personal records. Missing out were those who had previously run 100 yards or more, Sam, Merijn and Phil. The biggest increases, unsurprisingly, came from the second and third-placed runners. Ihor improved his best by a mammoth 40 yards, Bartosz by a similar 39. In

March 2024, Ihor would consolidate his claims to being a new star of ultrarunning, winning the Barkley Marathons at his first attempt. The story of Big's 2023 was that the established stars were now being surpassed by a new generation, with one notable exception.

Harvey, the establishment runner, the ultimate veteran, improved by 'only' 19, but then again, he'd stopped because he had to. How far could he have run? We will never know, but afterwards he was confident that he could at least have run through the night, which would have taken him to lap 120.

With the race now over, I was disappointed not to have the live feed and online chat to follow. It had been a fun few days where much of the running world had turned their attention to the race. I dare say employers breathed a sigh of relief that productivity would now return to usual, as I knew far too many people who had been following while at work.

For me, the timing was fantastic, as I didn't have to wait very long for another fix of Backyard drama. It was only two more days until I was off to compete in my next race.

8

Running Forever

EVER SINCE MY first Backyard, I'd been looking forward to my next event. All year I'd had the next team Backyard Ultra at Rocklea in my diary: 14 October 2023. This time, instead of being called States of Origin it would be the Last Team Standing. The format was the same, an individual race like any other Backyard, but with a team component to see which group could go furthest.

Again, I attempted to persuade as many people as possible to join a team. I was slightly more successful this time, with five people competing, although only four were in our official Runners Jam team. We joked that if we did well, we might still be running when Big's started, a week after our event would begin.

More realistically, I had a few goals for the race. I would love to win, of course, but knew the competition would be tough. I desperately wanted to reach 24 yards, as having fallen three hours short the previous year still stung. If everything went well, then maybe 30 hours would be possible, and 200 km had a nice round look. Given my injuries had gotten worse over the last year, I figured that the most I would be able to do, if everything went perfectly, would be 36, then stop at 9 pm on the Sunday night. Of course, I also knew that everything might fall apart, so I also set myself a minimum goal of 60 km. Surely I could do at least nine yards?

I had been looking forward to the flat track of Rocklea again and had done as much training as I could on flat surfaces. My injuries seemed to flare more on hills, so I'd completed a more boring training schedule, often doing endless laps of an oval. I'd recruited a support crew, updated my instructions for them, and started packing my gear a week in advance. I'd been tapering for two weeks, keen to extract every last bit of potential out of my body.

On the Sunday before it began, I told everyone at my church that I wouldn't be there the following week, as I'd still be running a race that started Saturday morning. Or so I hoped, anyway.

On Monday, we received an email from Alun Davies, the race director, announcing with great sadness that he had to cancel the race. With only seventeen people registered, it was untenable for the council to give such a small group exclusive access to public land.

I was devastated. A year of planning, hoping and dreaming, all gone. Countless hours of training focused on this one particular event, now flushed down the toilet.

We started throwing around ideas about what we should do instead. My first thought was to just do a 50 or 100 km training run around Daisy Hill Forest. That might be enough fun for us. Then I wondered about heading over to Rocklea and pretending the race was still on. We could do as many laps as we wanted. The problem with that idea was that we wouldn't invite support crew or spectators to come along to simply a training run, so we would be without atmosphere, help or any motivation to push hard when it started to hurt. We thought about last-minute entries to the Blackall 100, which was scheduled for the same weekend, but I knew its hills would be punishing for my under-prepared and still-injured legs.

Then my sister, Rachel, who had been planning to compete at Rocklea, had a bright idea. She noticed that Nicole Jukes, who had beaten us all the year before, was planning to run Smurf's Backyard Ultra in Cairns, and that perhaps we also could do that. The timing didn't suit Rachel, two weeks after Last Team Standing's date, but maybe it was an option for the rest of us.

At first, I wasn't keen. Cairns is a beautiful tropical city in my home state of Queensland, but it's nearly 1,700 km to the north. While I'd enjoyed visiting there many times, and loved running around its beautiful mountains and waterfront, my previous visits had been in the southern hemisphere's winter. Cairns in July and August was stunning. No cold gear was required, and I could run in a singlet, enjoy swims and feel like it was summer. The idea of running there in late October did not sound pleasant at all.

I'd also heard about the previous instalment of the race. It had been called Old Mates' Backyard Ultra and was described as Australia's toughest Backyard. It was won in 2022 with only 19 yards, with finishers reporting incredible heat and humidity. This year the event had been relocated to a much more suitable location, close to the airport, but it still had some decent elevation. Half of the course would be on a mountain bike track, meaning uneven ground and constantly changing terrain. It sounded like a much harder course than we were used to.

It would also require taking the Friday off work to get there, buying some gear in Cairns, plus booking flights, car and accommodation, all of which would make the trip a lot more expensive than driving half an hour to Rocklea.

However, the more we thought about it, the more exciting the idea became. The heat could be managed. I made contact with their race director, Josh Duff, who was brilliant. He promised to supply whatever we needed: tables, portable coolers, chairs, a gazebo and more. He was the one whose podcast I'd found so valuable the previous year, and he was even more helpful in person.

Mark Morton, who had run with me the year before, and Peter Jones, our friend who had helped with support, all signed up. It looked like a great boys' weekend away.

The big problem, apart from the heat, was that we would not have any support crew. We didn't want to ask anyone to take the day off and fly up, but figured we could support one another easily enough. We would have to adjust our expectations, as presumably there was some advantage to having support crew, but we had no idea how much benefit that was. We should be fine; I'd heard of Akihiro Maeda completing 67 laps at the Race of the Champions in Germany with no support crew, so it was worth trying.

Next came the problem of booking flights, as we had no idea how long we would run for. For Rocklea, I had felt confident about running 24-30 hours, and Mark and Pete were both running better than I was. How different would the conditions in Cairns be?

As it turned out, Pete had family commitments on Sunday afternoon, and it did seem unlikely that we would run past them into a second night. We reluctantly booked Sunday afternoon flights, which meant that the absolutely latest we could stop was after 32 hours. Even that would be cutting it fine, with no chatting after we finished, no traffic delays, and us finding an easily accessible shower before we boarded the plane. In the back of my mind I dreamt of phoning family, work, car hire company and airline while still running. I'd explain to them all that I had to change all my plans as I was running well and was probably going to win.

Training was interesting for the two weeks before Cairns. We'd been tapering for the cancelled race, so couldn't have a proper rest now, as five weeks of lower mileage would be counter-productive. We increased our training again, and I tried to do as much as I could in the heat. On any day when the forecast was for temperatures above 30C/86F, I would start work early, then disappear for a run in the hottest part of the day. I was keen to do whatever I could to acclimatise to higher temperatures. Unfortunately, while running in the heat the Monday before the race I had a mild hamstring tear, which became a convenient reason to have another taper until the day of the race.

In the weeks before the race, we kept on watching the weather forecasts, and they didn't look too bad, with most predictions in the 28-31C/82-88F range, not much hotter than we were having at home. We could handle that, and were as ready as could be. Most importantly, our tutus were packed, ready for lap 22.

By the time we got to Cairns on the Friday afternoon we were excited for a great weekend and a fun race. We picked up our last-minute supplies, found our budget accommodation, checked in at the race and enjoyed the pre-race pasta party. We hoped to get the gear that we'd been promised, and that the chairs wouldn't be rock hard, the gazebo tiny and portable coolers too small to be useful. However, we found that we couldn't yet get any of it, as all was being used for the dinner.

We did see that the gazebos had no sides, and were sceptical about whether it would be best for our base. Fearing the sun might come blasting in, we wandered around the nearby trees looking to see if any of them would provide better shade for us. However, each time we found a location that looked good, as we stood there admiring the position, we noticed ants crawling over our feet. In fact, all of the trees had large, vicious, black ants around them, which we quickly learned knew how to bite well. We decided to start with the gazebos and see how bad the sun was on them.

The next morning, after a typically disturbed night-before-race sleep, we arrived back at the venue just before 6 am. We were elated to discover that the gazebo Josh had reserved for us occupied the closest possible position to the start line, only about 10 metres away. This would mean only the shortest walk would be required to get to our area between laps, and we could avoid unnecessary movement.

With the sun low in the sky, the gazebo roof offered almost no shade, so we asked Josh if he had a spare sheet and rope. He was again happy to oblige, and we soon rigged up a moveable wall that would block out most of the sun.

Even better, the chairs were flexible and comfortable, exactly what we hoped for. We were given two large portable coolers and offered access to anything else that we needed. We realised how fortunate we were, and how well we were being looked after.

Right next to us were several other tents for out-of-towners. On one side was Rhys Williams, who had driven 1,000 km from Rockhampton.

On the other was Sam Gardener, who like us had flown up from Brisbane. Past Sam was Nicole Jukes and her amazing team, also having flown up. We were pleased we weren't the only ones silly enough to have travelled so far for a race in sweltering weather.

We lined up for the 7 am start, with no idea what was ahead. We were keen to run at least 24 hours, even with the tough conditions. To save money, we had no accommodation booked for that night, as we expected to be running well into the next day. Much of the conversation between ourselves and the other runners was about Big's, which had only finished three days earlier. Many joked about the race going for 109 hours to get the new world record.

The cowbell rang, and then reality hit. Rather than the dead flat course I was used to, there was hilly, rocky terrain with loose rocks, roots and all kinds of hazards. The first kilometre or two was on a dirt road with a couple of hills before we entered the Smithfield Mountain Bike Park. From there the course was mostly single-track paths designed for bikes. Gone were the smooth trails, replaced by ever-changing ground under our feet. We had to watch our every step and were constantly going either up or down small gullies and ridges. The environment was beautiful, running through tropical rainforest and eucalypt woodlands. It was the sort of place I'd love to run in training, but perhaps not for endless hours, and it was definitely a lot harder than my normal training routes.

By the end of the first yard, about 53 minutes later, we realised this wasn't quite Rocklea. Although the temperature was only 23 degrees for the start of the lap, by its end, with us not running particularly hard, our shirts were drenched with sweat. We took them off, squeezed them out, and hung them on coat hangers to dry before the next lap. Soon it would hit 33 degrees and 85% humidity.

The lack of support crew began taking its toll straight away. The course itself took a lot longer to complete than Rocklea, we estimated around five minutes more per lap. Instead of finishing most yards early with ten to twelve minutes of break, we had five to seven. Instead of a support crew offering food, drinks, massage guns, pain relief, band-aids, ice, water tank top-ups, or whatever else we needed, most laps we would spend three to four minutes getting these things ourselves. So instead of ten to twelve minutes of valuable rest, mostly sitting down, we had between one and four minutes. That provided significantly less recuperation and rejuvenation before the next lap.

Even worse, it meant that we had little margin for error. If something went wrong in a lap, there would be a lot less time to recover. If we slowed down, and we knew we would slow as our legs fatigued, it would not take long before we would time out on a lap. It felt like we had hit a death spiral from the start.

Mark and Pete were both a lot faster than I was, so after running together for the first few hours, once we would hit the forest they started running on ahead of me. It made sense given how much slower the course was, but it was a lot less fun running alone.

Fortunately, we made a number of friends early on. We adopted our neighbour Sam into our team, and would often run with him. Luke Raffles was walking a lot, and running slowly, so he was often near us at the back of the pack. I assumed he would be one of the earlier finishers, but he joked that he might finish every lap last until he was the only one left. It was great to see Nicole's smiling face there again too, although again she was mostly at the faster end of the field.

The spectators added a lot to the race. On the first yard we saw some runners' children cheering and offering hi-fives to their parents and everyone else who ran past. Lap after lap we would run out of our way towards wherever they were to get their hi-fives. We thanked them for their cheering, and told them how helpful their encouragement was. It made the laps more fun, and increasingly they would look out for us and cheer us on excitedly. They would be just hanging around, notice we were coming, then run over to the course to cheer us on. This happened three times most laps, and our mobile cheer squad soon became the highlight of each hour.

Even though we had no crew ourselves, others were helpful. On several occasions a gust of wind blew our sheet off and tipped much of the gear off our tables. Each time someone from Nicole's crew would come over and fix it all for us. Given the tiny margin we had between laps, it was massively appreciated.

Despite all the fun, after about four or five laps, though we hated to admit it, we knew our hopes for big totals were gone. We were still having a blast, but Mark and I both found that our appetites had disappeared. I'd drink a cup of water and feel full instantly, and not want to have anymore. We kept eating and drinking, but probably not as much as we should have. We weren't getting enough calories, nor replacing the water we were sweating out. I'm a prolific sweater, and the high humidity was claiming a toll. I thought I'd done well to train in the heat, but it was the extreme humidity that I wasn't ready for. It didn't make me feel better when one of the locals said, *I thought it was going to be worse than this.* This was tough enough for me!

I tried to stretch out my recovery time by staying in my chair later and later. With two minutes to go, most runners would assemble in the corral, but the more tired I'd get, the later I'd arrive. Given that our gazebo was so close, I'd often leave it until twenty or thirty seconds before the start of the lap before I'd pull myself out of the chair and stumble over. Often, I would just get to the start and then would leave a few seconds later. I could see from the looks of the other runners that they thought I was on my last legs, which was a bit embarrassing so early in the race. *Perhaps I might not win after all.*

I fell over twice in the first six yards, both times needing Mark to help me back to my feet. By now Mark was slowing, and I appreciated having him to run with more often. Fortunately, I avoided any new injuries, just a mild cut to one knee. Even so, I was shaken, covered with dirt and scared to fall again. Several of those who dropped out early did so because of falls, so I knew I had to be more careful from now on.

After nine laps and 60 km, Mark decided he'd had enough. He'd been feeling ill for a while, and knew things weren't going to turn around for him with the heat we were running in. He told me on his final lap that he'd finish then, and I knew I wouldn't be able to persuade him to go further. If he'd been a few laps short of his previous best, or another significant milestone, I'm sure he could have been prodded to go further. But with it still six hours until 100 km, and eight hours until his best of 17 yards, he didn't have any such hope to motivate him.

By then I'd started slowing too. Having up to seven minutes break between each lap had decreased to two or three, which meant I had no margin for rest once I grabbed some food and drink. Mark was a legend in instantly transitioning to support crew, but I was still cutting things fine. He was even kind enough to do things like removing and replacing my shoes, which were pretty disgusting.

I chatted to Nicole for a while on lap ten. I thought it amusing that once again, as happened at the States of Origin in Rocklea, we were the only two runners out on the course. Unfortunately, this was because we were coming last and second-last this time, not first and second. Injuries had been hitting Nicole hard for some time, and she didn't manage to finish the lap.

Without Mark, and with the race numbers thinning rapidly, I found myself running alone even more. Pete felt a lot more comfortable at a faster pace, but he was generous enough to start running the pre-forest section with me. He helped me get through the start of each hour, and the later trail sections were narrow and tricky enough that conversation was harder anyhow.

By now, I wasn't getting back to the gazebo most laps, finishing with only a minute or two to spare. Each time I would run into the final straight and see the others standing there ready to go for their next lap. I could see the pity in their eyes, as I was only just making it back. I got even slower, and the spectators and runners began to cheer as I came in for the effort they could see it was taking me to get in. Strangely, it was a lot of fun to be so close to the cut-off and have the encouragement. Each time it gave me a fresh jolt of adrenaline, enough for another lap.

As I approached, Mark would stand right next to the corral with a variety of food and drink waiting for me. I would cross the line, step back to where he was, take the provisions with me for the next lap, and step back into the corral. Then, before I knew it, I'd be off again.

Once it turned dark, I wore my headlamp, but kept it switched off. I occasionally would run in Daisy Hill Forest with no light, and thought it would be a good challenge for me to go more carefully and let my eyes adjust well. Mostly, that worked, and I enjoyed the fun of running in the dark during lap 12. I felt peaceful and relaxed, almost like having a rest while I was running.

All of a sudden, I ran onto a road. This was strange, as the course didn't cross any roads. Somehow, perhaps it had something to do with me running in the dark with a switched-off light, I had missed a turn and was now off the course. I had no idea where I was. Panic begin to set in, and I recalled a recent 24-hour rogaine Mark and I had competed in, where we ran several kilometres in the wrong direction. Hopefully I hadn't gone that far off again. I didn't know what my mistake was, and feared — given I was only just finishing each lap — I might not get back in time. Now that would be an embarrassing way to finish, dropping out due to not turning a light on.

I turned around and began running away from the road back towards where I'd just been. When I rounded the corner, I saw a light off in the distance; fortunately, it was another runner. He was coming out of a water station that I'd missed, and I followed his light back onto the track. I had no idea how much time I'd lost, and still had a fair way to go, so ran back as fast as I could. I sprinted in the final straight, enjoyed the applause of the crowd, then realised I still had two entire minutes to spare, more margin than I'd been having for previous laps. But now, I was exhausted, and the adrenaline surge that came from being lost and sprinting home was fading.

As I started yard 13, my legs felt worse than ever. The aches and pains that had been there for most of the day went to a new level after the effort of the previous lap. I was dripping with sweat, short on energy and tired from having to concentrate on every step for so long. My pace, already on the sluggish side, dropped even further. Around the halfway point I did some calculations based on my pace and position, and realised that I was probably going to finish the lap about two minutes too late. Things were deteriorating so quickly that it was unlikely I'd be able to reverse the trend. With no support crew, a much harder course, and the unrelenting humidity, I was in trouble.

But I didn't want to finish this way. I calculated that if I could finish this lap on time, then just do three kilometres on the next, I would clock up 90 km of running for the day, and 13 official yards. I determined that I'd put absolutely everything I had into finishing this one lap, then just walk until I hit 90 km on the next. I could live with that.

I increased my pace as much as I could. I skipped a water station, figuring it would slow me down too much. I tried to balance running swiftly with my aching legs and a desperate desire not to fall over in the dark on the still-difficult terrain.

With a massive smile on my face, I ran in at the end of yard 13, my slowest lap yet, with 45 seconds to spare. I stepped in to the corral, back out to grab some Coke and lollies from Mark, then back in, now ready to start lap 14.

I told Pete what I was planning, and he walked with me for a while. He gently asked if perhaps after walking for a while I might start feeling better, and just maybe I could finish this lap too. He was happy to stay with me and encourage me through, but if I was going to pull out, he'd run on alone. It was the perfect approach, and I was very, very tempted. I tried running with him for a while, and I started to think that it just might be possible.

Then suddenly, my right big toe began to hurt, and I could feel a massive blister. Given my existing complaints, this was the final straw, and I told Pete to go. I kept walking, and they were some of the slowest kilometres of my life. I'd lost any motivation to move, knew the race was over, and I just needed to get to a turnaround point and get back to the start to click over 90 km. After a while Mark came out to walk the last part with me, and that was a welcome relief. Eventually, with great joy, I crossed the finish line, having done just over 90 km.

I spent some time sitting, resting and feeling sorry for myself. After half an hour, Pete came running in, having completed his lap. Soon our neighbour Sam returned too. For the next few hours, I did whatever I could to support them both and encourage them to go further.

They were looking fantastic, running strongly, and I thought they would get through the night. But much earlier than I expected or hoped, they suddenly stopped, Sam with 16 yards, and Pete with 18. Both had one much slower lap, then timed out on the next. Sam finished in ninth place, and Pete was sixth. Although we'd all run well, it was disappointing that none of us had gone as far as we'd hoped, and we'd packed our tutus for nothing.

After Pete recovered we had nothing to do. It was almost 3 am, and we had no accommodation booked, and no flights until much later in the day. We tried sleeping in our chairs, but the lights and whistles each hour made it difficult. We hobbled off to our rental car, tried to ignore the nearly overwhelming stench coming from our bodies in the confined space, and slept for a few hours.

In the morning, we made sure we woke up in time to head back to the starting line. We wanted to have our turn supporting the children who had served so well as our cheer squads, and who were now racing in a single lap of our course. They ran magnificently, and with much more energy than we ever displayed.

By now the race was down to three runners. Luke Raffles, the one with the theory about winning by completing each lap last, was still going slowly. It turned out that he was quite a strong runner, and finally finished at noon with 30 yards. The other two, Rhys Williams and Adam Fox, the defending champion, ran together for another four hours in the blazing heat, before agreeing to share an honourable draw, 34 yards and a DNF each.

We spent the rest of the day before flying home trying to find somewhere to shower, before settling on a wash in the Cairns esplanade's public pool.

In retrospect, this race experience gave me a new appreciation for the value of support crews. If we had dragged someone along to help us, I'm confident we all could have gone a lot further. We would have spent much less time on our feet while they readied our provisions, filled our water flasks and did anything else we needed. More time in our chairs would have allowed us to recharge much better and give us much more margin between laps.

But also, I suspect a support crew would have helped us in other ways. A crew can ensure that a runner eats well, providing a broad variety of options, and nag them until they do eat and drink properly. They can make sure we get in the right nutrients and care for us in ways that we wouldn't think of. I could have used my massage gun on my aching legs, put ice on my head between laps to cool down, and spent time sitting with my legs elevated. But with limited time, I didn't even think of these, or so many other beneficial things. I came home more grateful than ever for those who support us in our races.

Early in 2024, Pete, Mark and some other friends ran in Rowan Cassidy's ten-lap We've Gotcha BACKyard Ultra at Rocks Riverside Park. I had a turn in trying to support them, and I found it a lot of fun. However, I also left with even more appreciation for the crews, as I'd much rather be running.

The champions of the sport know well the importance of support crews. Gemma, Judd and Marina all make integral contributions to the performances of Phil, Harvey and Ihor respectively. They take their roles seriously, prepare like professionals and provide a noticeable boost to their runners. Even casual support crews, though, can make a substantial difference, and that's what we'd now discovered in Cairns.

Perhaps someone as good as Akihiro Maeda can get by without a support crew, but it was beyond us. I asked him how he did the Race of the Champions without such a crew. He explained that when the Mexican team and other runners saw he had no support they helped him a lot throughout the race. Without deprecating this generosity, I'm still incredibly impressed. There are limits to what people who don't know you, and don't speak your language, can do to help.

Even without the support crews, and with us all finishing with much lower totals than we'd hoped for, Cairns was still an amazing weekend. We had no regrets, and thoroughly enjoyed our experience. There's something special about the Backyard concept that makes every event an adventure, every race far more fun than you would ever expect.

As I was writing this book, I noticed that another new event near me, Glasshouse Standing, was just about to begin. Competitors would start at 5 pm on New Year's Eve, so most runners would get to celebrate the new year by running. It was a great idea, an adventure for all involved.

And that may be a suitable way to bring this tale to a close, reflecting on what it is about the Backyard that is so attractive to so many. What is so special about these events? What has led to an explosion in the number of events and competitors around the world?

For starters, the race allows you to run a lot. Whether you like running for the feelings of euphoria, the relief of stress, the scenery or the serenity, the longer you run the more you can enjoy all of these. Personally, given that running is one of the great joys in my life, the idea of a race that allows you to run indefinitely seems perfect.

It may also suit me because it's a good sport for slower runners. All those people with fast-twitch fibres, and whatever other genetic advantages they may have, can still participate, but none of those gifts are helpful in a Backyard. The fastest person in one lap cannot build up any kind of a lead over the other runners, as everyone starts the next lap at the same time. Sam Harvey can run a lap as fast as he likes, but Claire Bannwarth will still be with him at the next start line. This is why Backyards are great for people who have good endurance, but low speed.

When you listen to interviews with Backyarders, you often hear similar stories about their pasts, albeit with exceptions. Often, they will tell how they weren't good at other sports, and many will talk about how they were on the slower side. I share both of those histories. The accessibility of the event for people with lower running speeds or sporting prowess is attractive.

The sport is also accessible to people who cannot yet run far. The fitness level required to run one yard within an hour is comparatively low. Most active people could do that without training. With even limited training, completing a few laps is possible. A few more, and suddenly someone has become an ultramarathon runner. It is a lot easier for someone to try for 'just one more loop', than to sign up to do a mountainous 50 km race. One of Laz's few regrets in creating the Backyard is that he put the word 'ultra' in the name. His fear is that the name dissuades people who don't want to run far from attempting the format. I've found that when I tell people I ran 141 km, they're less inclined to give it a try.

Accessibility may also explain the attractiveness of the event to older runners. It was remarkable that the runners at Big's 2023 had an average age of 41, and the winner was 47. Physical strength, flexibility and speed typically decline from your late twenties onwards. Gymnasts will often peak in their teenage years. Swimmers in their late twenties are seen as older. A sprinter in the mid-thirties is considered to be defying their age. Yet endurance, perseverance and strategic wisdom can all increase with passing years. With many of the benefits of speed removed in a Backyard Ultra, perhaps finally we have a sporting event where older athletes have an advantage.

Not being able to build a lead also means that people can have one bad lap, but still keep on going and not fall behind. Trip over on one lap and finish with not much margin? Just go a bit faster the next, enjoy some rest and you can get back to your normal rhythm. Second chances are available every hour.

The other consequence of not being able to build a lead is that it allows runners of different standards to compete together. At the Australian Backyard Masters at Dead Cow Gully, runners who could only do a few laps were able to start beside, then run along with, the likes of Harvey, Phil and Sam. There are not many events that allow for such a diversity of skill levels to participate together. It allows the newcomers to learn from the veterans, cautions the elites from thinking they're better than everyone else, and makes every lap more interesting. A below-average basketballer or baseball player might be able to stand on the same court or field as their professional idols, but they would have no chance of competing against them as even close to equals. Yet although the Backyard champions may run a few days longer than the rest, those toward the back can still enjoy starting and running with the best of the best.

That social aspect is also attractive. In a standard ultramarathon, runners quickly spread out. Even in a race with hundreds of participants, it is not rare to run alone for long periods, going for hours without talking to anyone except at the aid stations. In a Backyard, though, every lap you have the opportunity to run along with any of your competitors. If you run for ten hours, you could have three ten-minute conversations per hour, thirty in total, and still have half of the time by yourself. If you enjoy meeting new people, or chatting in general, it's a great opportunity to talk for as long as you like. In my races, I loved running with Rachel, Mark and Pete, who I already knew, for hours and hours. But I also valued the dozens of other people I was able to meet along the way.

Harvey often says that one of the things he likes about Backyards is being able to chat to his support crew, which normally means Judd Poindexter. They get to spend five or ten minutes every hour, for days on end, chatting. Not many friends get that much time together. For myself, I loved it when our friends and family visited us in Rocklea, and it was great to spend time with them all, and the support crew in particular. Similarly, Frank Gielen noted that chatting to his crew and fellow runners every lap was a highlight of his Big's experience.

Backyards are also good for encouraging teamwork and cooperation. Most runners will find that at some stage they start helping others during their races; as you run you often see an opportunity to help someone else. It might be a word of advice, sharing some drink with a parched runner, offering to split an energy bar, or just cheering them on to keep going. Often runners will see someone suffering and run with them for a while to get them out of their rut.

It also helps that most runners, in any given event, are not aiming to win. Most people are seeking to push themselves and go as far as they can. To do that, you know that you need others to do well too. So you help others, partly for altruistic reasons, as it's the loving and right thing to do, but sheer selfishness will also have you helping your fellow runner. If you want to be pushed to your limit, having others around you going further will enable you to do better yourself. This all lends the event to collaboration and teamwork, working with others to mutually achieve your goals. These are useful skills to learn for the rest of life too.

If you like eating, the Backyard is a great event. In Claire Bannwarth's pre-Big's video interview, she shared a common sentiment: *I love running and I love eating and a Backyard is the perfect thing to do both at the same time.* You hear something similar about other ultramarathons too, that people like them because they get to eat all day long. I've often heard ultras described as all-day eating contests that have some running thrown in. What makes the Backyard even more appealing to those with larger appetites is that the runners' access to food is unparalleled.

When I ran the Blackall 100, I carried whatever food I wanted in my backpack, which by necessity limited how much I took. I also put some food in drop-bags out on the course, and ate as much as I liked from the feast provided at the aid stations. They're not stingy, and the quantity, variety and service are all excellent.

But when you look at what is possible in a Backyard, the comparison becomes unfair. Some runners will place their orders before they leave on one lap and have whatever dish they asked for ready upon their return. Feel like a nice hot pasta dish, a bacon and egg burger, or heavily salted avocado on high-fibre bread? All you need to do is bring along the ingredients, cooking equipment, and a generous support crew, and it's all yours. When I ran a practice event at Andrew Southwell's house in 2024, as soon as I sat on my chair and started eating after the first lap I remembered how good Backyards are. What other excuse do you have to eat on the hour, every hour?

Jivee Tolentino's pre-race comment about what he likes about Backyards was more philosophical. He explained that the difficulties you endure help you to get through battles in the other parts of your life too. That is true, even if other endurance sports can make similar claims.

However, there is something that is different about Backyards, in how hard they allow people to push themselves. Because there is no finish, as the title of this book suggests, most runners will keep going until they get to the point where they perceive they have reached their limit. That is something rare and valuable. To encourage yourself to improve, to push your boundaries, to try to get out of the box your life has been in, these are crucial activities for healthy living. To have an activity that is safe, yet allows a radical exploration of one's limits, is a beautiful thing.

Tobbe Gyllebring, from Sweden agrees. He explains that in Backyards reaching your limit is a great gift, ironically one that you lose if you happen to win. He elaborates:

> *I used to say that the worst thing that you can do is winning a Backyard. What happens when you win a Backyard is that the adventure and the journey is taken from you, and the only thing that you get in return is a medal.*

In his 2022 book, The Sweet Spot: Suffering, Pleasure and the Key to a Good Life, psychologist Paul Bloom explores a key aspect of living related to this. He argues that the suffering people voluntarily endure in extreme sports, which I suggest Backyard Ultras could be considered one of, is useful to their thriving in life overall. He describes suffering as *an essential source of both pleasure and meaning in our lives.* If suffering, done properly, is helpful, then Backyards — a format literally invented by Laz to allow runners to suffer more than ever before — may well be a useful tool.

While I was writing this book I stumbled across a fascinating quote from the American Football coach Vince Lombardi:

> *I firmly believe that any man's finest hour, the greatest fulfillment of all that he holds dear, is that moment when he has worked his heart out in a good cause and lies exhausted on the field of battle - victorious.*

As I read that, I pictured someone having just pushed themselves to the limit in a Backyard Ultra, lying on the ground at the finish line, having gone further than they ever had before, having succeeded in pushing themselves to a new limit. Who cares in what position they finished? The triumph is in the personal victory.

And I do think that doing well in a Backyard can count as a Lombardian 'good cause'. Perhaps not quite at the level of helping the poor, but a good cause nevertheless. To achieve a personal victory in a Backyard can be one of a person's finest hours, a great fulfilment of dreams. It's that kind of drama, a magnificent success in a worthy pursuit that makes Backyards so attractive. To push yourself beyond your previous best, to go further than ever before, that is a great accomplishment.

Of course, this can all be taken too far. Pursuit of sporting glory or improvement can easily become an idol that we worship before everything else good in our lives. The incredible training that many put in for Backyards, a worthy pursuit of a good goal, can become something that pulls people away from family and community. It's difficult to get this right. But if other responsibilities can be fulfilled, and other people not devalued, the pursuit of self-improvement can be a great good.

At a far more mundane level, there are other basic virtues to Backyards. They are often cheaper to enter than other races, particularly those that allow you to run for long distances. They are safer than most too, with all runners in a relatively tight area. There will always be someone ready to run the next lap and find a fallen competitor. Medical care will never be too far away. Runners will never go hours without someone noticing that they are in need and should be assisted.

For organisers, they are also much cheaper and easier to organise than other events. The shorter courses, with runners repeatedly running around the same lap, allows for easier planning approvals, risk assessments, and traffic management. They require fewer aid stations and other volunteers out on the course. And of course, you can host it on a much smaller plot of land, often making the venue closer to home.

There is one final factor that Backyarders often list when they are asked what they love about the format. Lazarus Lake. Gary Cantrell.

The founder, host, race director and overall leader of the Backyard universe. There are the occasional critics of his style or leadership, and he makes no claim to sainthood. But within the Backyard community, affection for him is widespread. Listen to any Harvey Lewis interview and he will sing the praises of Laz for as long as you let him. Others have similar feelings. Once most Big's competitors finish their races, they will seek Laz out and thank him, repeatedly, for opening his home to them, for creating the concept, for the care he has shown to them all. Most will ask him for a hug; their affection is real and tangible. They admire his ingenuity, enjoy his humour, trust his judgment and appreciate his warm hospitality. For many, it is his charisma, his reputation and his record of running other remarkable events that first brought them into Backyards. Some started running Backyards and then discovered Laz, but many attempted the sport because of him personally.

With all the superlatives that have been written about Laz, perhaps the most apt word for him would be generous. It's not just his ingenuity as a race director that the runners respond to in their thankfulness, but his generosity of spirit and hospitality. Each year he allows waves of athletes to run on his property and always looks after them well. He's built an extra room on his house just to provide beds for international runners, and he's a prolific fund-raiser for charities. And charging as little as he does for his key races, to avoid money being the deciding factor in someone choosing to enter, is the height of generosity.

This does raise an obvious question, although one without an obvious answer. What happens to the world of Backyards when Laz decides to hang up his whistle? The events can theoretically keep on going forever. But currently, it all works well because of the trust people have in Laz. He is relied upon as the arbiter of all kinds of disputes about the rules. It is easy to say that the rules are simple and clear, but when a literal interpretation of them is taken to extremes, questions can arise. Sometimes, it appears as if runners are the lawyers, each arguing their case, race directors the local judges, and Laz a one-man court of appeal passing final judgment on how the rules are to be interpreted. Without Laz, there would need to be a more formal codification of the rules, and someone else, or some kind of governing body, making the rulings.

Similarly, every second year Big's serves as the world championships of the sport. At first, Laz introduced it as the de facto championship, but it now has official status. However, many of the other biggest events succeed because they are ways of getting to Big's. The off-year Satellite Championships, a true innovation, partly work because they offer the national winners the chance to compete at Big's the following year. The worldwide ranking system managed by Laz has value mostly because those who have gone the furthest are then also invited to Bigs.

If Laz moves to Florida, sells his Bell Buckle property, and stops organising Big's each year, what happens to the worldwide series of races? Again, a new system would need to be developed, with authoritative oversight or governance of the still-new sport. Would a systemised organisational structure with various stakeholder representatives allow the sport to mature? Or would that ruin its dynamism and choke its growth through typical bureaucratic committees, rules and policies? Perhaps the senior race directors could organise a collegial approach that retains the current status quo. Various events could then offer to host the world championships on a rotational basis, that event then becoming what every runner aims towards. Perhaps one or more of the event organisers, Naresh Kumar, Mike Dobies or Mike Melton, already heavily involved in Big's, could take over the reins of the event? Carl Laniak has already accepted leadership of the Barkley in 2024, which may be a hint of things to come. Until anything like that becomes necessary, which hopefully is many years away, Tennessee, and Laz, will remain the centre of the Backyard world.

What else may lie in the future of Backyards? Harvey thought he could have got to 120 hours, at least. Oriol has suggested 140 is realistic. Patto and Sam have both predicted people will get to 150. And many runners have talked about reaching some form of homeostasis, where they get just enough calories, food, sleep, drink, and social interaction each lap, that they could perhaps keep on running indefinitely. Although Phil felt he was running in that kind of a state at Dead Cow Gully, he doesn't think anyone can continue indefinitely. Most likely, people just cannot sleep enough each lap, or their stomachs process enough nutrients each hour, to make up for the sleep and calorific deficits they enter. Eventually, those deficits will grow too large, and bodies will force them to stop.

Hendrik proposed that perhaps the sport's rules would need some form of refinement to stop events from going on for weeks or even months. His suggestion was that once runners reach a certain point, perhaps 120 hours, they are then given one more lap where whoever completes it the fastest gets the win. The problem with that idea is that it dramatically changes the nature of the sport, so the attributes that promote a runner's success in Backyards become no longer helpful at the end. Assuming you could get there, speed would ultimately dominate.

Another suggestion comes from Patto. Perhaps at a certain point, the time allowed for each yard could start being lowered by one minute per lap. After say, ten more laps, the runners would only have fifty minutes to complete the yard. It would be a gradual shift and would slowly squeeze the runners out of the race. That seems reasonable, but until the possibly mythical homeostasis happens, such changes will be unlikely.

Another potential innovation for Backyards is in live coverage. Over the last few years, more events have had live video streams, allowing people to follow along from afar. Tens of thousands of people have accessed them, and the sport can be fascinating to watch. A weakness, if there is one, is that not much happens in a lot of the coverage. The start and end of laps are interesting, particularly if there is some drama unfolding. But while the runners are out on the course, there is often not much to watch, apart from recordings of the pre-race interviews.

If, somehow, commentary from informed analysts could be added to the video feeds, the interest could potentially skyrocket. The commentary could explain the sport to newcomers, set the context for each lap, and share fascinating stories about the race and runners. Commentary does happen already, but in a decentralised fashion through messaging apps and social media comments. If it could be organised well, commentary could potentially provide content-hungry television networks with 108 or more hours of quality sporting product.

What will happen to Backyards in the future? No one knows. Your fanciful guesses are probably as good as mine. What I do know is that as it stands, it is an exhilarating, adventurous, and limit-pushing sport. With things as they are, it is one of the best sporting stories of recent years. In its first thirteen years, its spectacular growth has been a lot of fun to follow, and even more to participate in. May there be many more magnificent Backyard Ultra stories to tell in the years to come.

A FINAL NOTE

Laz is an iconic character who has many layers and the ability to express himself like a modern Mark Twain. He's an artist of races, ultras of course. Laz didn't suspect the race he created in his backyard, designed for pure grit, strategy and endurance, over speed alone, would rocket to success in the ultra world.

I'm grateful for Laz's creativity, and for the Backyard Ultra. There are elements to the race which pull me back again and again. It always seems we can improve ourselves, whether building more physical endurance, our nutrition or pace, sleep or otherwise; we can grow.

The race is special to me because the format lends itself to runners running together. I'm competitive but I also love the camaraderie. I've met people all across the globe who have run a Backyard and it inspires me to see others sharing in the same format, pushing themselves. I really love nature! While you're finishing the same loop or on an out-and-back in the race day after day, you are outside and observing the world slowly.

It's also important to note, Big's is named after Laz's iconic dog Big. Big was a rescue, a pit bull who was abandoned with a gunshot in front of Laz's yard. Big lived far beyond the normal age of a large pit bull, living to a mighty 14 years of age. If you ask me, it was due to the love between Laz and Big. Big was fully dedicated to Laz, and Laz's affection for Big was clearly visible. To be successful at surviving long in Big's Backyard or otherwise you have to pour in a level of love.

Go run a Backyard Ultra! You'll discover something new about yourself, meet people, take in the nature and have a memorable adventure!

Some principles to go far! (1) Vegan foods are best for digestion and lowering inflammation. (2) Having a reliable crew member who stays positive & supportive can be invaluable. (3) Focus on the next snack, the next tree, the easy spot you enjoy! (4) Enjoy the people you will meet! All the best!

Harvey Lewis
Backyard Ultra world champion and world record holder.

ACKNOWLEDGEMENTS

As with any book, there are many people to thank. Gary Cantrell's encouragement and time have been absolutely crucial. He has created an amazing event which must take far too much of his time to maintain worldwide. To me, and to many others, he has been generous, kind and patient.

Thanks to Gary Dalkin for serving as my editor, Mike Trimpe for his front cover photo, Ben Taylor for his graphic design, and to Charlotte Parker for her chapter heading design.

David 'Patto' Patterson, and his Backyard Ultra Podcast, have both been magnificent. Patto does a wonderful job of helping guests to share their best stories from their Backyard experience without getting in the way. His is by far the most extensive oral collection of stories about Backyards. Through his podcast and overall helpfulness, he has been a great encouragement.

Tim Moffatt (@backyardstats) has compiled a massive database to analyse the data from Big's 2023, which he provided for my use. He also kindly, and patiently, answered innumerable questions about various results.

Many runners and Race Directors have been very generous with their time too, helping me to find and confirm the best stories. Alun Davies, Andrew Southwell, Bart Stes, Dave Proctor, Frank 'the Tank' Gielen, Hendrik Boury, Ivo Steyaert, Jacob Zocherman, James Blanton, Janne Svärdhagen, Jon Asphjell, Juha Seppälä, Lindley Chambers, Mark Owen, Merijn Geerts, Nicole Jukes, Patryk Świętochowski, Peter Clarke, Peter Munns, Phil Gore, Sean Sandiford, Stephanie Gillis-Paulgaard, Tim De Vriendt, Tim Walsh, Thor Thorleifsson, and Van Da Bui, have all been helpful in this regard.

Another group very kindly checked facts for me. For some this was a single sentence, for others it ran into thousands of words. Many of them discovered that my sources were incorrect and caught my mistakes. Each of these are greatly appreciated: Aaron Young, Adam Fox, Adam Keen, Akihiro Maeda, Amanda Nelson, Angelika Huemer, Angus Ward, Anna Carlsson, Bartosz Fudali, Bev Anderson-Abbs, Brett Standring, Chris Bosley, Chris Roberts, David Christopher, David Stoltenberg, Erchana Murray-Bartlett, Eric Deshaies, Fiona Hayvice, Frank Gielen, Greg Armstrong, Hendrik Boury, Heidi Berghammer, Helen Waterworth, Ihor Verys, Jamal Said, Jasmin Paris, Jennifer Russo, Jeremy Ebel, Jessica Smith, Jivee Tolentino, Johan Botha, John Kelly, John Stocker, Jon Noll, Josh Duff, Joshua Toh, Judd Poindexter, Karel Sabbe,

Katie Wright, Keith Russell, Kevin Muller, Kristin Tidwell, Levi Yoder, Luke Raffles, Maggie Guterl, Marco Poulin, Marcy Beard, Markus Isch, Matt Blackburn, Matt Shepherd, Michael Hooker, Mike Dobies, Mike Wardian, Naresh Kumar, Nazarii Hnat, Niki Micallef, Niklas Sjoblom, Oriol Antoli, Patrik Hrotek, Radek Brunner, Rhys Williams, Richard McChesney, Rob Parsons, Ron Grant, Ryan Crawford, Sam Gardner, Scott Snell, Shaun Collins, Shona Stephenson, Søren Møller, Steve Durbin, Tamyka Bell, Terumichi Morishita, Thembinkosi Sojola, Tim Englund, Tim Kacprzak, Tokimasa Hirata, Tomokazu Ihara, Tobbe Gyllebring, Travis and Ashley Brown, and Viktoriia Nikolaienko.

Thanks especially to Harvey Lewis, Dean Karnazes and many others already listed above for your kind words.

Thanks to Rachel Robinson, Elizabeth Parker, Peter Jones, Susan Herbert, Sandi Canuto and Ruth Parker for proof-reading the book.

None of this would have happened without my own experiences. Thanks to Mark Morton, Peter Jones and my sister Rachel for running and racing with me so often over the years. Thanks to Neil Bowles, my girls, Cameron Pope, Sandi Canuto and a host of others from Runners Jam who helped support us in our first race. Runners Jam has been a fantastic caring community of encouragement, wisdom and support, not just during a Backyard.

Speaking of support, my wonderful, non-running wife Ruth and our girls Elizabeth, Charlotte, Rebekah and Jessica have all been such a blessing to me as I've written this. They patiently listened as I shared yet another story—that I found absolutely fascinating—which I'd discovered earlier that day. They have improved my ideas and shared much wisdom about what might not work. Most importantly, they have been gracious and patient as I've attempted to focus on this book for much of the last year.

To you all, thank you, you are all appreciated more than I can communicate. What is good about this book comes from each of you listed above. The mistakes are mine alone.

A PLEA FOR HELP

Thank you for buying and reading this book. Independently published books don't have the weight of the big publishing companies behind them. There is an uphill battle for books like this to navigate the algorithms that affect what people will find. If you enjoyed reading this, could you please help by:

- Reviewing the book on Amazon and Goodreads
- Telling running groups and friends of runners about the book
- Sharing a photo of you with the book on social media
- Giving (or lending) a copy to your support crew, whether in paper, ebook or audio versions
- Asking your local bookstore if they can stock this title
- Signing up for (very rare!) email updates on future releases at www.runningforever.au

ABOUT THE AUTHOR

Stephen Parker has been running the streets and trails of Rochedale South, Australia, for over forty years. He adores his wife Ruth and four incredible daughters, and is the Associate Academic Dean for ACOM - the Australian College of Ministries. Since 1987 he has raced at least a half marathon every year, and since 2009 has been enjoying adventure races, rogaines, trail ultras and now Backyard Ultras. In 2016 he helped begin Underwood Park parkrun, where he continues to volunteer as an Event Director. He hopes his next book is *A Spirituality of Running*.

Printed in Great Britain
by Amazon